Anonymous

The Princess Daphne

A Novel

Anonymous

The Princess Daphne
A Novel

ISBN/EAN: 9783337027001

Printed in Europe, USA, Canada, Australia, Japan

Cover: Foto ©Thomas Meinert / pixelio.de

More available books at **www.hansebooks.com**

PRINCESS DAPHNE

"Why! if the Soul can fling the dust aside,
And, naked on the air of Heaven ride,
Wer't not a shame—wer't not a shame for him
In this clay Carcass crippled to abide?"

Omar-i-Khayyám.

BELFORD, CLARKE & CO.
CHICAGO, NEW YORK, AND SAN FRANCISCO
PUBLISHERS
1888.

Day after day we wandered—you and I—
Amid a labyrinth of thought, nor found
The answer to the problem that we sought.
Day after day we pondered, asking why
Our twin souls sought each other, and seemed bound
Together by some strange resistless tie.
And as each answer seemed nor wrong nor right,
But all inexplicable, I forsook
The quest, and sate me down to write this book,
That peradventure may contain some light
That; thrown upon our question, may explain
The bitter pleasure and the mad, sweet pain
That we have known together. I have done
This work for you ; look kindly on the flaws
That mar it, since it leads you to the cause
Why, when we met, we felt our souls were one.

SORRENTO, *March*, 1885.

In lands which the stupidity of civilization regards as barbarous, there are occult powers of which contemporary science is absolutely ignorant. The materialism of Europe has not the faintest conception of the spirituality which the Hindus have reached . . . their mortal envelope is but a chrysalis which the immortal butterfly, the soul, can abandon or resume at will.

. ˙ .

I have attempted to undo with magnetism the bands that join mind and matter. In experiments that were certainly prodigious, but which failed to satisfy me, I surpassed Mesmer, Deslon, Maxwell, Puységur, and Deleuze: catalepsy, somnambulism, clairvoyance, soul-projection, in fact, all the effects that are incomprehensible to the masses, though simple enough to me, I have produced at will.

. ˙ .

I have fasted, I have prayed, I have meditated so long, I have dominated the flesh so rigorously, that I have been able to loose the terrestrial bonds. Vishnu, the god of the tenfold incarnations, has revealed to me the mysterious syllable that guides the soul in its avatars.

I am not an erudite in the ordinary acceptation of the word; but on the other hand, in studying certain subjects disdained by science, I have mastered some unemployed occult forces, and I produce effects which appear miraculous, though they are perfectly natural. . . . By watching for it I have sometimes surprised the soul . . . . Armed with the force of my will, that electricity of the intellect, I vivify or I annihilate. Nothing is opaque to my eyes; my gaze pierces everything. . . . We Europeans are too superficial, too matter of fact, too much in love with our clay prison, to open windows on the eternal and infinite.

THÉOPHILE GAUTIER. "AVATAR."

[*Myndaert Verelst's Translation.*]

CONTENTS.

THE

PRINCESS DAPHNE.

PROLOGUE.

"THEN, if I understand you rightly," said Mr. Paul du Peyral, "the case lies thus. My late friend and benefactor, Casimir Préault, makes my enjoyment of the fortune he has left behind him, contingent upon my offering myself as the husband of his second cousin, Miss Daphne Préault of New Orleans?"

"Exactly!"

"And if she refuses me, I enjoy the income only so long as I remain unmarried?"

"Exactly!"

"And should I marry anyone else, it reverts at once to that young lady, unconditionally?"

"Exactly!"

"I understand—good morning."

"Good morning;" and the senior partner of the firm of Seligman, Searcher, & Certiorari bowed Mr. Paul du Peyral out of his office on the ground-floor of No. 195 Nassau Street, New York City.

"Well," said the latter gentleman to himself, as he proceeded up-town in a brown study and a cab, "I am in a pretty peculiar position. Prospectively a wealthy man, but my wealth contingent on my offering myself to a woman I have never seen. Well, they say she is beautiful. Daphne seems inevitable! and as the inevitable I accept her. I wonder if she will accept me?"

On reaching his rooms he straightway indited a letter, laying his hand and heart at the feet of the testator's nominee. This done, he dressed himself; and, with the air of one who has manfully done his duty, he sought Delmonico's and dinner.

A week later, he received the following reply:—

NEW ORLEANS, LA., *December—*, 18—.

Sir:

Your impertinent offer of marriage has reached my daughter, who has placed it in my hands to reply thereto. We beg, once and for all, to decline the offer with which I presume you consider that you honour us. We have already suffered sufficiently from the madness of my cousin, Mr. Casimir Préault, of Baton Rouge; we did not expect, however, that he would insult us by suggesting the possibility of an alliance between his second cousin and his body-servant. We congratulate you on the disgraceful success of your efforts to gain an ascendency over the enfeebled mind of an octogenarian, though that ascendency robs us temporarily of an inheritance which should be justly ours. Any further communications that you may wish to make to us must be made through the attorneys to the estate, Messrs. Seligman, Searcher, & Certiorari; any letter of yours to us will be returned unopened. I have but one regret, and that is, that my age and infirmities prevent my administering the chastisement that, in my opinion, you deserve.

Obediently Yours,

VICTOR PRÉAULT.

"Good!" ejaculated Mr. Paul du Peyral, as he turned to his breakfast; "I've got the money unhampered by the woman."

CHAPTER I.

A BOHEMIAN SOIRÉE.

Do you know Holland Street, Kensington? Yes? I wonder whether you do, or whether you answer me "in the air," the *prænomen* "Holland," as applied to streets, roads, parks, and gardens, in that expansive area known as "Kensington" to us, which comprises the Brompton, the Notting-Hill, the Hammersmith, the Fulham, and almost the St. John's Wood of our fathers, being so familiar as to call forth the affirmative with hardly a moment's reflection as to whether one is telling the truth or not. For Holland Street is not a very well known locality: it is hardly a thoroughfare: and unlike Holland Road, and Holland Park, and Holland Park gardens, it is not lined with the gorgeous abodes of fashionable Bohemia—but it is Bohemia all the same, Bohemia as *we* knew it, the Bohemia of Thackeray, of Jerrold, of Albert Smith, and almost of Dickens; and it is inhabited, or at any rate was, at the time of which I write, exclusively by "the boys." The men who lived there were "the boys," and wore the pepper-and-salt continuations, the velveteen or corduroy jackets, the open collars and quaint ties, the comfortable shirts and the uncompromising hats that distinguish "the boys" from their uninteresting but respectable fellow-men, all the world over. And the women, too—they too were of "the boys"; and since long before Oscar Wilde carried the costume of the *atelier* into every-day life and conventional drawing-rooms, they had worn the artistic folds and colours which have become familiar to us coupled with the adjective "æsthetic," and, in merry communion with the male artists, enjoyed a blissful immunity from the tortures of civilization, represented for them by high heels, tight waists, Mrs. Grundy, and the Nineteenth Century dress-improver.

Those were happy days in Holland Street, and its Bohemian glories have not yet quite departed; its red-brick walls and ramshackle studios have not been invaded or routed by "villa residences"; its pipes have not been banished by the the cigarette; it has hardly begun to be civilized, even to the extent to which Bedford Gardens and like localities have succumbed to the influence of fashionable Bohemianism, and there are many nooks yet therein, where the dress clothes cease from troubling and the opera hat's at rest. You know, of course, the church-yard of St. Mary Abbott's, and Hornton Street: those are the media of communication by which "the boys" sought the outer world when they wanted it—which was seldom. They took the little flagged footpath through the church-yard, or, when the carrying of a picture to or from an exhibition warranted or required the extravagance of a cab, they reached their classic shades *via* Hornton Street. Hornton Street is practically a one-sided affair looking due west; that is to say, throughout a greater part of its length it looks out over the gardens of Something Priory (I think it is called), and its inhabitants dread the day when this "open lot," as the Americans would say, shall be built over by greedy heirs, or by thrifty executors and trustees—for now, in the early spring, from their upper windows they can watch the birth of the year and the return of the song-birds, and later on they can open them and get the full benefit of the summer fragrance. A discreet little street is that called Hornton, where there is no danger of being overlooked by inquisitive "opposite neighbors," but not inhabited by a homeful little colony like Holland Street—or as Holland Street was in the autumn of the year 18—.

My story opens in the September of that year. Autumn seemed to have roused herself from her long sleep, and had timorously—tentatively, as it were—laid her chilly touch upon the great city, to warn it that ere long she would be fully awake, and strong enough to take it wholly into her grasp. Already the chestnut trees in some of the parks and squares seemed to have realized that they could not store up for another year the gold they had gathered from the sunshine during the summer, and had begun to squander it extravagantly, flinging it lavishly to earth in the brilliant bronzes and gilts of the leaves that strewed the grass beneath them ; the sparrows were beginning to seek the patches of sunlight on the tree-tops, or fluffed themselves into cosy, chattering feather-balls in the warm dust of the more deserted roadways. The summer was not gone, but it was strong with life only for a day or so at a time, husbanding its strength, as it were, during the intervening hours, to display it with the more arrogance at intervals, as a temptation to the world.

But the season of the year was a matter of indifference in Holland Street. Spring meant, in its eyes, one of the male "boys," flying into the studio of one of the female "boys," and dragging her out for a walk, out toward Hammersmith and Chiswick and Barnes and Ealing; summer meant half-a-dozen of them providing their own refreshments, and going up the river—to find that each had been struck with the same original idea, viz., to bring a chicken-pie ; autumn meant a cottage by a wood or by the sea, whence they should return laden with sketches and "studies" to be worked up in the winter; the winter, which represented only an increased expenditure of gas and coal, with tea and muffins at intervals during the day. How happy we were! and now that we are respectable fathers and mothers of families, a younger generation is doing the same thing behind the walls and windows of Holland Street.

Perhaps I am generalizing too much, for of course I have a particular house—a particular *ménage*—in my mind's eye. It is No. 141 on the north side of the street, one of those houses with no front to it, which gives one the idea that the builder was going to face it the other way, but changed his mind at the last moment, cut a front door looking into the back-yard, and filled up the road in front with a garden—which garden, in turn, the inhabitants had filled up with a studio. There are many such in Holland Street. Where the houses are, so to speak, right side foremost, there are little gardens in front of them, wherein old-fashioned flowers grow luxuriantly in defiance of the London smoke, and through which flagged pathways lead from the front doors to the wooden gates; and in one of these we shall seek some of the actors in this drama.

At present our attention is turned to No. 141, at whose uncompromisingly ugly door a young man is letting himself in with a latch-key. An artist obviously, by his velveteen coat, soft hat, and long hair; and a man whom one would remark wherever one might see him. His face is, perhaps, too finely moulded for a man's—there are those who declare him to be effeminate in appearance; his eyes are large and of a dancing brown, his nostrils clearly cut, his lips thin, the jaw is square, the forehead high, and the brows are straight, the whole being framed in masses of rather light brown hair. The hand and arm not occupied in opening the door are encumbered with parcels;—Gabriel Hawleigh has been shopping in High Street, Kensington. Whilst he fumbles with the key, the door is opened from the inside by a girl, dressed in a long, loose frock of chestnut brown, girt about the waist with a broad *moiré* sash, who stands on the steps and laughs at him. The front of her dress is concealed—protected rather—by a long apron, and calico sleeve-preservers are tied over her arms, from the elbow down. She is neither pretty nor plain, but her great, grave, gloomy gray eyes quarrel with the sweetness of her expression, and with the laugh which, parting her finely traced lips, displays two rows of dazzling teeth. Her hair, rather short, forms round her head an aureole of gold, which shimmers as she laughs at the "boy" on the door-step. In sooth a goodly sight are they, as she stands in the shade of the doorway, and he, with one foot on the step, looks up at her.

"Thanks, Maye," says he, as he steps into the house and she closes the door.

"Have you got the muffins?" she inquires, anxiously.

"Yes."

"And the plums?"

"Here they are; they had a narrow escape from squashing against Dick Lindsay, as I came through the churchyard."

"And the soda-water?"

"It's coming round—I won't carry soda-water bottles through High Street."

"And the coffee?"

"There!"

"And the cheese?"

"Rather!"

"Very well; go and finish clearing out the studio, and I'll come up directly;" and the girl disappears, whilst Gabriel hangs up his hat, and, passing through the little drawing-room on the right, steps through the window into the studio. Here he looks round him as one is wont to look round when one is "at home," and then produces from his apparently inexhaustible pockets a box of cigarettes, which he dumps down rather contemptuously upon the mantel-shelf, and a fat package of tobacco, which he empties carefully into a stone jar by their side.

The studio already shows signs of having been cleared somewhat, but now he continues the operation, carefully covering a half-finished picture on an easel with a cloth as he turns it to the wall, and lifting into a corner a smaller easel, the flower-painting on which, however, he does not cover up. Only, the bowl of Gloire de Dijon roses which stood on a table by its side he carefully carries out of the studio and up-stairs into his own room, taking pains that their arrangement be not disturbed, so that on the morrow Maye Trevethick may have no difficulty in finishing her study from them. When he returns, an elderly lady is sitting in a low arm-chair by the window of the drawing-room.

"Ah! madre," cries he, "how are we getting on?"

"I think everything is ready now, dear. Maye is putting

the finishing touches to the baked meats down-stairs, and I'm ready to receive the company, and have got all my stereotyped phrases ready to greet them with. We shall have quite an historic party!"

There was to be a party in the studio,—the reader has gathered that already,—and the little household at No. 141 Holland Street were quite excited at the prospect of the festival, which was to be one of those merry Bohemian orgies such as "the boys" delighted in. Let me present the host to you before the company arrives.—Stay! there is a ring at the bell—some one arriving? No, only a boy with the soda-water.

The lady in the window is Mrs. Hawleigh—a sensible, clever old lady, such as young men delight in talking to, very courteous, very correct, a great reader, but a wise old lady who, having passed her later life in poverty, by comparison with the affluence of her earlier years, knows her world thoroughly, and in the parlance of "the boys," has no nonsense about her. Hermippus the Sage it was who remarked that the society of young people keeps old people young; and this was the case with Mrs. Hawleigh—the artistic colony with whom we are concerned adored her. She was a kind of mother to them all, and returned their affection with impartiality: she had only two especial favourites, and they were her son Gabriel Hawleigh and her niece Maye Trevethick. She had married, when quite young, a lieutenant in the ill-fated Light Brigade, and soon after that fateful 25th of October, when the blue and black missive from the War Office had told her that the young husband to whom she had given her whole soul without reserve had ridden "into the jaws of death, into the gates of Hell," and had left his fair young body before the batteries of Balaclava, she had given birth prematurely to her boy Gabriel. His consequent delicacy was almost a source of solace to her, as a safeguard against his joining that profession which had already torn two-thirds of all she cared for in the world from her. Mrs. Hawleigh, though possessed of but slender means, lived only for Gabriel, and had refused to marry again ; had only watched with delighted solicitude the growth of her son's artistic taste, and had denied herself many a little luxury that he might cultivate it to the utmost ; for Gabriel, with all his softness and delicacy, had undoubted talent in the profession he had taken up, though that talent had not as yet proved very remunerative.

Gabriel Hawleigh was an artist and a fiddler, and spent his life in the companionship of his easel and his violin. His mahl-stick and his fiddle-bow were the twin sceptres of his autocratic power—in Holland Street. Often his mother feared that the one would interfere with the other, but it was impossible to make him forsake the one and cleave to the other, especially since Maye Trevethick had become a member of the household, with her enthusiasm for her paint-brush under the tuition—and the able tuition—of Gabriel, and her skilled, sympathetic touch upon the piano which stood in a corner of the studio, and on which she would often play rich phantasies by the hour, or accompany Gabriel when, for her delight and that of his mother, he would take up

"———this small, sweet thing,
Devised in love and fashioned cunningly
Of wood and strings,"—

interpreting the masterpieces of the composers for his instrument, or following Maye through the chords and melodies of some daring improvisation, in which he would plead to her in harmonious whispers of things unutterable. For they were very poor in this world's riches. Ah—yi !

Maye Trevethick, the orphan and only child of Mrs. Hawleigh's only sister, had joined the household some three years before, and was now a sweet woman of nineteen. Gabriel was twenty-two. By that you can approximately fix the date of my story. When her father, Claude Trevethick, had died in India, her mother had soon followed him to "that undiscovered country from whose bourne no traveller returns," and her worldly possessions hardly sufficing for the co-maintenance of body and soul, Mrs. Hawleigh had taken the girl to her heart and home, and the *ménage* in Holland Street had become triple instead of, as heretofore, dual. Mrs. Hawleigh had never regretted her good-hearted impulse, for the pure, sweet girl had brought a rare sunshine into the little house, and was as much one of the family as if she had been in very truth Gabriel's sister. Such were the inmates of No. 141, and such, one of them at least prayed that they might ever continue, for the mother's heart read truly in the clear pages of her boy's soul, and daily she wove happy visions of a happy future.

The hour approached for which, as Maye said, "the cards had been sent out." Mrs. Hawleigh was suppressing a tendency to doze, and Maye and Gabriel were having an active row about the framing of certain works of art that at present lay around the studio in a frightfully dissolute state, when the bell rang, and Eric Trevanion was announced by the "Empress," a good-naturedly obese person of uncertain age, who, progressing through the stages of Mrs. Hawleigh's maid, Gabriel's nurse, and general factotum in Holland Street, had enjoyed the names of almost every imperial Roman dame, and from Eudoxia, Theodora, Faustina, Aspasia, Poppæa, and a host of others, the morals of whose original bearers would have brought her gray hairs in sorrow to the hair-dresser's, had arrived at the simple appellative of "Empress," from her imaginary authority in the Bohemia of Holland Street.

Eric Trevanion, whom the Empress had just admitted, was a Bohemian of a class much commoner to-day than it was at the time of which I write. He was, as it were, an amateur Bohemian; that is to say, he had private means of his own, an ample allowance made him by his father, a wealthy Cornish squire, enough to prevent the necessity of his selling his pictures to live; and this was a most fortunate thing for him, for though a royally good fellow, Eric was not much of an artist, though he meant very well, and covered acres of canvas, in his very superlative studio next door, with what he called "Studies from the Impressionists."

"Mine is an untamed genius," he used to say; "I can't trammel it with purity of line and rules of colour; it is enough for me to know that my work elevates the thoughts and stimulates the imagination. The study of my pictures is a search after the hidden beauties of the Undefined. Look at *that*, for instance; if you look carefully but comprehensively at it for a little while and at a little distance, the subject will form itself for you, and you will be astonished that you did not see it at once. Since you are pressed for time I will tell you. This is 'A Discord in Aniline Purples—Jimmy Whistler struck by lightning in the middle of a sneeze.' The large canvas on the wall is a Theosophical picture. I think the idea came to me in a trance, I'm not sure; it looks, I admit, as if it had been painted by my astral double the morning after a drunk; but the idea is very sublime and Esoteric Buddhism-ish—'A Nocturne in Green Apple Color—Madame Blavatzky as a Priestess of Isis, pondering on the "Now-ness of the When," whilst Mohini and A. P. Sinnett play three-card *monte* in the distance.' Some day I shall grow a white curl and be appreciated—at present I'm happy enough as I am."

Such was the new-comer, the first arrival, a young man dressed with scrupulous carelessness in the costume of Bohemia. Son, as I have said, of a Cornish squire of considerable means, he had adopted art as a profession for the sake of its associations and its freedom. Tall and dark, and quiet in manner, no one ever knew whether he were serious or not, or whether, like the Æsthete of historic fiction who dined with closed doors off beefsteak and onions, he laughed at himself in the solitude of his own studio; but everyone liked him, for it was whispered that his right hand did many a good action of which his left hand remained blissfully ignorant, among the impecunious "boys" whose pictures he would buy, ostensibly on commission for his father, and this often with such a lordly disregard of their merits as paintings, that, when Gabriel Hawleigh ate things that disagreed with him, his grisliest nightmare was always one of incarceration in the elder Trevanion's picture-gallery. His especial cronies were the Hawleighs, possibly on account of their proximity, a proximity which lent itself to his continual appeals "next door" to have buttons sewed on, or especial delicacies cooked, or the wounds produced by his amateur carpentering bandaged. To-night he made an early appearance, with two chairs in one hand and in the other a basket.

"Do you want some more chairs?" was his greeting. "And look here; the governor sent me up a couple of brace of partridges yesterday, so I had them cooked and brought them round. I get very hungry later on and require strong meats, so I said to myself, 'Come early and bring your own birds.' How are you all, anyhow?"

"Now that's what I call having a proper regard for the ethics of the situation," cried Gabriel. "Empress, here is food! Give me the chairs, and now let's greet him. How are you, Mr. Trevanion?—so good of you to come!"

"Not at all—pleasure, 'm sure," replied the Cornishman, gravely. "And whilst I think of it—before the aristocracy of Camden Hill turn up—have you got a shoe lace? Hark! some one approaches—I shall go away and come back fashionably late. How are you, Miss Easton?—have you brought the latch-key? I've left mine on my dressing-table."

This last remark was made to the elder of two girls who made their appearance at this moment, Sylvia and Eva Easton, occupants of the floor above him next door, who were engaged taking off their hats, smoothing their hair, and giving themselves and one another little corrective pats and punches all over, in a corner with Maye, to an accompaniment of those hysterical whispers and bursts of suppressed merriment without which no properly constructed young women can greet one another after an enforced separation of—say—two hours. The elder, Sylvia Easton, was a student of "Still Life," and had been remarkably successful at getting five-pound pictures exhibited and sold in Suffolk Street, Pall Mall, and Burlington House. Her sister Eva was recently home from a two-years' sojourn in the Conservatoire at Leipsic, where she had devoted her time to the study of the violin. That accounted for the *papier maché* fiddle-case and roll of music which she dexterously concealed beneath her cloak, with one end plainly visible to guard against its being ignored.

"Let us go into the studio," said Mrs. Hawleigh, as another arrival announced himself by "tirling at the pin;" and the little nucleus of "the party" stepped through the window.

"Great Scott! Pouff!!" exclaimed Trevanion, flying to the ropes of the skylights, which he opened to their fullest extent. "Gabriel, what are you doing?"

The gaslights of "the flarer" were reinforced by half-a-dozen candles disposed around the studio, and seated on the floor before a brass Venetian lamp, Gabriel had succeeded in producing a perfume which, not having the pen of a Dante, I am powerless to describe.

"Well," said he, smiling apologetically, in defiance of the contortions of his face from his nose outward, "I thought this Venetian thing would look pretty, alight, but I can't get it to work. By Jove! if the merry Venetians always produce this effect when they try to illuminate the world, I don't wonder that they seem rather to like the Grand Canal at low water!"

"Take it out! Ouf!" vociferated Eric.

And amid the derisive laughter of the band, Gabriel removed his highly artistic but disagreeably pungent illumination; whilst Maye lit some incense in a *cinque-cento* thurible to neutralize the aromatic effects of his experiment.

Meanwhile the other guests begin to arrive. First Bernard Rawlinson, a grave, handsome creature with picturesquely dishevelled hair and an indumentary *désinvolture* peculiarly his own. Rawlinson would have been an excellent artist if he had not been a tolerable actor, and an excellent actor had it not been for his talent as a painter. As it was, he divided his time about equally between the studio and the stage, with the result that the one always interfered with the other, and precluded his reaching the summit of excellence in either.

He was followed by Dick Lindsay—a funny man. That was obvious the moment you saw him. His smooth-shaved and rather ugly face never changed its expression in the slightest degree; but from behind his light, gold-rimmed spectacles, his keen blue eyes seemed to watch everything around him, and discover the hopelessly ludicrous in whatever presented itself within range of his observation. He stood in the doorway and snuffed the gale suspiciously.

"Is anybody dead so far?" said he.

"Not at present," replied Sylvia Easton.

"Then I think I may venture," said he, stepping into the studio. "What has happened?" he queried.

"Gabriel has been making sacifice of a sweet savour, and has just disappeared, like the ghost in the 'Antiquary,' 'with an aromatic perfume and a melodious twang.'"

"Oh! I thought someone had had an accident with the chemicals;" and he subsided by Mrs. Hawleigh's side as Gerome Markham, an artist attached to the permanent staff of a comic paper, made his appearance. A small, fat man with a large income and a supremely careworn and worried expression, clothed in the most superlative evening dress, with a gardenia in his button-hole.

"Apothecary! an ounce of civet," cried Bernard Rawlinson, as Markham stepped round on tip-toe, making his choicest salaams to the company, and diffusing a faint, sweet perfume of chypre as he went.

"Yes," said he, as if in answer, "I perceived a weird aroma before I left Phillimore Gardens, and as the wind set from this direction, I thought you would appreciate my delicacy in providing a counteractive."

Others followed him, and at last about a dozen genial souls had shaken their hosts by the hand, had turned from Gabriel more in sorrow than in anger, had congratulated Markham on the picturesque splendour of his appearance, and joined in the tea, coffee, and gossip of the studio. Suddenly Trevanion, who occupied the music-stool, swung round and said:

"Where's the Princess?"

"Echo answers where," said Gabriel.

"Then Echo is a liar or intoxicated," rejoined Lindsay, "for Echo ought to answer 'cess.'"

"But where *is* she?" persisted Trevanion.

"I saw her to-day," said Eva Easton, "and she said she was coming."

"I think," said Rawlinson, "that the President's dining with her;" and at this intelligence every tongue was hushed, for "the President" dining in Holland Street was an event that brought throbs to every Bohemian heart. And yet it was not uncommon, for Sir George B——, President of the Royal Something-or-other of Painters, with his fine, handsome face and silver-gray hair, was "a boy" among "the boys," and, often looked in on the colony, and smoked cigarettes whilst he made suggestions that accounted for many an admission to the holy precincts of the Academy on Varnishing day.

"Well, he's in good company," said Mrs. Hawleigh, "and Sir George is likely to stay there."

"No!" said a voice on the threshold; and most of the men rose to receive the great man himself, who stood smiling for an instant at the colony, and then bent low over the hand of Mrs. Hawleigh.

"May I come to the party?" said he, as he settled himself by Mrs. Hawleigh's side.

"Rather!" said Gabriel.

"Coffee?" said Maye.

"Thanks—both of you," said Sir George.

"I come as an ambassador or advance-guard," continued he, "to say that the Princess Daphne will be here directly; she stayed to interview someone for a moment, and sent me on—there's a ring! Perhaps it's she." Maye rose and went quickly to the door; the next moment Miss Daphne Préault

—called unanimously by the colony "The Princess"—stood in the drawing-room window and looked round the studio. The men rose again with one accord, and a little murmur of satisfied "Ah's" went round.

That Miss Préault should have been dubbed "The Princess Daphne" never caused a moment's surprise to any who saw her. Who she was, and where she came from, no one knew for absolutely certain; and the combined and persistent curiosity of the entire female colony had not as yet elucidated the problem. Meanwhile they bowed before her; and though she often seemed unconscious of her empire, the sceptre she swayed was that of a rule which, all agreed, was highly beneficent to her subjects, and very genuine indeed.

A dim rumour existed in the colony to the effect that the Princess Daphne was a Creole. No one, however, dreamt of pressing the idea heavily upon her, and when suggested lightly, she would equally lightly set it aside. Since then, however, I, the writer of this narrative, have been far afield, and among the beauties who stroll of a summer's evening along Carondelet Street, or on the Levée, or in the old Rue Royale, in New Orleans, or who lounge on the piazzas of Baton Rouge and Mobile and such semi-tropical cities of the New World I have seen many a finely moulded quasi-Amazonic figure that reminded me, as nothing else has ever done, of Daphne Préault. The reader may as well be let into the secret that a Creole she was.

Daphne Préault was tall, or at any rate held herself, as many women have the trick of doing, so as to convey that impression; and this dignity of stature was still further enhanced by the grand proportions of her body, by the half-Spanish lines of the neck and shoulders, the finely rounded bust and non-atrophied waist, the curves at the hips, and the purity of the lines down to her feet, which, like her hands, were not too small. Her hands especially were a study for the artist or sculptor; not too small, as I have said, and of a respectable breadth, the flesh firm and lightly colored, the thumb not weak, as it so often is in a woman's hand, the fingers smooth and slightly tapering to a delicate squareness at the tips, the nails long and curved, the finger-tips rounded on their surfaces into that little cushion of flesh, sure sign of sensitiveness in a hand; the whole exquisitely flexible, the

> "Gentile morbida leggiadra mano
> Cui fer le proprie mani d'Aurora"

of Paolo Rossi. And, above all, her head, which for very fear I have left until last! A head not too small, covered with masses of hair that would have been black but for the reddish lights that flashed through it when she moved, hair that came low on a broad, clear forehead, bounded by straight and rather heavy, dark eyebrows, from beneath which a pair of great dark-brown eyes looked straight into one's soul. The nose straight as we see it on a Greek coin, the mouth firm, but finely, almost sensuously, curved, the jaw square and strong, the whole complexion pale rather than coloured —and there you have the portrait of the Princess Daphne. Yes! to the *cognoscenti* she could never be anything but a Creole; but nature had been kinder to her than to most of her race,—she had not, in producing perfection of form, exhausted her creative energy, but had endowed this imperial woman with a brain no whit behind her physical development; and though she was equally amiable to the entire colony among which she lived, her especial cronies realized —and fully realized—that they were lucky indeed.

"Am I too fashionably late to expect absolution?" said she, as she surveyed the group, "or has Sir George prepared a gracious forgiveness for me?"

"The Princess can do no wrong—*sta felice alla casa,*" replied Gabriel, gallantly, as the girl stepped into the studio with a little laugh, and greeted the company with a series of "nods and becks and wreathed smiles."

"I have been doing combat with our natural foe, the art-dealer," said she. "The particular specimen of to-night thought to catch me in a good humour after food, and buy a miscellaneous lot by gaslight, for ready but insufficient cash. I am proud to say that I resisted, and told him to come back to-morrow, when I shall probably be suffering from this evening's dissipation, and be in too bad a temper to make him any concessions."

"There is no doubt about it," said Bernard Rawlinson; "if Art-dealers were not as a class—well, let us say—stupid, they would buy pictures on gastronomic and barometric principles. Take my own case, for instance: '*Metiri se quemque suo modulo* what's-his-name,' as the classic has it. If I have looked in on Gabriel in the morning, and feasted on half-cooked muffins, I spend the afternoon meditating an essay on the meaning of the word 'Remorse.' At such times the dealer has no chance; nor has he any luck when the weather is on my nerves; but if it is a fine day and I have had tea at the Princess's, I become kindly disposed towards him, and take his paltry shekels in exchange for works of art worth treble—in my estimation,—and merely smile a wan smile of pity when he declares that he is ruining himself to save me from starvation, on strictly philanthropic principles. To paraphrase Byron, 'Now Barabbas was an art-dealer.'"

"But why talk of funerals, physic, and art-dealers?" cried Lindsay; "let us rather make music. Miss Trevethick, won't you twankle on the harpsichord for us?"

"Certainly," replied Maye; "I'll play you a little thing of my own. I call it 'Funeral March of the Hanging Committee,' and I am going to dedicate it by special permission to Sir George B——;" and she began to run her fingers over the keys, first in playful, catchy fantasy, drifting thence into pure tunefulness, and ending with a grand, rich fugue that left the assembled crowd wondering at its meaning, so strange and suggestive was the *leit-motif* that crept into the harmonies at every moment, or anon would stand out by itself in a bit of exquisite melody. When she finished, a dead silence had fallen on the gathering, broken only by the Princess's ejaculation of, "Thanks, dear; it's very sweet of you to exhaust yourself like that for our selfish, but appreciative edification."

"What I like about Miss Trevethick's music," remarked Lindsay, "is that she gives no chances to the social fiend, the man who beats time, or whistles the air if he knows it, or insists on turning over the music."

"Poor Lindsay!" said Markham; "one would think he had been himself a sufferer, though I doubt whether he knows the difference between a piano and a penny-whistle."

"True! I have not suffered from the musical fiend; *my bêtes noires* are the Story Fiend and the Introduction Fiend. Some day I shall write an essay on Social Fiends, and clear off old scores. Yet, after all, the Social Fiend is only a product of high civilization and cultivation, and will increase, I suppose, rather than decrease."

"Explain! Define! Speech! Speech!" was the cry; and Lindsay, after looking helplessly around for a few seconds, thus held forth:

"What I mean by my introduction," said he, "is that the fiendishness of the Social Fiend generally results from the perversion of some high quality, which, kept within proper limits, would inspire our respect, *e.g.*, musical, literary, or dramatic talent.

"The social fiend is of two classes—or declensions—the *active* and the *passive;* or perhaps it would better express my meaning if I were to say, *transitive* and *neuter.* To the former fiend one stands in some measure in the light of a foil; one's presence, and to a certain extent one's coöperation is necessary to him; one inflicts him on one's self, so to speak, and consequently he may be avoided with care, and discretion, and practice, and presence of mind. The latter, on the other hand, is a fiend all by himself; he can sit alone and exercise his fiendishness, disseminating it quasi-unconsciously all around him; he cannot be avoided; in his case, absence of body is preferable to presence of mind; you must get up and go away!

"Thus much by way of introduction. We can now, in the

words of the classic, 'cut the dialogue, and come to the figures.'

"On mature reflection I think that the most drastic and damnable kind of musico-social fiend is the man who taps with his foot when music is being played. The man* (his brother *cadet*) who hums the tune in an undertone, or gently whistles an accompaniment, pales into insignificance before him. The affliction arises from a diseased musical ear, a pathological condition, I believe, unknown to the aurist. I once knew one of this class who tried to beat time to Wotan's fifty-minute recitative in the 'Siegfried' of Wagner (the sin was its own punishment—he was carried out in convulsions); but it is the slow waltz or quick march that principally draws forth his natural corruption. An air is being played;—suddenly you become aware of a little measured thud on the brain repeated at regular intervals; you tap your ear and reconcentrate your attention:—in vain! the tap, tap, tap seems to become a kind of devil's tatoo on your inmost soul: the rest of the audience also gradually wake to the fact, and a scared expression spreads itself around, whilst the entire *assistance* ignores the music, and begins searching for the fiend. At last you find him, a mild-mannered youth with a wisp of hair bristling at the crown of his head, with large hands and a pale face—absorbed, concentrated in the music; his right foot is merrily accompanying the melody; he is as unconscious as a *young* organ-grinder of the grief that he is causing; he doesn't see the cyclonic glares directed at him, not he! He is only mildly surprised that he alone applauds at the end of the performance; the rest of the audience is only waiting for the end of *his*, and merely regards the musician as a kind of accomplice. The tapper has 'queered the show,' but he doesn't realize the fact. The only person who is similarly self-satisfied is his brother fiend who has been softly whistling the air between his teeth all the time; and this improvised drum-and-fife band forms a kind of link of brotherhood—hitherto unrecognized—between them. These fiends have, as I say, fallen from a high but uncultivated musical taste, like the fiend who insists upon turning the leaves for the *pianiste*. His radius of iniquity is often more circumscribed; it may extend only to the lady playing, her chaperone who doubts his capacity, and the man who wishes *he* could perform this office for the fair *artiste*: if the leaf-turner is sure of himself it is all right for the others; but as a rule he isn't. He only does it 'to show off'; and his anxious, conscience-stricken face, as he stares blankly at the page, wondering where the deuce and all the player has got to, gradually betrays his mental state to the audience, and they sit writhing with apprehension till the *artiste* makes a convulsive bob of the head, the fiend makes a wild dive, and it is five to one he drops a leaf on the floor and replaces it upside down. If he doesn't the audience breathes freely for another five minutes, and so on at intervals, until the fiend perspires, apologizes, is frigidly thanked, and retires into his pristine insignificance to reflect upon the impression he has produced.

"There are other musical fiends that we all know:—the man who insists on being told the name of the piece played, and the man who tells him—wrong; the man who, in the dead silence that follows a performance, is heard remarking that he heard Rubinstein play—or Sims Reeves sing—that particular thing; the man who tells the lady performer, at the conclusion of a carefully learnt English song, that he is 'so fond of those weird little Arabic chaunts.' And so on—and so on—and so on!

"The musical fiend, of whatever sort, is the best specimen of the neuter declension. The most perfect exemplification of the *transitive* class are the story fiends, whether active or passive. Among the active ones, of course I will not refer to the retailer of 'chestnuts,' the man who tells you the original story for telling him which Caín killed Abel; or the man who tells a story inside out, *i.e.*, gives you the point seriously, and wonders that you don't laugh as he concludes with the introduction thereto; or the man who tells you a story that you know of old, and leaving out the point altogether, gets mad when you bring him safely onto the track once more. All these are too common for the esoteric profundity of this sermon. The story fiend I *hate* is the man who with much pantomime tells you a pointless old yarn for the purpose of impressing with his wit and eloquence a girl across the room whom he *hopes* is looking at him and taking in his performance.

"Similarly do I hate certain story fiends of the *recipient* variety. For instance, the converse of the last fiend, who, whilst you are telling *him* your latest and best, is making eyes across the room, and gauging the effect upon *her*, and when you come to the point where you should be interrupted by a smile, and wait for it accordingly, turns an absent-minded, lack-lustre gaze upon you and ejaculates spasmodically, 'Oh! ah! yes! Haha! very good—and what became of the boy?'—or some tom-foolery of that sort. Only one degree removed from him is the man who, instead of listening to your yarn, keeps his eyes fixed on the ground about six feet in front of him, racking his brain to think of a story on his *own* account, and at the conclusion of your effort, instead of grinning appreciatively, chips in like an east wind chased by lightning with 'Ah! yes, and that reminds me of a story,' etc., etc., etc. Ugh! there's a brute for you! And yet how common!

"Then you have the fiend who tells you a long yarn, usually concerning his own prowess in the Camp of Mars and the Court of Venus, when you are dying to skip over unconcernedly and take the seat just vacated by *her* side. You are like the Pool of Bethesda; whilst the descended angel troubles you, someone else steps in and reaps the benefit.

"And again, what a fruitful field for abstract and experimental objurgation is the introduction fiend—the man who insists on being introduced to you, and the man who insists on your introducing him to So-and-So!—the man who grasps your hand with an eighty-one ton crunch and says, 'We have a mutual friend in Mrs. X.; she has often spoken to me of you.' You have never heard of Mrs. X., and don't believe in her existence, but you daren't say so, for fear that he will queer you with some pleasant acquaintance whose name you haven't caught; so you put your head on one side like a contemplative parrot, and say, 'Oh yes! And how was Mrs. X. when last you saw her?'—praying inwardly that you are not, both of you, constructively, liars.

"And then the man who says genially, 'Oh! is this Mr. X?' in much the tone of voice in which Uriah's wife is said to have remarked, on her first introduction to David, 'Is *this* the youth who slew the great Goliath?' Or the man who says treacherously, 'Oh! Mr. Z., I've heard so much of you;' you break into a cold perspiration and wonder what he's heard about you, and from whom. But, good heavens! I've been lecturing for half an hour—believe me, I apologize—somebody else do something to wipe out the memory of my harangue!"

Lindsay stopped, and the laughter which had rippled through his discourse culminated in a storm of delighted applause, in the midst of which Maye set forth the more solid baked meats, and the company proceeded to picnic.

Whilst they ate, Bernard Rawlinson recited to them, and at the conclusion of the little repast, Gabriel, with much pomp and circumstance, asked the Princess on behalf of the men to permit them on behalf of the ladies to smoke.

"Well," replied she, "of course it is understood that we all dislike smoke exceedingly, and regard the use of tobacco as wholly vile; but on this single occasion we will not only permit, but countenance, the proceeding."

So saying she produced a silver cigarette-case and selecting a cigarette for herself handed it to Sylvia Easton, who did the same and passed it on to the other girls. This was carried through with the utmost gravity, and the symposium continued amid the soft blue fumes of the weed nicotian, unsupported, however, by Sir George and Mrs. Hawleigh, who had slipped away softly, for fear of breaking up the party by their departure.

It was one of those delightful evenings in which everyone does something. The two Eastons played a duet, and after that Gabriel and Maye were persuaded to do likewise. When Gabriel played in public it was a thing to hear, for it seldom took place: his fiddle was to him his confessional, his confessor, and his confession; and if we are to accept Neil Gow's axiom, that "a mon's a player when he gar himsel' greet wi' his fiddle," Gabriel Hawleigh was a player indeed; for his playing was the very soul, the very agony of music, and often, when he had a melancholy fit on him, he would bring tears to the eyes of his small but appreciative audience, consisting, as a rule, of Maye and Mrs. Hawleigh.

To-night, however, he was in his more enthusiastic, fiendish mood, and tore out of his fiddle a brilliant suite of wild Czardas, drawing Maye irresistibly along with him as she played the piano accompaniment, and winding up with a wild, triumphant solo of barbaric melody, that roused his audience as if it had been a thunderstorm of harmonies.

This solo terminated in a roar of enthusiasm, during which he recovered his senses, as it were, and when it subsided he seized the opportunity to fall on one knee before the Princess Daphne, saying:

"Like the King's minstrel I crave a boon, Princess."

"It is granted, Ser Menestrel—what is it?"

"That *you* sing for us."

"Oh, you wretch!" exclaimed she. "If I had guessed—but I've promised, so I suppose I must;" and amid the delighted acclamations of the crowd, Daphne Préault moved to the piano.

"After that gorgeous performance of Gabriel and Maye's, I can't sing any of my French *repertoire* to you; here is a little Cuban suite of melodies, in the Cuban dialect; it is supposed to be a triumphal song of a woman's self-sacrifice."

She began in a low, soft minor key, a weird, half-monotonous melody of which every note seemed to thrill the very souls of the listeners; then, just as the depth of despair seemed to have been reached in the music, the major inversion of the chord was heard in the bass, the treble took it up, and the lament became a grand, almost military chaunt, that ended abruptly with an unheralded minor harmony. Daphne Préault had the pure, rich contralto of the south, and threw herself into her music in a way that used to make her listeners tremble. Like Gabriel, she seldom flung the glories of her art before the public, which made it all the more an event to remember when she did sing; and to-night undoubtedly she eclipsed herself.

On one at least of the company she had made an impression not likely to be soon effaced: he sat on a long, low, carved chest, with his head resting in his clasped hands as he leaned against the wall, his soul far away on the wings of the music, forgetful of everything save the grand orgy of sound. When the music ceased his eyes turned with an expression of dumb wonder in the direction of the singer, and, attracted perhaps by the intensity of his gaze, her eyes sought his. The Princess Daphne resumed her seat quietly. The man was Eric Trevanion.

And so, amid music and conversation, light tobacco and light refreshments, the evening wore on. To an historian much latitude and meanness and betrayal of confidence are allowed, but I do not propose to divulge the tale which was told by the clock as the last guests—Gerome Markham and Dick Lindsay—concealed about their persons a stirrup-cup proffered by Gabriel, who then, turning out the gas and contemplatively munching a biscuit, wandered up to bed. The Princess had been the last girl-guest to go, escorted by Eric Trevanion; and then Maye Trevethick had softly and silently vanished away, leaving a small male group to talk unrestrained "shop" into the small hours of the morning.

The Bohemian *soirée* was ended, and the Empress, on the following morning, expressed a hope that there might not very soon be another.

CHAPTER II.

UNE MAÎTRESSE FEMME.

FROM Holland Street, London, to Forty-first Street, New York City, is a far cry,—three thousand miles or more,—but though we have transported ourselves, Aladdin-like, across the site of the submerged continent of which Ancient Egypt was a colony, and Yucatan a young dependency,—according to Ignatius Donnelly,—and have reached the commercial capital of that "great aristocratico-oligarchical democracy where all men are equal and none of the women," we are still in Bohemia, though it is Bohemia of a very different order from that which we have left behind us in the old world.

The American autumn was much like the English one in temperature; only its outward and visible signs were different. In the squares, the asphalt was strewn thick with broad golden and bronze leaves, and the water drawn off from the fountain-basins had left hideously bare the roots of the lilies and lotuses and other semi-tropical water-plants, whose flowers had been so good to look upon during the empty summer months, and whose leaves, decaying, were watched with almost vulture-like impatience by the municipal gardeners, who were waiting for their death to lift bodily the great square boxes of roots, to be put away for the winter, or to cover them with the fallen leaves. In Central Park, and in the open lots up beyond One Hundred and Fortieth Street, the crimson awns of the sumach were beginning to bow reverence to the autumn winds, and save and except that now and then summer seemed to have left a day behind, and to have come back to look for it, the new world, like the old, was preparing for winter.

In one of the lower rooms of a house on Forty-first Street, whose number lay in the first hundred, but is immaterial to our story, the morning light streams in upon a small, supple figure which lies curled up on a low divan,—a divan so colossal in its proportions that the figure looks even smaller than it is,—and illuminates a picture that tells its own story to the inquisitive sunbeams. The room, which is large, though furnished in the main with the faded elegance that announces the lodging-house, shows by a few of its more prominent objects that its occupant has come thither from haunts of luxury and taste. The observant eye can pick out at a glance the objects that are the property of the woman who lies on the divan in the reckless *abandon* of sleep, relics of former years when her footsteps fell in softer places. An inlaid piano by Steinway, a screen of rare Japanese brocade, a proof-etching or two, a masterpiece of Meissonier, and an unfinished sketch by an artist whose name gives market value to a line drawn across a sheet of millboard, some matchless Satsuma and Kâga porcelain, and some scraps of rare stuffs thrown across chairs of bastard design, in a vain attempt to conceal their illegitimacy—all bespeak the *artiste*, the woman of refined taste. The floor is covered with a matting of scented Indian grasses, that fills the air with a quaint, pungent odour, and over it are strewn tattered but glorious Persian and Turkish rugs.

But what catches the eye and holds the senses, taking prisoner the imagination, is the divan on which the little immobile live thing rests. It is very large and very low, covered in brown satin and furs, and cumbered with huge cushions of varied but harmoniously combined coloured silks. A great sheet of rich brocade is drawn in a crumpled mass to a corner, and is falling on the ground over the edge of the divan; the cushions are doubled up and punched into numberless odd shapes, their corners sticking out in all directions; and *blottie* among them is the small, supple, sleeping form of the woman, whose individuality harmonizes to admiration with her surroundings. Her attitude, which would strike the ignorant observer as intensely uncomfortable, so curled and twisted does it seem, looks, in her case, perfectly natural and easy. She is but half undressed, and must have fallen asleep almost unconsciously, when, in the conflict of Morpheus and Eros, exhaustion had overtaken her unawares. At least it appears so; every line of the dormant figure and its minutest details reveal a delicious lassitude. One little foot, in a slipper of gold brocade, rests on the floor; the other slipper has fallen off, and the foot is drawn up under the figure. The light silk covering has slipped away, revealing a stocking of open-worked gold-green silk stretched over curves to which it clings as if fearful of marring their beauty by the slightest suspicion of a wrinkle, and heightens the dazzling tints of a glimpse of the satin-like skin, that sleep has indiscreetly revealed above the stocking.

It is only a glimpse, for a "mysteriette" of pink silk covers the rest of the figure, without hiding its delicate, sensuous curves—only making the picture more indefinite and more alluring by adding the subtle charm of the unseen to charms which the imagination grasps without difficulty.

She lies deep among the cushions, her head thrown back in a mass of shiny hair of a bronzed, burnt gold, which, uniting with the purple brown of the divan, makes an exquisite background for the pale shell-pink of her skin. The stream of light which steals into the darkened room lies in a solid ray across the divan, shedding over the sleeping figure a glow which seems not to illuminate it, but to be shed by the figure itself upon the surrounding brocades; and so, a perfectly natural effect of light seems to become a weird, spectral mystery. The dead stillness of the world, the halo environing the sleeping woman, the dim light pervading all else in the room, combine to make a picture which embodies all that there is of sensuous poesy in real life.

The delicate brows, the finely-curved lips, the curved nostrils, and subtly-rounded chin, betray the woman's Oriental origin; and if any doubt remained on the point it is dispelled when, without any start or visible effort of awakening,

Mahmouré di Zulueta opens her grand, brown eyes and, with a movement of intense, unconscious longing, stretches out her arms to the empty air, and encountering naught save a tumbled cushion, grasps a fold of it with a little feverish clutch as, using her arm lever-wise, she gives her whole body a comprehensive voluptuous twist that hides the scrap of skin that dazzled the sunbeam, beneath the falling folds of silk, and sinks back into the cushions with a scarce satisfied sigh. As she does so her hand encounters something hidden among the cushions: she draws it forth and recognizes it with a smile of happy recollection. It is a portrait—it had been her last thought as she sank to sleep, and is her first on waking; and as she holds it before her, it brings a warmer tint to her cheek, a brighter glow to her dark eyes. The face before her, be it by reason of the photographer's art or of the individuality of the original, is one of great beauty, intense, delicate, and very youthful, so youthful indeed that at a first glance it might be taken for that of a mere boy, but on closer inspection one discovers in it a firmness, enhanced by the high intelligence of the brow; and the woman gazing at the picture through her half-closed eyes sees there the self hidden behind the mask. To all else he may be and is what he chooses; to her his inmost being is revealed, and through the changeless, senseless reflection, she sees the thousand flashes of the master passion which she, and she alone, has bred within him—a passion of which he had always laughingly declared himself incapable.

And concerning the woman herself, the supple Eastern woman with the strange Eastern name—Mahmouré di Zulueta? There is, I know, something inexpressibly tedious in the "previous histories" of heroes and heroines of romance. Perhaps I ought to have made a former chapter of that of Mahmouré, for it is quite quaint enough to spur a biographer to his highest effort in this particular branch of natural history. I am not going to enter into a discussion of whether her history was stranger than her nature, or whether her nature was stranger than her history; whether her history was the result of her nature, or *vice versâ*. Without the remotest tendency to mediocrity she was neither very good nor very bad; she was always rather both, and often very much one of them; the world being divided, admittedly, into men, women—and Mahmouré di Zulueta. Probably it was an effect of her home training, the tender influences of a father and mother who worshipped her, that prevented the bad in her from developing to its fullest extent. It is thus that many great characters in history are spoilt, are, as it were, still-born. Without the refining influences of her home Mahmouré would have been historic, but whether as a Vallière, a Brinvilliers, a Bradamante, or a Lola Montez, far be it from the present historian to hazard a conjecture.

Her early years were monotonous, spent between the English home where she found her level in gentle, commonplace family affection, and the continental *conservatoire* where she laboured from an early age for the development of the talent that should some day make her famous; for her father, himself an artist of great enthusiasm and judgment,—two rarely concomitant attributes,—strained his every resource to fit her for the position which he felt she was bound to attain. She rewarded him for all his bitter struggles (and God alone knows what privations he had endured for her) in the usual way. Developed to womanhood at an age when most of her sex are hardly out of the nursery, she chose to fancy herself in love; and she married, when barely fifteen, a complicated concentration of the lowest qualities peculiar to half-a-dozen nationalities. The name of this mongrel was di Zulueta. A friend of the family, expert in variegated genealogies, asserted that his father was a Greek and his mother an Italian, that he was born on board a Spanish ship in French waters, and was a naturalized American citizen domiciled in England!

It is hardly worth while to attempt the impossible, or to describe the abysmal depths of blackguardism to which this gutter-bred cur had sunk by the sheer specific gravity of his own cowardly vileness; but he oozes into my narrative at this point, for he married this child—for not only in years, but in everything else save physique, she was a child; and thus her first folly, the launch of her "inconsequent" career (in the Balzacian sense), was committed. Art for art's sake, which might have been to her a gracious, generous protectress, was thrust aside, and the first step in her progress was taken.

And what a progress hers should have been with the materials at her command! A gorgeous voice, of great range and power, and, above all, of that quality so rare, a perfect sympathy—that one gift of blood and race without which the finest voice becomes "as sounding brass, or tinkling cymbals." Fantastic but dazzling personal beauty, the matchless health of a perfect constitution, were all factors in a personality that should echo her fame from world to world—and the first exercise of her will had been to fling the whole treasure of herself into the grasp of a foul-mouthed, underbred ruffian.

The first era of her life may be said to have commenced with her marriage, which, though uneventful in itself, was a fitting probation for what was to follow. He was a hard taskmaster to his child-wife, but, brute though he was, he treated —from motives of policy—his golden goose with some show of affection: but his coarseness killed the goose. Had he been a clever rascal he might have kept the girl; as it was he never spared her, feeling sure of the obedience she dumbly gave, never looking deeper when some greater exaction than usual struck a flash from the highly-charged personality he was trifling with. He was consequently not a little astonished when, one night, in the presence of her father, she remarked coolly and with no passion or quiver in her voice:

"I am not going to live with you any longer."

Her father, who had refused his sanction to the marriage, and loathed her husband, still did what he believed to be his duty, and urged her to reconsider her decision.

"Better let me go now, when there is no man in the case,

If I wait six months longer, there will be," she had said, calmly but quite characteristically.

It was not long before this that she had made her début on the stage, and that début had created a furore. Men about town had but one topic of conversation—this new girl with the great, wondering, innocent eyes; and a Great Personage (as novelists love to call libertines of the blood-royal), on his first visit to the theatre, had sent for her. She had no idea of the importance of the attention, and kept the G. P. so long waiting that the G. P. indignantly retired. This was much commented upon in the theatre, and doubtless did not escape the observation of intelligent managers. Throughout this period that husband of hers was her execrated monster; but for her father's sake she endured the burden, until month after month added feathers by the ton to her load, and at last the result came in the calm, dispassionate words that terminated her married life.

With the advent of this relief departed every moral reserve, and her vagabond, Bohemian imagination began to expand. She had no lover and wanted none—later on she had lovers and still wanted none :—liberty seemed so glorious. Experience had taught her that man would steal away from her this newly attained possession; and the word "Freedom" was emblazoned upon the oriflamme that led her into and out of every scrape that ornamented her life. She had vowed never to be enthralled again; and she all but kept her vow.

She became the fashion. Her little rooms, just close enough to Belgrave Square to swear by, and avoid the ambiguity of the euphemism, "South Belgravia," were the cherished haunt of the smartest men in town. I say "men" advisedly, for no "man" could boast one jot of possession. Her own income gave her independence, and she laughed at the Richelieus and Rochesters of the *foyer* and the *coulisses*. Of course, one or two men more enterprising than the rest sought by every means to capture what, by reason of its impossibility of capture, appeared a hundredfold more attractive than it possibly was, and by force of constant pressure came very near breaking, if not wearing away, the stone; but, on the whole, there was no getting over the fact that Mahmouré remained, through sheer disinclination, her own mistress—and nobody else's. She had plenty of "episodes" but no "histories."

Why follow her amid the thousand scenes of passion, real and pretended, that, like every beautiful theatrical Bohémienne, she passed through—amused sometimes, excited sometimes, disgusted often, but touched, never. She kept the foremost rank in her profession until, weary of the reiteration of unsought conquest, she sought the New World. With all London at her feet, she travelled three thousand miles to find the Pygmalion who should quicken this worldly Galatea of European Bohemia.

Just before she left London, a celebrated journalist, who led a light-hearted life of libel and lickings, said to her:

"Dear child, why don't you marry Lord Blank? Acting as the Countess of Blank over the water, you would make your fortune—besides, it would be such fun writing paragraphs about it; I haven't had such a lovely chance since my wife bolted with D——."

"Thanks," she had replied; "sorry I can't oblige you—but never mind. Get my obituary ready for an emergency, and I'll leave you my diary to work from."

Thus she reached New York; and there, shutting herself up, she abandoned the world which she found took such vast amusement out of her, and gave her none in return, living a life of the closest retirement, a retirement from which she only emerged from time to time with some old friend of her earlier days.

By this time Mahmouré's age was—well, never mind; I didn't intend to begin the sentence.

And thus four years sped by, during which she worked hard and successfully as ever. She was the very incarnation of health, the wonder of all who saw her, so fresh and girlish was she; for all the world judged her life—of which they knew nothing—to be what it might have been had she so willed it. For in the New World, as in the Old, she inspired deep, wild passions which to her were mere pathological curiosities. She had caprices, of course! but they were not what she wanted; and at last she became resigned and made up her mind that love, the crowning joy of womanhood, was not to be hers.

* * * * * * *

The end came terribly and suddenly. The wild, irregular years of artist life succeeded at last in undermining the gigantic constitution, and one day, in the middle of a peal of laughter, she fell to the ground, dyeing the white frou-frou of laces, the folds of silk, her white satin couch, and the masses of heavy exotic flowers with which she loved to deck herself, with the crimson life-blood that welled from some unseen injury. The picture was an apposite termination to her unconventional life, as it appeared when, lying unconscious, they found her an hour later, incarnadined as if with her very soul's self—the poor little feet now so limp in their pink satin slippers, with the crushed mass of sensuous flowers, their waxy whiteness scarce whiter than the lifeless features of what had been an hour before—Mahmouré di Zulueta.

For five long, weary months she lay between life and death, and then, her lovely figure, her overflowing vitality, her voice,—all, save her beauty, which remained, chastened and refined by her interview with the Dark Angel,—things of the past, Mahmouré realized that the end of her artist-life was come, and relinquishing the Bohemia of Thespis, she turned to that of the Muses, and drawing upon her rich store of experience, adopted a life of literature, seeking the acquaintanceship and companionship of its masters.

It was shortly after this that Paul du Peyral was presented to ber in the foyer of the Metropolitan Opera House—and the introduction was a complete success.

When first Paul du Peyral had met Mahmouré di Zulueta they had immediately cemented between themselves a merry bond of good-fellowship. Each respected the talents of the other; on her side there was a certain curiosity to examine the handsome young Southerner who had led such a laughing, conquering life among the women of two continents. They had taken up their cues the first time he took advantage of her permission to call upon her, and had engaged in a brilliant little battle of epigram, in which they had talked much irresponsible philosophy and cheap cynicism, and had scoffed at love right merrily, though, in the minds of both, there arose Balzac's axiom, "*qui parle d'amour fait l'amour,*" to talk of love is to make love—she, amused by the contrast between his looks and his speech, the one so young and the other so old; and he, delighted at finding that the woman he had known by sight and name so long, was gifted with a mental freedom so essentially identical with his own. And so their first interview had passed, leaving nothing but an interest inspired by each in the other's mind, with enough danger mingled with it to make them await with impatience their next.

It soon came, and was soon repeated. She used to curl herself up on the divan, whilst he walked about, and, half seriously, and half laughingly, talked about himself or exchanged epigrams with her on platonic friendship, which they professed a belief in outwardly and confessed to ridiculing inwardly. They resembled nothing so much as gymnasts delighting in their own danger, as they danced on a tight-rope of platitude stretched across the gulf of passion.

This operation was actively proceeding one evening when a footstep and a knock announced the approach of some guest or other. As she rose to open to the new-comer, almost unconscious of the significance of her words, she said hurriedly, "Sit him out, whoever he is!" and admitted an old and evidently harmless "family friend." He was one of those good, innocent creatures who attach themselves to beautiful women in this capacity, regretting every moment of their lives their harmlessness and innocence, but clinging to these attributes feverishly as their sole excuses for existence.

His entry hastens the *dénouement*. She has held herself in check when alone with the man who, in her soul, she has begun to long for with all the passion of her wild Oriental nature, and has purposely held herself at something of a tension, from pride rather than from prudery, so anxious is she not to let the wooing appear to be hers. But now she revels in the luxury of "letting go," protected as it were by the presence of Unnecessary Respectability. Her wondrously supple body, following the dictates of her scarce-formed passion, now writhes itself upon the divan into a thousand unconsciously exquisite *poses*. Slight though it is, Paul du Peyral, deeply versed in the ways of woman, sees the change, notes the deeper colour on the lips, the brighter light in the dark eyes, and he knows that the end is not far off now. She talks to the Unnecessary Friend with a freedom, an utter disregard for conventionality, and a reckless gayety that make the Unnecessary Friend's mental hair stand on end. He also cannot make out why the youthful stranger does not go away, according to the rules laid down in the "Complete Manual of Etiquette for Gentlemen," but finally, after having made several heroic attempts to dislodge him, all of which are epigrammatically parried, and leave him doubtful whether the youthful stranger is a paragon of politeness or of impertinence, he resigns himself, takes up his unwilling hat, and leaves them.

Now that they are really alone a fear arises in the minds of both lest by precipitation the analysis may be spoilt—to borrow a phrase from the laboratory. He knows thoroughly well how one false note would jar her beyond possibility of re-established harmony, so, adopting the tactics of Fabius Maximus Cunctator on an historic occasion, he waits. She has thrown herself back on the divan and signed to him to sit by her side.

"May I?" says he, and sinks among the cushions at a virtuous distance.

Why can she think of nothing clever to say? All she *does* say is, "Is not this a lazy lounge to lie about on?"

"Delicious!" he answers; "but then everything about you is so restful, so soothing. Do you know, for a nervous man, as I am (though it doesn't appear), it is an exquisite pleasure to be with you, to sit near you, to touch you?" He has taken up one of her hands, and is softly, nervously, playing with the fingers. "Do you mind my playing with this? it is so pretty."

"Oh, not at all!" in the same tone as she would refuse another cup of tea.

"Have you ever been magnetized? do you believe in electro-biology?" he says, gently passing his fingers up to her elbow and drawing them back with a sensuous, lingering pressure.

"I don't know—see if you can do it."

He is apparently wholly and entirely taken up with his experiment, giving her a chance to raise her guard, as it were. He does not look at her, and so, after awhile, she relaxes; a languor born of his wonderful magnetic touch envelops her, and she looks at him, as she thinks, unseen. His face is so tranquil, she cannot decide if it is science which at each magnetic pass leads his hand nearer to her shoulder. Her sleeve is loose, he has raised it—for purposes of his scientific experiment. He draws his sensitive fingers down her arm very slowly as he says, "How lovely these little blue veins are! see this one, for instance."

He is evidently very much interested in "this one," for his head gets nearer and nearer till his lips touch the extended arm, and rest there warm and moist. A deadly stillness prevails, as, with an intense difficulty, she suppresses the tremor caused by the pressure of his lips; but she forgets that the very suppression has caused a contraction of the muscles that he has felt and interpreted. When he raises his head there is a humidity about his eyes which makes it very difficult for her to preserve her impressive appearance. He makes no movement, but only looks, with that sweet, damp look, till she can endure no longer. She raises herself a little from the cushions as if to speak, and then sinks back, a little nearer to the silent, imploring face.

He will not advance one step apparently. Suddenly, after a little movement, as if of pain, she takes the comb from her hair, and the glorious mass falls all over her, reminding him of the picture of the Magdalen in the Pitti Palace. Its subtle perfume seems to envelop him, and, plunging his hands among the glistening threads, he buries his face in it, almost with a sob. She remains very, *very* still. At last he whispers:

"How exquisite!—and how sweet of you to let me!" And he fills the mass of bronze gold with wild kisses, till she, with a rapid movement, clasps her hands around his neck and draws his lips to hers.

He seems all entangled in her sweet, sinuous embrace. At last he takes his lips from hers for a moment, and gazes through her half-closed eyes, and then, with a little cry, he gathers her up in his arms and clasps her, panting, and almost senseless, to his bosom.

* * * * * * *

"If you would only love me a little! I know I don't deserve it; all men say that, I believe; but in my case it's true, for I was always worthless. Won't you help me to a new life?"

As he spoke he crushed the little figure again in his arms; her answer was scarcely audible, so close had she laid her head against his heart: "Do you know how near to death I am?" and, as he pressed her closer to him, the wan light died out of her face and she seemed transfigured. A moment before, when he had wound his arms about her, her features had been worn and weary, scarce showing a trace of reason for the worship that had been hers, and was hers still. True hearts had ached to see her look as she looked now, and to hear her confess the wealth of her passionate love in every quiver of her rich, low voice.

For now her face lit up with the glory of a passion hitherto unknown in her wild, brilliant life; the veil of sadness and sickness faded, and left a face, whose charm we are powerless to judge—can only feel. It is not beauty, but something so fascinating, so strange, that even the fresh young face of a beautiful girl might remain unnoticed beside it, though she is on that borderland between youth and age so dreaded by a woman who has had a far greater portion than her share of the world's admiration and man's homage at her feet.

And he who holds the little figure in so close an embrace—look at him as he stands, glorified by his perfect youth and strength. Tall, heavily but lithely built, a strong head set massively on such shoulders as woman loves to look upon, and fears, in spite of herself. A hero to the backbone, though born in some little village of Louisiana, with his long, fair hair and blue-gray eyes, handsome as a man of his size should be, though not formed on the perfect lines which constitute an artist's ideal. His mouth, soft, gentle, and sensual, is too heavily formed for beauty, though it is in keeping with himself, for it seems to promise so much in the way of individuality; the chin is firm but not too heavy or coarse, with a good-natured dimple in it which is one of the principle charms of the face. He is much older than his age; many who have lived his years are boys, but he is a man in every sense of the term. How he can have absorbed so much life as he has is a mystery, as yet; but judged, even as she judges him, by the fierce critical light of the greater world which she knows exoterically and esoterically so well, he comes unharmed through the ordeal. "*Si jeunesse savait, si viellesse pouvait!*" said the Sage. Well, his is a *jeunesse qui sait et qui peut!*

A great fire of joy is in her eyes, for she had honestly believed that no power of man could bring her back to life and love in the world, and all this shines in her face as she answers him once more: "Do you know how ill I am?" For she would not take advantage of the impulse of a moment, though fraught with such insane happiness and intoxication as this.

"I know," he answers, kissing her senses away, "I know; but you shall live again and your veins shall throb with the pulses of my love. I will give you life in which to forget your foolish fancies."

"Why have you come to disturb my life?" she says, after a pause. "I know how much older I am than you. I am not strong enough to love you as I might. *Don't* play with me." This, almost imploringly.

"What is age to us who have only just begun to live?" he answers.

And so she resists no more, but lies in his arms, just as he had lifted her up and laid her on the cushions of the divan; her lips are close to his, and then she knows of nothing save of that wild embrace, is conscious of nothing save the soft touch of his finely moulded hands. At last, as if to wake himself from some exquisite dream, he rises to his feet and looks down upon her.

* * * * * * *

At parting, whilst he holds her in his arms, he says, almost malignantly:

"Never let us injure one another by word, or deed, or thought; for two such enemies as we should be, this world is far too small."

No other words, no protestation of devotion could have given her so full a measure of joy; for a savage love is the only one possible for her, gentle though all her life has seemed to be. She stands before him, looking up into his face, on hers a wonder, a curiosity, a questioning that seems to say, "Why did you seek me? what can be the reason? How have I won you?" After a long look she murmurs, as her hands cling to his arms that are clasped round her waist:

"I think you are right—there is no middle course for us."

There is nothing very clever, or original, or significant in the few words, but a look creeps into her face which does not fit the soft features—it is the expression of some beautiful wild animal, fraught with all the jealous intensity of passion, revealing—dimly, though indeed revealing—a cruel, wild love that kills rather than relinquishes its object.

Fascinated, both of them, their lips meet and part silently, and leave them quivering—and so he goes out into the night leaving her transfigured.

She looks into the glass critically, searchingly : she hurries away an instant and then, returning, looks again. The bronze-gold wrapper she had worn has fallen off, leaving her swathed in a gown of soft, clinging white silk, which is bound around her in sinuous folds—even illness has been powerless to rob her of the supple grace that she inherits from her Greek ancestors. She looks at the reflection, evidently satisfied ; then a doubt grows up within her and she turns to another glass, thinking the first may have flattered :—no, the reflection is still good to look upon ; her lips are crimson with excitement, and give greater beauty to her dazzling, perfect teeth : she looks fixedly, without conceit, as if appraising to its exact value each feature, seeking to justify in her dreadfully wise mind all that the last six hours have brought. With the memory, her knees give away beneath her and she stumbles into the cushions of the divan, and as she almost unconsciously continues to balance the pros and cons, the last remaining spark of reason dies amid the ashes of memory, and, with a big sigh, Mahmouré di Zulueta sinks to sleep.

With the practiced indiscretion of the romancist and historian, I have betrayed the confidence of the early sunbeams, and already the reader has assisted, in the spirit, at the waking of Mahmouré. Little by little she roused herself, and began the indolent and luxurious operation of clothing her little, fantastic body, whilst she sipped her coffee, and at intervals embarked on the arduous undertaking of crunching an atom of toast ; for, like all Oriental women, it was with the greatest difficulty that Mahmouré could be induced to feed like a Christian—which she was not and had no intention of becoming. She preferred to spoil her appetite and ruin her constitution with sweets and strange groceries, which later called forth Paul's dictum that "Mahmouré lived in a state of chronic *hors d'œuvres*, physically, mentally, and morally!" It was nearly one o'clock before she was what she called dressed, and, robed or rather wrapped in crossing and recrossing folds of white china silk, with a little Greek jacket of gold embroidery on a burnt-sienna ground, she punched the cushions of the divan into a comfortable nest, and settled herself among them with a scrap of embroidery, the last novel sent her from Europe by its illustrious author, and a writing-pad whereon to make a show of writing letters that never got written.

She was cuddled up thus, diffusing around her a quaint fragrance of sandal-wood, of myrrh, and of Tonquin, when a card was brought her: "*Mr. Paul du Peyral.*" "Ask him in? Certainly!" And it was thoroughly characteristic of the woman, that, instead of arranging a fold here, a ribbon there, and giving a precautionary touch to her hair, to receive the natural enemy—man, she merely stretched herself out a little more comfortably among the cushions, and held up her hand to be kissed by Paul, who had almost to kneel on the divan by her side for the purpose.

"I'm so glad you've come," said she; "it proves at any rate that it's all real. I was beginning to wonder if I hadn't been sent to sleep by the 'family friend,' and that you had both left me to a pleasing, but wearing kind of dream."

"No," replied he, "it was all exquisitely real—and, being so, what do you think of it?"

"I don't know what to think. I never felt like it before—it's all new to me. Suggest something, please."

"I wonder whether you would act on my suggestion."

"Certainly—if it's feasible."

"And supposing it isn't feasible?"

"Well—I should try;" this with an air of lazy but interested curiosity.

"Let us marry one another!"

With a sudden movement she started into a sitting posture, and thus, her arms clasped around her knees, she remained, her brown eyes wide open and gazing into his with an expression of lively amazement.

"You suggest to marry me—you who know three things that would 'make the heart of the stoutest quail,' as they say in inexpensive fiction? First, my age; second, the whole of my inconsequent life; and third, that my illness has left me a mere shattered wreck of womanhood."

"Certainly—and those three things I meet with three incontrovertible facts. First, a woman is as old as she looks, and you look about my age; besides, your real tale of years give you an experience that makes you more maddeningly fascinating to me than any girl between seventeen and five-and-twenty could be. Second, your 'inconsequent' life is at an end, for I shall be your last love, just as you are my first. Speaking properly, a woman's last love is the only kind of love that can satisfy the first love of a man. Besides, your love for me can only be terminated by the death of one of us, for I shall love you till I die, and if you were unfaithful to me I should kill you without a moment's hesitation. And third, true, your health is shattered, therefore it is necessary that you should not only be taken care of as only a husband can take care of you, but also that, should I die, you should inherit what little property I have, as only a wife can inherit. I might almost say to you, in fact, as M. Le Comte de Nocé said to Mlle. de Pontivi, '*Voulez vous être ma veuve?*'—will you be my widow?—for my life is full of dangers, and I might die any moment."

"Paul, you overwhelm me! A man of the world, such as you are, cannot be blind to the fact that marriage with Mahmouré di Zulueta would be ruin to your scheme of existence, which depends, as you yourself have told me, on your social position."

"*Chère amie*, your words are like those of a printed book with the leaves in it. What you say—as I expected you would say—is perfectly true, but why and how, you can scarcely guess. Curl yourself up among your cushions; I am going to expound my plan with a long story."

"Go on, *mon ami.*"

"I, Paul du Peyral, aged twenty-eight, descendant of a Franco-Spanish alliance, rejoicing, as few of us Creoles do, in the possession of a certificate of legitimate original birth and ancestry, live, move, and have my being by a caprice—the caprice of a cranky old Southern gentleman whom I had the good fortune to please at a moment when he had had what the Irish call "an elegant row" with his entire family. I was left an orphan at sixteen, and, more from pity than from anything else, was adopted as companion, assistant, secretary, steward, or whatever else you like to call it, by an old bachelor who lived a few miles from Baton Rouge, by name Casimir Préault, and who led a solitary, woman-hating life, engrossed in the studies of the indigenous mosquito, the cosmopolitan house-fly, and the naturalized London sparrow. He was very wealthy, and the premonitory symptoms of his demise were consequently watched with cheerful solicitude by his only living relations, the Préaults of New Orleans, of Louisville, and sundry other cities of the South. Now, this old gentleman's nearest living relative was a cousin, by name Victor Préault, whom he cordially hated, and for whose benefit he used continually to devise irritating and ingenious schemes of disappointment. The interest which I educated myself to take in the morals of the mosquito, the haunts of the house-fly, and the pathology of the common sparrow, in spite of my more absorbing interest in psychology, suggested to him a scheme for the disinheriting of Victor Préault, which, however, was tempered by a more or less genuine affection for his cousin's only daughter, Daphne Préault, whom he adored in spite of that young lady's aversion for him, an aversion which rendered futile a cherished scheme of his for the marrying of the said young person to his *protégé*, Paul du Peyral. He consequently made a will, the ingenuity of which has always inspired my profoundest respect. He made a disposition of his entire property to trustees, in trust to pay the entire income to me, on certain conditions and hampered by certain directions. First, I was directed to marry Miss Daphne Préault, whom I had never seen. If she formally refused to marry me, the said income was directed to be paid to me, so that I might be in a position to prosecute his and my hobbies in elegant independence—to wit, psychology, and the studies of the mosquito, the house-fly, and the sparrow. But the will further contained a proviso that, should I ever marry anyone other than the young lady aforesaid, the said income was to be paid thenceforward to Miss Préault; and in the event of my death the same thing was to take place, she being meanwhile invested with a power to dispose of her reversionary interest in the estate, by will, in case of her pre-deceasing me. Now, I am prejudiced against, rather than in favour of, this young woman, and this is one of the reasons I have never married, in spite of the conspiracies of designing mammas, ignorant of the provisions of my benefactor's will. The other reason is, that until I saw you I never loved any woman sufficiently to make her my wife—you alone have the mentality, apart from your exquisite personality, which tempts me to throw up everything; but I have thought of a plan that obviates this latter very painful necessity, though I have, by this time, money enough of my own to render me mildly independent. My plan is this. I am naturally very carefully watched, both by my trustees, and on behalf of Miss Préault, who is, I believe, in Europe somewhere, having gone thither on the death of her father some years ago. We must elude their vigilance, and it may be done in this way: we will go away somewhere and be married very quietly, and then we can return here and go on as we should go on anyhow, only that in the eyes of the world, should they ever guess the completeness of our connection (which is unnecessary, if we are careful), you will be my mistress, whilst between ourselves you will be my wife, and will assert your position after my death, in respect of my separate personal estate. I ask this because I love and admire you—two very different things, and seldom concomitant—from the bottom of my soul, and I verily believe that the knowledge that you *are* my wife will have an excellent effect on both of us. Only, before the world I shall be still Paul du Peyral the scientist, and what is of far greater interest to the world—the bachelor; whilst you will continue to reign in the Bohemia that is so dear to you, as Mahmouré di Zulueta. Say, then, darling, will you take this new lease of life from me?"

The womam, at the conclusion of this speech, had buried her head in the cushions. She kept her face thus hidden for a few minutes, during which neither of them spoke, then, raising her eyes to his, she encircled his neck with her arms—he had sunk among the cushions beside her—and drew his head down to hers, whispering:

"Paul, Paul, my darling, are you sure you will not regret this?"

"Never, sweetheart."

"But this other woman—it is not fair to her."

"Ah—bah! she is nothing to me, and you are everything. Sooner or later this property must be hers; at present she is ignorant of all; let her continue so. I wrote immediately I came into the property and offered myself to her; she refused me insultingly, and her representatives have never ceased trying to harass me; fortunately, however, though an amateur, the old gentleman was too good a lawyer. If you love me, do not let any thought of these horrible people interfere with our happiness. Tell me, is it 'yes' or 'no'?"

The "Yes" was felt rather than heard; and radiant with hopes, and looking younger than ever in her new-found happiness, Mahmouré di Zulueta lay almost unconscious in her lover's arms.

CHAPTER III.

"L'AMOUR EST ENFANT DE BOHÊME."

Many are the pros and cons of London weather. It has been said of us Londoners, and I fear with truth, that we have the most horrible weather in the world, especially in autumn and winter; but we can boast with equal truth that nowhere else in the world do we find an in-door comfortableness that renders even a foggy day delightful, as we do in London—nowhere else can one be so unspeakably cosy as in a London snuggery whilst the elements practise for another Deluge, or the world outside grows white and soft with snow. Well, the day after Gabriel Hawleigh's party was "a foggy day"—and by this I mean a day as foggy as London knows how to make it when she gives her mind to the subject—a day that reminded one of the pictures of London by Leech in the early numbers of *Punch*, wherein link-boys flit like the familiar demons of the fog.

It was useless for the Princess Daphne to attempt to work, for the fog lay on the glass of the skylight in her studio roof like a curtain; so she drew an arm-chair close up to the fire, lit the gas, and took up a book—one of those cynical modern romances of immoral psychology which combine the somniferousness of the old-fashioned novel with the innocuousness of the nursery-rhyme. The warm red and brown lights flashed by the fire amid the encircling gloom, the gas-jet with its shade, and the girl's brown dress made a charming picture in the stillness of the fog; but the Princess was not sorry to have it disturbed by a ring at the bell, closely followed by the appearance of Eric Trevanion. He also had been driven by the "murk" from his soul-elevating easel, and his thoughts had brought him to the door of the Princess Daphne's cottage.

"Ah! Mr. Trevanion," said she, as she saw who it was; "to what am I indebted for the honour?"

"To the weather, Princess, which gave me an excuse I was ardently desiring."

"I'm sure you require no excuse to call on me; if you're let in, it means that I am glad to see you—or anybody. If I'm busy I 'sport my oak'! To-day I am honestly dull, trying to read this miserable production. I've formulated an axiom this morning, which is as follows: 'Modern literature is the apotheosis of truism.' Formerly everything was paradox; a writer thought he had only to state the glaringly improbable or contradictory, to catch the popular taste: to-day he says sapiently, 'To put on one's hat wrong side foremost is very uncomfortable;' and instead of saying, 'Well, what of it? we know that!' his readers hold up their hands and cry, 'Dear me, how *true!* what an *observer* he is! why, we've often noticed that ourselves!' Yes, modern literature is the apotheosis of truism, and the criterion of its excellence is piracy in the United States. If a book is clever enough to say nothing that we don't know already, it is clever enough to be stolen in America. Such is fame!"

And the Princess laughed a little, silvery laugh, which stopped short as she saw the smile die away on the face of Eric Trevanion.

"Why, Sir Knight of the Rueful Visage," said she, "what ill news shortens the smile which I expected as homage to my tirade against the novelist of to-day?"

"No ill news, Princess; only I'm puzzled. I can't make you out; you're so brilliant, and clever, and—all *that*, you know—and you're so absolutely by yourself in the world, I can't account for you; you're a kind of Sphinx to us all, and yet you talk more freely about yourself than anyone I have ever known. But it's never to the point. You know what I mean, though I can't say it," concluded he, helplessly.

"Well, are you another Davus, or will you be Œdipus?"

"I don't know who Davis is, unless he's the man who bought that academy picture of yours, and I never heard of the other gentleman," replied Eric, mendaciously, so as to hear Miss Préault's definition, which was bound to be interesting if not funny.

"Well, the Sphinx, you know, was a bewildering lady with a taste for cannibalism and conundrums."

"Yes, I know that."

"Davus was the journalist of the time, the regret of whose life was that he was not Œdipus, who was the contemporary Irving Bishop, and read the lady's thoughts."

"And what good did it do him?"

"No good; he would have married the Sphinx, or what was human of her, and killed what was animal and bad, and no doubt, like many a modern husband, would have been rather sorry for himself. As it is, I believe he married his mamma."

"But you are not the Sphinx really."

"Yes, I am. I am half-human and half-animal," returned the girl, gazing abstractedly into the fire. "There is a great deal in me that is terribly human, and there's an underneath side to my character which is terribly savage. I don't know which side troubles me most; and I don't know whether they will ever be separated from one another, and if they are, which will remain incarnate in Daphne Préault, and which will fly off into space;" she raised her eyes as she finished, and found Trevanion leaning forward in his chair, his wide-stricken eyes fixed upon her with an expression that fancy had often placed there for her before, but intensified, feverish, yearning.

"Princess! Daphne—you gave me my choice a minute ago whether to be Davus or the other man—let me be the other man—let me solve the riddle of your life for you. Surely you have seen how I worship you. I never thought I should dare to tell you of it, but I can't help it—I love you." He had taken one of her hands in his and was covering it with kisses; she did not try to take it away, but merely looked down with a gaze of infinite pity at him as she replied:

"Yes, I knew it, but it isn't to be. I would love you in return if I dared; but I cannot, I dare not, trust myself to love anyone: sooner or later you would discover all my badness and weakness, and then it would be all over. The unknown is always a goal for one's ambition; I am a goal for *yours*, which is, I fear, more than half curiosity. So long as you see me from a distance you wonder and do not question; touch me, and you would soon criticise; and when we criticise we soon despise. Eric, my dear friend, I like you far too well ever to show you that weak under side of my nature. Be a companion, a friend to me, if you will,—you are the only man who ever had the chance to be,—but a lover—never! Come, *mon ami*, we are merry Bohemians; don't let's trouble our life with the silly emotions of the outer world."

He had risen to his feet, and laying one arm upon the mantel-piece, was looking into the fire, leaning his head upon his hand. Her words troubled him; troubled him with a sensation that was neither pleasure nor pain, but confusion of thought. He brought her the armor of gold, but she refused it, almost inviting his offer of the armor of brass: she had offered him a kind of emotional Platonism, that made his heart beat high with hope, but refused his avowed love on the one plea that flatters a man whilst he will not accept it—her own unworthiness.

"But I want something more," he said; "I want your love."

"No, boy," she replied; "come to me for sympathy, for friendship, for assistance, for confession; but love—real love—only comes to a man once. It has come to you, but you don't see it; some day you will, and then you'll be very grateful to Daphne Préault for not engaging your heart, your soul, but only your brain."

"What do you mean?"

"I mean that I know a girl who loves you with her whole

heart. Ah! no; I am not going to tell you who it is, if you can't see for yourself: but when you are married you shall come here with your wife, and Daphne Préault will continue in the sunshine of your life the friendship that she inaugurated with you in a London fog. Now leave me alone, dear boy, and come here to tea with me to-morrow—you will have thought it over by then, and realized that it was for the best that I advised you."

So saying she gave him her hand to kiss, and with her little imperial gesture dismissed him. He stood looking at her humbly, helplessly, for a moment, and then—he was gone.

The Princess remained in the house just long enough to wrap herself in a cloak and put on a hat, and then started forth to call at the Hawleigh's. Here also she found work at the easel suspended, but Gabriel and Maye were lost in a cloud of harmony that seemed to make the very fog that had filtered into the studio vibrate with its passion. Daphne Préault did not disturb the musicians, but stood at the entry to the studio till the music should have ceased. When this moment arrived, Gabriel, violin in hand, flung himself onto the lounge, whilst Maye merely bent over the keys and seemed lost in reverie. It was Gabriel, in turning over on the couch, who first saw the magnificent figure standing in the flickering light, and springing to his feet, exclaimed,—

"*Princess!*"

At the word, Maye turned also and greeted the visitor, and then they all drew chairs to the fire and began to talk with daring originality about the weather.

"You have the advantage of me here," began Miss Préault, when this subject had been exhausted. "When you can't work you can play— sounds like a truism, doesn't it? but you know what I mean. Now *I* simply have to read or receive visits until I get tired of both, and seek congenial society here. Which do you prefer, Gabriel, the fiddle or the easel?"

"Well, really I hardly know," replied he; "sometimes I

wish I'd been brought up a professional musician instead of a painter, and at others I wouldn't give up painting if the triumvirate of ghosts of Stradivarius, Tourte, and Paganini came down and implored me to become a violinist by trade."

"And who are they?"

"The Trinity of the Fiddler's worship, the Princes of Fiddle-making, Bow-making, and Fiddle-playing. I invoke their names every time I take up my violin, and beg their shades to inspire me. Ah! I should never be an artist on the instrument; I should always remain a virtuoso."

"And what is the difference?"

"Well, it's the difference between the active and the passive: the artist is master of his violin, the virtuoso is its slave. Joachim, Viardot, Vieuxtemps were and are artists; Sarasate, Wilhelmj, Paganini, were and are virtuosi. Don't you see the difference? The artist can read at sight the most difficult music, and plays by note; the virtuoso plays more, as a rule, by ear, than otherwise. The artist strives after perfection of *technique* for the interpretation of the works of the great composers for the instrument; the virtuoso, on the other hand, aims at brillant execution for the interpretation of his own moods, his own thoughts, his own fantasies. That's what I do; and there are days when I wish I had given my whole time to it."

"Then, I suppose," remarked Daphne, "that, just as you are a virtuoso with your bow, Eric Trevanion is a virtuoso with the brush. Certainly he doesn't aim at perfection of *technique*, and certainly he tries to interpret his own moods, thoughts, and fantasies—and does so to his own satisfaction doubtless!"

"Well, yes; I think we may call Eric a virtuoso of the camel-hair; his impressions are hardly what one would call artistic—are they?"

"And what do you think about it, Maye?" queried the Princess.

"Do you know, I never thought of Eric as an artist. I

look upon his profession as a colossal joke, and an excuse for keeping untidy, artistic rooms."

"What do you think of him as a man?"

"Good gracious, Daphne, what an indiscreet question! Why, I think him a very worthy person, very bright and kind and all that; but I never made a study of him. Why ask *me?*" The girl did her utmost to make her light reply as meaningless and casual in tone as possible; but the flush that came over her face as she answered told the Princess the story she wanted to know.

"I wonder he has never married," she went on, vivisectionally.

"On the contrary," broke in Gabriel, "the wonder to me would be if any girl would ever be bold enough to take him, and be painted continually as a 'Note in Black and White,' 'A Crochet in White Worsted,' 'A Quaver in B Minor,' or something eccentric of that sort."

"I think," returned Miss Préault, abstractedly, "that he'd make some girl a perfect husband. He'd be so tender, and gallant, and chivalrous, and delicate."

Maye looked at her gratefully, and would have spoken, only Gabriel cut in, remarking:

"Well, I'm glad you think that, because he's madly in love with you."

"Of course he is—so are you," replied the girl, without turning a hair.

"Of course I am, but I'm not so badly bitten as Eric; I'm only at the stage of telling you so whenever I have a chance; he's got to the point of thinking it continually."

"Don't talk nonsense, Gabriel," replied the Princess, sharply.

"I am not talking nonsense: and look here; I wish you'd marry him and take him back to Cornwall or Dartmoor or wherever it is; he's ruining me—here am *I* painting nightmare pictures now."

"Oh! *where?* Show me."

"Under the seal of profoundest secrecy, I'll show you the great work for the next Academy."

So saying, Gabriel uncovered the canvas on which he had been at work. It represented a London street, in a dense fog. In the foreground, lighted by a yellow blotch of street lamp, a blind itinerant fiddler was playing, apparently unconscious of the state of the atmosphere. A man and a girl were passing, wrapped up snugly, and laughing at one another. Under cover of the fog they had twined their fingers together as the girl held the man's arm tightly in hers; whilst the blind fiddler played on, in apparent ignorance of all. The painting was unfinished, hardly, indeed, more than roughed in, but the composition of the oblique vista of street was perfect, the balance of the figures was masterly, and the whole thing was toned in a manner which showed high artistic skill.

"But, my dear friend," said Daphne Préault, gravely, "this is really a great work if you finish it as you've begun. What shall you call it?"

"'Sunshine in the Fog,' I think, or perhaps, 'It's an ill wind blows nobody any good.' You see, I want to convey the idea that the blind fiddler is unconscious of the fog as well as of the happiness of the young couple flirting under his blind old eyes and under cover of the darkness. It shows that it might be an advantage to be sightless sometimes—you see, to him it's apparently an ordinary day, for the sunshine is in his soul as he hears the two go laughing by."

"Gabriel," said Daphne, "this will be a great picture—mark my words."

"Well, I hope so," said the boy; "it's time my undoubted talents were recognized by the Hanging Committee and the art-dealers. If this goes well, it will make a rent in the cloud, through which I may be enabled to shove some of my lesser masterpieces—known to the vulgar as pot-boilers."

"Well—a thousand congratulations! But I must go back to work, for the sky's clearing a little."

And with this she left them. In the drawing-room she found Mrs. Hawleigh.

"What do you think of the boy's picture, Daphne?" said she.

"I think it is going to be very great. What accounts for his sudden stride?"

"Can't you guess, dear?"

"Ah! And does *she* care for *him?*"

"Yes, I think so. Gratitude would make her do so, but I don't think it is necessary. He has worked hard enough for her, poor boy! I hope nothing will happen to disappoint him; it would be his death-blow, I think."

"Mrs. Hawleigh, forgive me, but has it never occurred to you that she might care for anyone else?—Eric Trevanion, for instance?"

"My dear, I have *feared* so sometimes, but when I see Eric with you, I feel easier about it. You know he adores you, I suppose."

"Yes."

"He has told you so—no doubt?"

"Yes."

"And do you care for him?—pardon me for asking, but I'm so anxious on Gabriel's account; do you care for Eric Trevanion?"

"Yes"—this almost in a whisper.

"And have you told him so?"

"No, I have not told him so."

"Oh! why not, dear? Think a moment—if you love Eric and would tell him so when he asks you, how happy we all should be—you—he—I—and those children in there."

"That boy, you mean, Mrs. Hawleigh?"

"And the girl too, dear; she knows Eric doesn't care about her, and if she knew that you returned his affection, she would give her whole heart undivided to Gabriel, and uninfluenced by that terrible thing, gratitude."

"I hardly know myself enough, Mrs. Hawleigh. Sometimes I am afraid when I think of marriage. There are two sides to my nature, one human and the other savage"—she was unconsciously drifting back to what she had told Trevanion—"and I know that marriage would kill the one and develop the other, and unless the man were a great, strong creature, I am terribly afraid that the human, womanly side of me would disappear. It's the way with all of us Southern American women; we can rule others, but require to be ruled ourselves; and I doubt if Eric Trevanion has it in his power to rule me, to keep me in his power when he gets to know all about the real Daphne Préault, with whom the Daphne Préault *you* know is hardly on speaking terms herself!"

"Oh! you do yourself injustice. All girls do when they are in love. Go and think it over, dear; I am sure you will see that what I say is for the best."

"Very well—I'll think it over."

"That's right—and remember that by making yourself and Eric happy, you are giving a new life to Gabriel and Maye, a new encouragement to him in his work, a new bulwark of defence to Maye, against the whims of her silly little heart."

The two women kissed one another, and the Princess Daphne walked back to her cottage.

It was situated at the other end of Holland Street, and was one of the little houses with a patch of garden in front of it to which I have alluded, in describing the street. When her father, Victor Préault of Baton Rouge, died, leaving her an income which, computed in American dollars, was statable in four figures, of which the first was only one remove from an unit, Daphne, alone in the world, strongly inclined to art, and averse to governess-ship, had struck her camp, and migrated direct to Holland Street, where her income warranted her in furnishing the little semi-detachment in which the scene I have described between her and Eric had taken place.

Her originality of invention and daring touch had quickly assured her artistic success, and her personality had gradually made for her a throne from which she ruled the colony with a beneficent and almost motherly sway. A better friend "the boys" had never had, and rumour chaunted a variegated though monotonous Iliad—paradoxical though it may seem, written down—of the way in which everyone had been obliged to go through the tortures of unrequited affection and refusal, before settling down into the ranks of the Princess's adoring subjects. The little house was charmingly furnished, and the studio into which the goddess of the place now stepped was characteristic of its denizen as only a studio can become. It was very large, and its general appearance reminded one more of a Roman *atelier* than anything else: its solid furniture consisted of a lounge covered with an enormous bear-skin, a rosewood writing-table, a miniature grand piano by Chickering, and a renaissance cabinet filled with a collection of the silver, ivory, and porcelain toys of the eighteenth and preceding centuries. Daphne Préault painted, as regards touch and subject, with the weird independence of the modern French school; and it seemed as if into her work, which had the minutia and detail of Meissonier, combined with the sensuous fantasy of Vedder and Blake, she flung without reserve the infinite shades of her complicated personality. One of her finest works—which she refused to sell—hung over the high oaken mantel-shelf; it represented Gabriel Hawleigh in his silk working shirt of morning, and "*autres choses*" of afternoon, his collar lying open, his feet thrust into morocco slippers, reclining on the bear-skin of the lounge, with his fiddle under his arm. Evidently he had got up in the middle of his work, seized by some musical whim or other, and, at the conclusion of his performance, had flung himself exhausted onto the fur; the Princess had insisted on painting him thus, and called it after Tourguenieff's marvelous story, "*Le Chant d'Amour Triomphant.*" It was an admirable specimen of her skill, and a great favorite among "the boys."

To-day, however, she did not paint, but lay till evening

almost motionless on the bear-skin, "not at home" to any-one, and revolving in her mind the events and conversations of the morning. A black woman—a negro servant who had accompanied her across the ocean four years before, brought her tea at five o'clock, and at half-past seven she went forth to dine in Queen's Gate, returning to bed and to sleep soundly till the sunrise woke her next morning.

What the result of the previous day's cogitations had been not even the practised indiscretion of the novelist is entitled to impart to his readers. It is enough for them to know that, to-day being bright, she worked hard at her Academy picture until Clytie, the darkie woman, bringing in the tea-tray at five o'clock, announced:

"Mr. Trevanion."

Daphne Préault rose, and extending her hand, said:

"*Bon chevalier!* sit down and drink tea and eat things, and then I'll tell you a programme I've made out for our amusement this evening, if you're disengaged."

"I'm always disengaged for you, Princess."

"Very good! that's as it should be. You must go away at six, and come back at half-past seven; I've got two stalls for the Parthenon, and want you to take me to see the new play. *Vi piace cosi?* Does my plan suit you?"

"Certainly," replied Trevanion; and they chatted easily and merrily on different subjects, avoiding the one which was uppermost in their minds, until the stated hour, when the young man, with a joyful "*Au revoir,*" left the girl to her important meditations, her more important dinner, and her most important toilette.

At half-past seven he was at the door with a hansom; and Eric Trevanion and Daphne Préault were bowled along in what Lord Beaconsfield, plagiarizing from Balzac, called "the gondola of the London streets," past Kensington and Knightsbridge, and down Piccadilly to the doors of the Theatre Royal Parthenon.

People may say what they like to the pyschological con-trary, but there is certainly something deliciously "*intime*" in the fact of driving alone with a woman, whether it be in the family coach, the discreet *coupé*, or the ordinary hansom. We are told that when the American young man "goes courting," he lavishes his substance on innumerable buggy rides with his young woman. I have passed much of my life in what Mr. Carnegie has called the "Triumphant Democracy," and have not observed this to be the case; but there is no denying the fact, that when, in the depth of the transatlantic winter, the snow is packed in a polished layer upon the face of the world, the transatlantic young man and the transatlantic young woman do eagerly patronize the sleigh known as a "cutter," wherein the pair sit very close together indeed, and the young man drives; or better still, the roomier form of sleigh in which, if I may be allowed the expression, they "snuggle" beneath the buffalo-robes, and the young man prevents the young woman from falling out when they turn sharp corners. The spring is consequently the season of love and marriage in America—as is, I believe, the case elsewhere, according to the poet; and the Englishman who said he preferred—as being less dangerous—sitting in a draught in a rocking-chair, with his feet in a tub of ice-water, jangling a bell, to the national winter pastime, must have experienced the joys of sleighing with a well-meaning, but *male*, companion. In Canada they toboggan, and this is a still more ingenious invention (or rather collaboration) of Eros and Hymen; and these things have their efficient counterparts in England, no matter what may be the vehicle that enforces an intimate physical propinquity.

Love is to a great extent a meteorological phenomenon, that is to say, it is largely a matter of atmosphere. Who has not experienced, on entering a woman's boudoir, the sensation that the whole atmosphere is deliriously saturated with her physical as well as mental personality? To a much greater extent is this noticeable in a brougham or *coupé*, where the area is even more circumscribed. How keen an observer have we considered to be the French author who describes the sensations of an amorous swain on finding himself reclining in a box upon wheels, practically enveloped in the draperies of his inamorata! Such *séances* are often, like spiritualistic functions, carried on in darkness and silence; but the mingling of atmospheres produces a mental excitement that has hurried many a domestic drama to its *dénouement*. And the Londoner who understands his hansom will agree with me. *She*—the She with a capital S—not unfrequently becomes as fascinating as the "She" described by Mr. Rider Haggard (even if she was not so before), when, with a flash of ankle and whiteness, she has stepped into the expectant hansom, and we have followed her, and then, by closing the doors, have covered our knees with the outlying regions of her opera-cloak and other "things." The celibate philosopher will agree with me that to order the "cabby" to "put down the glass" is fatal; the hansom then becomes worse than a *coupé;* the half-doors are bad enough! It is not necessary to talk; we have most of us observed that She leans more heavily upon our extended hand in getting out than she did on getting in.

Eric and Daphne were in love with one another. They said but little during the transit, but lounged, rather than sat, crushed against one another by the narrowness of the cab, and gave themselves over to the unrestrained enjoyment of their thoughts, trusting to the rattle of the vehicle to drown the almost audible beating of one heart, if not of two. Arrived at the doors of the Parthenon their eyes flashed strangely bright in the darkness, and both felt almost relieved that the ride was over, and that the play was there to obviate the necessity of conversation.

But between riding with a woman within the confines of a cab and sitting next to her in the stalls of a theatre there is little to choose; indeed, for harmlessness, I think the palm might be given to the former. We enter and take our seats, and then, passing an arm behind her, we help her to remove her wraps and reveal—for ourselves—the ivory skin, the rounded arms, and the delicious dress which has been hitherto hidden from us by the aforesaid wraps; and, in so doing, we envelop ourselves, as it were, in a cloud of the delicate fragrance of the perfumes with which women in all parts of the civilized world love to heighten the fascination to themselves. We settle ourselves luxuriously in our seats, and the play commences; after a moment the spirit moves us to rest our elbow on the arm of the stall; we find it already occupied, and draw our sleeve away again with a thrill! Next time we are more successful; the arm is unencumbered; she has leaned foward interested in the play: in a minute or two, the strain of attention relieved, she, in turn, rests her elbow on—well, on the arm of the stall, after we have apologized *sotto voce* and once more vacated the position. Then something in the play calls for a whispered comment, and a lovely head is bent close to our own to listen, and to require the remark to be repeated; then our heads separate, and for a few seconds we haven't an idea of what the play is all about. Next, the opera-glasses fall down, and we dive amidst a maelstrom—so it seems to us—of laces and stuffs to recover the same, whilst the prettiest hand in the world holds the maelstrom aside to facilitate the search, and the glasses are gently laid back in the place whence they originally fell. Next minute, the act-drop falls, the lights are turned up, and we chatter volubly about the play, uttering commonplace platitudes against which our intelligence would revolt in broad daylight, ask stupid questions which require and expect no answers, and answer at random questions that have not been asked.

The curtain rises on the next act—the act in which the love interest of the play develops. It is getting interesting; and now—quite unconsciously—both our elbows rest upon the intermediary arm, which has by this time assumed the *rôle* of the wall which separated Pyramus and Thisbe—not touching one another; that only happens—unconsciously also—about half-way through the act; and we are almost surprised to find that it is the case, when the act-drop falls once more, and turning to one another simultaneously, each reads in the other's eyes what each—we, that is—would have done under circumstances similar to those in the play. Between the second and third acts we chat reasonably, almost confidentially, on subjects quite personal, quite unconnected with the play we are witnessing, leaning back in our stalls, our shoulders almost, if not quite, touching one another. We are interrupted—almost surprised—when the lights in the house go down, and the stage lights up once more. There is little or no pretence during the last act; we sit as close together as circumstances—*i.e.* the people behind—will allow. As the story before us draws to its climax, and everything ends happily, we fancy we can hear one another breathe; and when the concluding sentence, often the best-written in the whole play, is drowned by the rustle of people struggling into their outer garments, and groping for hats which have somehow gone off on voyages of discovery by themselves, we carefully and with procrastination—which is the soul of business, in spite of the proverb—wrap her up, in dire terror lest the night air should attack that beautiful throat, and we are rewarded by ever so slight a pressure of the hand that rests on our arm as we reach the outer world and embark once more in the insidious hansom, which we direct, with an air of luxurious proprietorship, to drive to *her* house.

On the application of the above analysis to the circumstances of my story I offer no comment. Eric Trevanion and Daphne Préault witnessed the performance at the Parthenon—and drove home to Holland Street.

"Waters, both strong and mild, with biscuits and a fire will be in the studio," said the Princess Daphne; "won't you come in for an instant before you stroll down the street?"

"Thanks! with pleasure;" and they went in.

Clytemnestra, or for short, "Clytie," the ebony tirewoman of the Princess Daphne, had removed her opera-cloak, her fan, her gloves, and other impedimenta, and had left the pair alone. Whilst Eric busied himself with the innocuous comestibles that stood on a little table by the fire, Daphne threw herself onto the lounge and sat, lazily watching him, and prosecuting a search after conversation. Between them there had sprung up a sudden restraint which was quite unusual; the pauses in the conversation were longer than necessary, the stray remarks were mostly irrelevant, the observations were spasmodic and impersonal. They who had been accustomed to compare their feelings with perfect frankness seemed conscious that a tacit understanding had been raised between them, had grown up without their knowledge, and forbade a word that might invoke—they knew not what! Who can say which hand-pressure, which tremor of the eyelid, which quiver of the lips had shown them that a chapter of their lives was ended? Who can say which lightning-flash of passion had riven the cloud of their happy *camaraderie*, showing the heaven of love beyond? Whatever might be their future, the unconscious carelessness of their past companionship was left behind forever.

And now she leaned forward and gazed into the fire, and he could look at the exquisite lines of her neck and back. Her hair grew exactly to the "beauty line," and being drawn up rather high on the head left a few lovely little soft curls at the back of the neck, their dusky warmth making her white skin still more dazzling and cool. After a moment of eloquent silence she said:

"Eric, come here."

He approached her, and impulsively he sank on his knees on the hearth-rug, at her side and a little behind her, and, feeling as though it were too good to be true—some deceitful vision that he feared to dispel—he remained in rapt wonder looking at her, scarcely breathing.

Was it a simple accident, or the unconscious magnetism of love that drew Daphne's head back toward him, back until his lips almost touched the little curls? and then, he breathed rather than imprinted a kiss, as if by accident, upon the beautiful neck. As he did so, with a strong shudder she leant back in the lounge, and with little more than curiosity in her face, though a delirious weight lay on her heart, she said in a steady, clear voice:

"My poor boy, you will only be more miserable if I kiss you—and some day you will blame me—"

Before she can say any more, he has construed her words for himself, and such a torrent of kisses rains upon her hair, her eyes, her lips, that she is unable to frame a thought or utter a word, but gives herself up to the moment. The subtle charm of the tender violence little by little overpowers her, a stifled sob breaks from her, and she turns deathly pale. If he had understood women better he would not have taken his arms from about her, as he does for an instant, and ask her if she feels faint! The sound of his voice destroys the spell; she puts him from her almost roughly, with a nervous force that surprises him, and says:

"Go—go—or I shall never forgive you;" and as he tries to speak, she interrupts him, saying, "Eric! I know I am in your power—but I am only a woman—go, for God's sake! go, and don't take advantage of that power."

It is a terrible temptation to him as he holds the gorgeous figure in his arms, and he hesitates: then his manhood conquers; he rises with a little stagger, and without daring to look at her, he hurries from the studio. The front-door slams, and he is gone. And is she grateful to him for his obedience? Ah! who knows?

With the sharp click of the outer gate-latch, distinctly audible in the stillness of the night, Daphne awoke, as from the influence of a dream. She rose, straightening and smoothing the folds of her dress as if to brush away the touch of the man, and, walking to the fire, stretched out her icy-cold fingers to the blaze. As the warmth began to circulate in her veins the softness faded from the great brown eyes, and in its place came a calm, questioning, introspective look, which would have done more to pull Eric Trevanion together, could he have seen it, than the radical brandy-and-soda that he gave himself on reaching his rooms.

Then, turning from the fire, she lit a cigarette and began

pacing up and down the studio. It was characteristic of her to vivisect herself with far less mercy than she would have shown to another woman; her code had ever been, "mercy and extenuating circumstances for her feeble fellow-creatures; but for herself!—the hard, uncompromising Truth." So she figuratively placed her inmost being in a sort of glass case, put it upon the piano, turned up the lights, and proceeded to examine its intricacies critically. No flaw escaped her—no weakness was condoned—no excuse of sex was pardoned. What were her feelings as regarded Eric Trevanion? —*this* was the burden of her investigation; did she wish he had remained?

Yes, she would answer herself truthfully, she wished he had not been so obedient—or so English. Why had he not forced her to say she cared for him as she had never cared for man before? Should she marry him? Was what she now felt the love she had so often read about, and had never believed in or sympathized with? Hardly. She had no more desire to marry him now than she had had before the events of the night which was now shivering with the chill of approaching dawn. No, she wanted to be free—but she wanted Eric as the companion of that freedom; but even with all her independence of spirit, could she stretch the mantle of Bohemia so wide as to cover *that?* Hardly. But the weird confusion in the glass case said plainly, "I want liberty, and what is liberty without him?—a mere simulacrum of independence." This strange Creole girl, against whom no word of reproach had ever been breathed, was sensible that before morning her vital choice would be made. She could do as she pleased on payment of the cost—Liberty and Eric. But the cost was enormous; in this one venture she was called upon to sink the entire capital of her womanhood. She brought the whole of her faculty of mental concentration—so rare in woman—to the solution of this point.

The recklessness and fatal danger of the choice attracted rather than repelled her. Her savage nature, once aroused, found an added charm in the thought of thus gambling away her most precious possession; in her perfect chastity she could look upon the commission of a sin in the eyes of the world without a shock. Why do I continue? In seeking to show the complicated nature of Daphne's personality I cannot escape being either minute to weariness or vague to incomprehensibility. It was this very confusion of characteristics that was one of her greatest fascinations.

For hours the brain battled with the heart—the spirit with the flesh; and as the bell of the neighboring Carmelite Monastery roused the monks to Lauds and Prime, Daphne Préault seated herself at the writing-table and wrote to Eric:

"I have fought, and I have conquered. I am yours—come to me."

CHAPTER IV.

MESMERISM.

In the society of every city in the world, I suppose there must be, by some inscrutable law of nature, *some* nasty people—probably to make us appreciate the nice ones. Whatever may be the reason, however, there is no doubt that New York, at the time that I chronicle, was no exception to the rule; and even in the fascinating cosmopolitan society of the modern Gotham there were a few nasty people, of whom undoubtedly the nastiest were by common consent the Van Baulk'ems. Mrs. Odious Van Baulk'em regarded herself as handsome, and as select in her strife after social position. I have often observed that people who refuse to recognize those of their own class in life, and seek to entertain their social superiors, usually find themselves reduced to entertaining the sediment of a class superior to their own—the impecunious and shady ones, who will go anywhere for a dinner and daughters with money—and so entertaining, fondly imagine their society to be "select." Well! select it is; but it is a selection of the riff-raff of a class into the solid substance of which they would give their eyes to be admitted. The Van Baulk'ems were of this complexion, and this was the kind of society that one would meet at their house on Fifth Avenue should one be so imprudent as to pass through its portals on the strength of one of the innumerable cards that Mrs. Van Baulk'em was in the habit of flipping all over New York, *via* the "Society List," and especially among the young men who might possibly feel justified by their constitutions in "going in for" the angular and highly-coloured charms of Miss Van Baulk'em, or the clever, pretty vulgarity of Miss Parthenia Van Baulk'em, a young lady suspected of society journalism, who had been hawked round Europe and America for years, in search of an adventurous swain. But such had not turned up; and though it seemed likely that the millions of the elder might attract a penniless European of doubtful antecedents, the younger, Miss Parthenia Van Baulk'em, showed no inclination to "go off."

From this very slight sketch of a very unpleasant family, the reader will have gathered that the Van Baulk'ems' house was hardly one where Paul du Peyral would elect to spend much of his leisure time; but as, on his first arrival in the city, he had dined at the house on Fifth Avenue, and had allowed himself to be mildly lionized as a social *savant* by the family; and as, moreover, there was something essentially *piquante* and refreshing about the ready repartee of Miss Parthenia, he would periodically drop in on Mrs. Van Baulk'em's reception day, and converse with that young person for a space. One of these occasions took place about two months after his marriage with Mahmouré di Zulueta, and, in obedience to the laws of cause and effect, that visit materially influenced the course of the history I am recording in these pages. The opera season had recently commenced, and Paul had unconsciously made himself very interesting and instructive on the subject of the German school of opera, with Wagner as the text of his homily.

"Why don't we see you more at the opera, Mr. du Peyral?" had queried the fair Parthenia.

"Because I have but little time for such pleasures. My work is of a kind that appreciates, nay requires, the peacefulness of the night hours; and again, the conversation for which one goes to the opera in New York is so cruelly interrupted by the music that one has no chance of appreciating it and profiting by it."

"But don't you think it is possible to divide one's attention?"

"No, I don't, Miss Van Baulk'em. To appreciate a melody in an opera, one must have followed very carefully the harmonies which have led to it. An isolated melody is like a proverb in a foreign language, which one knows by heart, and of which one admires the meaning and sound, without knowing its literal translation."

"Well, I quite agree with you, only I wanted to get at your sentiments on the subject."

Miss Parthenia was accounted a brilliant conversationalist, and deservedly so, for she had fully realized that, in woman, conversational brilliancy consists of little else than an appreciation of the conversing man; and Paul left the Van Baulk'ems' house that day—he was but human, after all—with a pleased conviction that the girl was not so bad as she was painted perhaps, and as he stepped onto the avenue, recorded in his note-book an engagement he had made to visit the Van Baulk'ems' box at the opera on the following evening.

Two months before this, he and Mahmouré had fled New York and hidden themselves in a little Canadian village on the banks of the Niagara River, and beside that grand, placid stream, that gives so little indication, save by a dull murmur on a very quiet day, of the agony of turbulence with which it has rushed over the falls a few miles further up, had become man and wife, in the presence alone of a couple of parishioners, the parson, and God. There had followed a few weeks of pure, lovely delight, in contemplation of the turquoise water, with Ontario in the distance, reminding one by its colour and placidity of the Trasimene Lake; and then they had returned to New York to a life outwardly unchanged, but new in every thought, both to Mahmouré in her nest in West Forty-first Street, and to Paul in his bachelor apartments—not so very far off. The world remarked that they seemed to be "very good friends," and looked at them with uninterested curiosity when they appeared in public together, according to the custom of the Bohemia in which they lived; but not on that account did disinterested mammas cease to play upon Paul the shrapnel of invitations to every kind of entertainment where marriageable daughters do congregate.

The light of life seemed to be returning to Mahmouré's pale cheeks, the fire of life began to shine, as of yore, from her eyes; but Paul was unchanged, save in the eyes of one or two of his most intimate friends, who told one another that he seemed to lack in a measure his old enthusiasm, to enter less eagerly into the somewhat exhausting schemes of amusement they put before him; that his mouth was less determined, that his eye was less bright than of old, when they disturbed him at his books and at his weird calculations, at hours when domesticated New York has sought its virtuous couch.

Nevertheless, ten o'clock on the evening of the day following that of his visit above recorded found him entering the Van Baulk'ems' box, to be greeted warmly by Mrs. Van Baulk'em, who was chatting with a man on the sofa in the ante-loge, and to be "sent forward" in order to be seen talking with the dear girls in front. It was during an *entre-acte*, so that Miss Parthenia had no compunction in proceeding to draw him out, an operation in which that young lady excelled, and in deference to which Paul subsequently wrote an article dedicated to her and entitled "The Conversational Corkscrew—a study of Platitudinous Periphrasis!"

"Mrs. Lexington Park has told me," began the siren, "that you are most interesting, M. du Peyral, if one can get you to talk about transmigration of souls—metem-what's-his-name—you know."

"Metempsychosis?"

"Yes, that's it—and I have been thinking how it would be if one could suddenly change places and souls with one of those people up in the gallery. How strange it would be to find one's self suddenly full of new ideas, perhaps wondering if one can afford to come again on Friday, and whether the people down here enjoy themselves more than they do up there."

"I think, *mademoiselle*, that if you could make the change

you desire, you would probably find that you were in an atmosphere of genuine appreciation of the music, whilst in your place here would appear, by the exchange, a stupid, unsociable creature who actually wanted to *listen*, and might even go so far as to say 'Hush!' when your neighbors talk 'small talk' and 'scandal' to the music of the 'Götterdämmerung.' Think! how terrible!"

"Do you know, I think I should rather like it."

"Are you sure?"

"Yes."

"Then look at me for a moment."

She did so, and almost immediately closed her eyes, and Paul smiled a little self-satisfied smile. Unfortunately Miss Van Baulk'em, observing that her sister had sunk from scandal to silence, and fearful lest she might rise from silence to snores, tapped her with her fan and exclaimed,

"Thenie! you're going to sleep!"

She opened her eyes, and looking at Paul, said, "How odd! I just closed my eyes, and there I was in the gallery when Nell disturbed me." And then, seeing the smile on Paul's face, she exclaimed, "You wretch! I believe you had something to do with that."

"Not at all!" returned he; and then, rising, he added, "Alas, I must be very dull to-day; you were nearly asleep! *Au revoir;* when next we meet tell me what you think of—the opera."

"You will come soon—very soon?"

"With pleasure—good-night."

As he made his *adieux* to the mother in the ante-loge he caught sight of the man sitting by her side. A dark, handsome man with straight brows, a coarse mouth, and square jaws. Paul looked at him inquisitively, and the man returned the gaze without flinching: the next moment Paul had left the box. Outside, in the corridor, he stopped still for a moment, and then, looking on the ground, began pacing up and down, muttering the while—"Who is he? Who is he? Where have I seen him before?"

From another box, during the next *entre-acte*, he saw him again, talking in the front of the box with Miss Parthenia Van Baulk'em. Then the whole drama came back to him. Act 1. A country village, a beautiful woman, a handsome stranger. Act 2. A dishonoured wife, a wagging tongue, a hurried flight. Act 3. South Belgravia, a "scene" or two, and an outcast. That was all. And there was Charles Sturton Baker, in superlative costume, displaying his handsome face in the Metropolitan Opera House. The Van Baulk'ems had got him!

Paul remembered the example of the eminent firm of soap-boilers who made a large fortune by attending to their own business, and strolled home in the moonlight, Baker, the Van Baulk'ems, the opera, everything dismissed from his mind by a mental picture of a little, lithe figure that lay curled upon the huge divan, in Forty-first Street, looking at the clock, and wondering whether "Götterdämmerung" was one of the long operas, or whether he would be there soon.

A footstep in the hall-way, a rap at the door, and he is there, kneeling at her feet and playing with that wondrous hair, of which he used gayly to say, "the sunshine, when it kissed it, turned to darkness for very envy."

"You are tired, my poor Paul—the room is hot," she says, passing her ridiculous handkerchief across his forehead.

"No, no, sweetheart—it's not that—I don't quite know what it is; it has come on quite suddenly." He looks into her eyes until she seems to draw his very soul into hers, and then, suddenly rising with an exclamation almost of pain, he says:

"Do you know, Mahmouré, I don't think I'm as strong as I used to be? These mesmeric experiments I've been doing lately seem to take a great deal more out of me than they used to—I've been feeling tired and distracted. But never mind about me; there is something I wanted to ask you—what was it?—oh, yes. Do you know anything of a man named Charles Sturton Baker?"

"Good heavens! yes—what of him?"

"He's here, in New York. I was in a box at the opera with him to-night. What do you know about him?"

"Well, not much that is definite beyond that affair about poor little B——; you know all about that, I suppose. After she went to grief, he used to hang about the theatre, and played '*Inferno e Tommaso*' among the girls. He once had the audacity to make love to me, and I had him thrown out of the place by a scene-shifter. What's he up to now?"

"I think he's going to marry Parthenia Van Baulk'em—or rather, her money."

"Well, let him; they about suit one another."

"No! After all, she's only a fool—and he's a knave; and though, according to the dictum of the philosopher, the two would make an interesting little microcosm, she doesn't deserve such a fate as that. I'm sorry for her."

"Well, what can you do about it?"

"Nothing. But, after all, Miss Parthenia knows I've been all over the world, and perhaps she may ask me about him."

"And if she does, *cher ami*, don't know anything about the animal."

"That would hardly be fair, would it? If a fellow *can* protect a woman, surely he ought to do it—eh?"

"Yes, of course he ought; but if you undertake to protect a woman against an unscrupulous blackguard who happens to be her lover, you will probably find yourself in a most enterprising little mess. But *sapristoche!* Paul, since when this concern for the little Van Baulk'em?"

"Oh, I don't know. I think she's a clever little thing, for all her vulgarity; at any rate she's sharp, and I'd sooner talk to her for half an hour than to nine out of ten of these society women. Now, make me a scene of jealousy."

"Certainly! Kiss me immediately!"

* * * * * *

"Paul," said Mahmouré, presently, when their conversation had turned into a more reasonable channel, "this mesmerism of yours is killing you; I'm certain of it, and you must stop it. Every time you make your experiments with me as a 'subject,' I feel stronger and better than I did before them; but simultaneously you look paler and more worn. *Mon cher*, with a physique like yours, you require all your vital force to keep it going—you musn't waste it on me. What is the use, dear heart? I am a dying woman; your absolute influence over me shows it, if nothing else; reserve your force for some fresh young subject who won't sap your energies as I do."

"*Tiens!* listen to her! here is Mahmouré posing as a charming little vampire! Why, darling, I've a great deal more strength than I want for myself, and if I can make over the surplus to you by mesmerizing you, you ought to be as glad of it as I am. But come, we waste time. You remember that experiment we made when I sent your soul across the sea, and you told me what was going on in a house in London—well, I want to carry that experience still further. I am going to mesmerize you and to try to identify your soul with that of someone over there, and learn what that someone is *thinking* about as well as *doing*."

"But, Paul, it's not possible."

"Perhaps not, but we can try. If we succeed, after all it's only a progression in the clairvoyant experiences with which we have been so successful. It depends, I think, only on one thing, and that is, the existence of a personality over there identical with your own or mine; if such exists you will be able, if my will is strong enough to direct you, to identify yourself psychologically with some man or woman over there, for whom, if you knew them in the flesh, you would feel an affinity that would make *me* madly jealous. Come, let us try; the result, if we attain it, will be an enormous one."

"Very well, Paul—but promise not to over-exert yourself."

"Bah! what a timid little woman it is! Now, make yourself comfortable."

And Mahmouré du Peyral—to call her for the first time

by her new, real name—settled herself among the cushions of the divan.

"Look into my eyes—there!—be quiet—quiet—ah!—so;" and Paul put his hand on the forehead of the woman, who sighed deeply and closed her eyes. "So—you are asleep, are you not?"

"Yes."

"Where are you?"

"I don't know."

"Who are you?"

"I cannot say."

"You are in a room?"

"Yes."

"How is it furnished?"

"As a studio."

"Is there a looking-glass in it?"

"Yes."

"Look into it and describe yourself." [A pause.]

"Well?"

"A tall woman with dark hair—a man is by my side—*Eric!*"

"Who is Eric?"

"Oh! don't you know? he is my lover, my good, brave Eric."

"Is there a writing-table in the studio?"

"Yes."

"There are letters addressed to you lying on it. Read me the address of one of them."

"Miss Préault, The Cottage, Holland Street, W.

"*What* is the name?"

"Miss Préault."

"*Daphne?*"

"Yes—yes—who called me? Eric! my darling, there is some one in the room; oh, my love, help!—" and the little figure on the divan began to writhe as if in terror.

Paul du Peyral, trembling with the effort and excitement, took the beautiful head in his hands and blew softly upon the forehead once or twice. The convulsions ceased slowly, and Mahmouré opened her eyes. Seeing Paul leaning over her, she threw her arms around his neck and, in the terror and excitement of the moment, burst into tears.

"Come, come, sweetheart," said he; "I have tried you too much. Ah! but this is horrible—wicked—dangerous! Do you know where your soul has been?"

"No, dear, only I thought you were changed, over there, or here, or wherever it was, till I felt a terrible pain and woke up."

Paul was the first to recover himself. "Mahmouré," said he, "we have trifled with a great power, and its working has been more mysterious than I anticipated; more strange, more marvellous than I ever could have dreamed. Do you know that your soul found that of Daphne Préault?"

"What? of the woman you were to have married?"

"Yes."

"Oh, Paul, never let us do this again; it is not right."

"On the contrary, with your help I shall at last be able to find out something about this strange young woman—but not now; you are tired, and I must leave you. I have much to do, much to think of, to-night; to-morrow we will talk of this again. Now, good-night; in half an hour you must be fast asleep—do you hear?"

"Yes, Paul;" and after a last wild embrace, he was gone.

"At last! at last!" he cried to himself, as he reached his own rooms and began rapidly jotting down some notes in a little book with a lock-clasp. "Through Mahmouré I shall have this woman—this Miss Préault—in my power; what does it mean? Is it that the same blood runs in both our veins, as old Préault used to tell me sometimes. What it that old story of our common ancestry were *true?* How else account for the identity of our personalities? for, unless my researches have led me astray, it must be that which caused Mahmouré to single her out as the object of her search for a sympathy in Europe. Oh, Grand Principle of Life! if you are indeed capable of obedience to command, solve me your secret; whisper the solution of this mystery to me—to me, Paul du Peyral!—if only to reward me for the sacrifice to you of the best years of my life, of my health, of my very soul."

He rose and began pacing the room; suddenly he stopped, and raising his arms in the air, cried:

"Daphne Préault! if you and I are indeed one in soul, and breathe with the same life-current running through our veins, show yourself to me—to me—to me!"

Then, suddenly a wild pain gripped his heart, the room grew black around him, and there stood before the eyes of his super-excited imagination a woman such as we have described Daphne Préault, but having the features, almost the face, of Paul du Peyral. Then he fell senseless upon his face, in which condition his body-servant found him next morning.

"Not a word of this to Madame di Zulueta," said he; and the magnificently trained menial gave him an assurance, which his long experience of that individual's inflexible mendacity told him was to be implicitly trusted.

And so, for the next few days, he went about as usual, nothing altered in his manner to Mahmouré or to the world, but now and then catching his breath for an instant, and looking a trifle whiter round the eyes.

On Sunday afternoon he paid his promised visit to the Van Baulk'ems.

He had not been there more than a few minutes when the fair Parthenia, corralling him into a corner, asked suddenly:

"Do you know Mr. Baker—an Englishman?"

"Mr. Charles Sturton Baker?"

"Yes."

"Well, *no*, I can't say I do. I came across him some years ago, but though I was presented to him, I can hardly say I know him."

"He is very charming, is he not?"

"Well, that is a question entirely for you to answer; you

know the English are a queer people, and have a different standard from ours; many actions which we look upon as blackguardly, they, I believe, look upon as quite the right thing to do. I am hardly a judge; Mr. Baker has done things that I think infamous, but he may be charming 'for a' that.'"

"But he moves in the best society in England—or might, only that he is a quiet, domesticated kind of man, and does not care about it."

"Well, I should say that you have formed a misconception concerning him; he is distinctly what I should call a 'fast.' man. But, after all, he only takes up the opportunities afforded him by human nature in the class of society in which he moves. As for his going into 'the best society,' I should hardly say that was correct; I believe that my 'set,' in London, is pretty good, and I never met him there. I have only come across him in a rather 'rowdy' country-house, where he was having a desperate flirtation with a child of sixteen."

"Is he not very well connected?"

"No—I think not. In fact, I think that he is rather by way of being an absolute nobody; I may be wrong—if you like I'll find out for you."

"Well, I should rather like to know; but you won't mention *me*, will you?"

"Of course not!"

And so the conversation dropped, and presently Paul sought "fresh teas and houses new," and thought no more about the ten-minutes' chat that was to have such an influence upon the fortunes of himself and Mahmouré di Zulueta.

It was not till that evening that an idea on the subject occurred to him. Said he to himself: "That little girl is evidently crazily in love with Baker; I wonder if young Hawleigh knows anything about him." And the practical form his idea took was to write and ask full particulars concerning the handsome adventurer from Gabriel Hawleigh, whom he had met in a little French village some years before, and whom he recollected as a young English Bohemian, who seemed to know everybody who had ever lived, by sight, name, or reputation.

He wrote, merely asking if Gabriel knew anything definite against the man, and if he did not, to send a "kind" letter, "not as a guarantee of good faith, but for publication."

Whilst it passed across the sea, he continued his experiments with Mahmouré, learning by degrees, with an accuracy resulting from the marvellous coincidences of their three personalities, almost as much about the Princess Daphne as the Princess knew about herself.

And so the world wagged, day following day, and causes developing eternally into effects.

Now, Gabriel Hawleigh's recollections of the days he had spent in a French village on the Biscayan coast were not as distinct as those of the young American who had shared his self-imposed exile, and on receiving Paul du Peyral's letter it took him an appreciable time to remember who Paul du Peyral *was*. Gradually, however, the memory of those half-forgotten days returned to him, and he turned his attention to the object of the enquiry. Charles Sturton Baker was one of those mysterious individuals that one comes across periodically in the more careless section of London society; —one of those young men who, clustered about the doorways of semi-public or subscription balls, compare offensive notes on the wives and sisters of their friends; who wear ribbed shirt-fronts and single studs, cylindrical collars, satin ties, and self-satisfied smirks; and who, when the hours of labour in the far-eastern "City" are at an end, take the Underground Railway, and are swallowed up by the deserts of Belsize or Bayswater, by inaccessible North-Western suburbs, miles beyond the comparatively civilized spots "where omnibusses turn round."

We have said that he was handsome; add to this that his mysterious occupation in the murky orient supplied him with the wherewithal to satisfy the lower cravings of his sensual nature, and hide the essential feebleness of his mind behind the venal adulation of impecunious clerks, and caused the said clerks to regard his triumphal progress along Piccadilly on Saturday afternoons, in a hansom, with some Lottie or Tottie of the ballet, as evidence of his claims to the titles of "devil of a fellow" and "rare good sort." The frisky matrons of his inaccessible suburb, "the squaws of the north-west frontier tribes," as Dick Lindsay used to say, hearing of his reckless lavishings in the matter of Gaiety stalls and five-shilling cab-fares, got up quite a little excitement about this provincial Lothario; and the ladies whom he honoured with dishonour were looked upon almost with reverence by the compulsorily virtuous remainder. And, by-the-by, he had crept into a calling acquaintance with the Holland Street colony, *via* the Miss Eastons, whom he had met at a subscripto-suburban ball, at the Kensington Town-Hall.

Therefore Gabriel, though loth to commit himself, could hardly profess entire ignorance of the swain, but could not be said to know anything either for or against him. He had seen him a member of a party of men at a music-hall, and paraphrasing the saying of the French philosopher, "*La nuit tous les hommes sont gris*," did not regard as a crime the fact that he had been disorderly, and, in vulgar parlance, "chucked out." That he was over-dressed did not matter much. After all, if one cuts one's coat according to one's cloth, one wears it according to one's income and education; and to him Mr. Baker was a tasteless young man who wore very good clothes very badly. He therefore replied to Paul du Peyral, that he knew nothing against the man as a man, and that he was a harmless, stupid kind of thing who couldn't do anyone any harm; and armed with this non-committal reply, which he thought would close the matter satisfactorily for all parties, Paul strolled up to the Van Baulk'ems', and showed it to the fair Parthenia. She received it in silence, thanked M. du Peyral for the trouble he had taken, and the incident, as far as he was concerned, was apparently terminated.

"After all," thought he, "abuse of one man by another is very much like mud splashed up by an unconscious cart; a modicum of it is sure to stick, according to the proverb; but even that modicum, black and sticky as it is when it's wet, turns white or at any rate gray when it's dry, and is easily brushed off; and I've no doubt the fair Parthenia will rather enjoy the process of brushing than otherwise. Besides, it is possible that Baker has become steadied down, and has repented the rascalities of his fevered youth."

And so he returned to his solitude and to Mahmouré, and to his absorbing interest in his psychical experiments, which he concealed beneath the ostensible search after knowledge in the studies of the Sparrow, the Mosquito, and the House-fly.

The constantly recurring "Psychical Romance" may be described as an intellectual nightmare resulting from the literary indigestion of the day, an indigestion produced by a surfeit of Wilkie Collins, Stevenson, Hugh Conway, and Mrs. Crow; and lest I lay myself open to the reproach of swelling the mass of "weird" literature of the past decennium, I beg the reader to skip the following exposition of Paul's discoveries in Mesmerism and Telepathy, but to remember that I have set them out, and to recur to them for an explanation should the spirit move him presently to fling aside the book with the exclamation, "Bah! another attempt to panoply platitude with the dim magnificence of mystery!" if he is in the habit of using this sort of language to himself.

Shortly, the result of his investigations, arrived at after months—nay years—of wasted tissue and brain-power, was as follows. The whole matter resolves itself into one of sympathy. Two persons are presented to one another: the one has a personality—a vital force—represented by the numeral *six;* the other has a vital force represented by the figure *two.* Very well! They try to converse: at first the conversation is spasmodic, choppy, uninteresting, carried on at cross purposes as it were; gradually, however, the mere physical propinquity lessens this mental discrepancy, and before long they get interested in—*i.e.* they understand—one another. The higher force lowers itself in proportion as the lower force rises, till at last the two are said to be "in sympathy with one another." They almost know one another's thoughts; each can almost guess what the other is going to say next: they no longer require to explain their respective meanings minutely; an unfinished sentence, a word, a look, conveys a whole thesis on the point under discussion. They are reciprocally charmed, for they feel themselves to be on an intellectual level with one another; in a phrase—to recur—they no longer represent the contrast of six and two, but each giving to and taking from the other, they represent at the end of the conversation the uniform vital force of *four each.* Mesmerism is an acceleration of this process by an effort of will; Telepathy is a higher development of it. And in Mesmerism *or* Telepathy the one mind conveys to the other, to be acted upon, the thoughts that are uppermost at the moment within itself.

In the almost clairvoyant experiences of Paul and Mahmouré, this had occurred to a high degree, and had been very powerfully assisted by the coincidences of the personalities of Paul and Daphne Préault, united as they seemed to be by some distant tie of Creole ancestry. Mahmouré being powerfully attracted to, and acted upon by, Paul, there was no doubt but that Daphne would possess the same influence over her; and, following the natural laws of attraction, it was not surprising that her spirit should seek that of the Princess, living as the latter did amid associations doubtless familiar to Paul, and being, beyond all, the soul in which Paul's interest was principally centred in Europe.

People who "see ghosts" are generally looked upon either as mystics or as rather weak-minded subjects by the rest of the community; this is because we always feel a certain uneasiness in the presence of an eccentricity. If that eccentricity is one beyond our comprehension, we revere its author; if it is one that we can criticise and examine, familiarity breeds contempt, and we despise him. Reverence and despite are merely developments of fear. Ghost-seers come under either the first or the second category, according to their talkativeness. The uncommunicative ghost-seer is feared—nay, he is thought a trifle mad; the communicative ghost-seer, on the other hand, is laughed at, and considered a *raconteur* or an ass, according to his powers of eloquence. Now, following the theory of Paul du Peyral, a ghost is nothing more than a coincidence of condition occurring between two persons at the same moment, by which coincidence the illusion —or rather phenomenon—of the appearance of the one to the other is produced.

To recur to the doctrine of sympathy established between two people who are conversing with one another:—At a given point, maybe, their personalities find one another in absolute or perfect coincidence. The result of this is, as a rule, love : courtship is a continual search after a renewal of those conditions; marriage a more or less successful effort, as the case may be, to establish a new sympathy on a new plane.

However, to return: The sight of another person is merely the effort of a certain excitement on the visual segment of one's brain; when the sympathy, perfect, absolute, of which we have spoken has been established, that excitement becomes a very strong one. Two persons look into one another's eyes, and through their eyes into their souls; the impression made is necessarily very forcibly stamped on the memory, and it is not so much an impression of the outer form under contemplation, as one of the inner soul that shines out in the gaze. Now if, at any future time, by reason of the one person thinking of the other with any strong effort of cerebration, by a rare coincidence that other person finds himself in the same vital condition—at the same numeral of personality, in the same state of sympathy and degree of attraction—as he did on the occasion when the sympathy was originally established, then, the conditions of the mind being the same, the same impression will be conveyed by the optic nerves to the brain, and the effect is produced of the appearance of the one person to the other, which, for want of a better term, has become called "a ghost."

It is rare for each to appear to the other at the same time; the coincidence of thought, effort, and personal condition is *too remotely* possible: it is the person who makes the effort who either sees the object of his mental strain, or, if his thoughts are centred upon its present occupation, appears to that object.

And so, every effort of thought of which Paul du Peyral was capable being concentrated upon the woman whom, in the body, he had never seen, he was wont to call up her mental picture with a vividness that gave to her spectre all the attributes of substantial form; and adopting her as a subject for his experiments, which chance, coincidence—call it what you will—had flung in his way, he pursued his investigations with all the devotion of a *savant*, and at the expense of his life.

CHAPTER V.

DAPHNE AND ERIC.

THE "*tempora mutantur*" principle, as far as this story is concerned, holds good in Europe as it does in America and elsewhere; and whilst Paul du Peyral and Mahmouré led their separated though identical lives in New York, time had wrought its changes in the Holland Street colony, though that time was measured by months only, and not by longer periods. Spring had arrived and was growing old; already, at intervals of a week or so, the sun shone so brightly that the shades were closed on the sunny sides of the streets, giving them the appearance of having been struck blind with astonishment at the fine weather, after the fog and rain and slush of the metropolitan merry spring-time.

In Holland Street, grimy persons had appeared, and had borne thence carefully protected canvases, to deposit them for approval or rejection at the doors of Burlington House; in a word, "Show Sunday" had come and gone, and hearts beat high with hope or apprehension; whilst "the boys" who had sent in their Academy pictures rested a little on their oars,—or rather brushes,—and awaited the official in timation of—what? Most of our personal friends—if we may call them so—had launched an argosy on the sea of public appreciation; but all of them awaited with some anxiety the fate of Gabriel Hawleigh's picture, "Sunshine in the Fog," which had fulfilled its early promise of excellence, and was regarded as the *chef-d'œuvre* of the colony.

To Gabriel himself, though he said but little on the subject, the acceptance or rejection of this picture by the hanging committee meant everything—a large word, but the only one which properly expresses the case. Into it he felt he had put the very best work of which he was capable; he knew that he could do no better, and that if this were "found wanting" he had better abandon art as a means of livelihood, once and for all; and this reflection occurring often to him in the midst of his wildest rhapsodies with his violin, he would drop his instrument from his shoulder and sink for hours into a revery on the Future—and Maye. She, on her side, said but little about the picture; but the Princess Daphne was an angel of hope to him, and never for an instant assumed anything on the possibility of the rejection of his masterpiece, but urged him to work in anticipation of his popularity as an artist, which she regarded as a very proximate certainty.

"There will be a great demand," she used to say to him; "mind the supply is ready to meet it; and, for heaven's sake, don't sell your old rejected trash on the strength of this big work of yours. You can do that later, when your hold on the public is strong enough to defy the dangers of dilution with inferior work. Remember, Gabriel, and keep Maye's happiness in your mind as the lodestar of your energies."

Maye herself was placidly content with her existence—or outwardly so, at any rate; deep in her heart, if the truth must be confessed, lay a gnawing agony that had usurped a place there ever since the "engagement" of Eric Trevanion and the Princess Daphne had been announced. Their *liaison* had been published to the colony under the title of a betrothal, though it was as impossible to get anything out of Daphne concerning her future marriage as it had been to extract information on the subject of her past history. Eric practically spent all his time with her, and seemed to have abandoned his profession of *flaneur* of the studios; and men spoke still more reverently of the Princess in his presence, standing unconsciously in something like awe of the man whom Daphne Préault had selected as her future husband—if not, as was whispered, as her present lover—from amid the army of aspirants.

He seldom touched his palette or spoilt good canvas now-a-days. They had been but an occupation for idle hours at best, and now his occupation was Daphne; and, as he had but one pleasure, and that was to sit with her whilst she worked, she had fitted up a second and more substantial writing-table in her spacious studio, and tried to make him take seriously to literature, and make some use of his undoubted cleverness, his knowledge of the world, and his very exceptional education.

Unfortunately, as a *littérateur*, Eric was an epigrammatist rather than a word-painter, and he seldom got beyond titles of striking and remarkable originality, for essays, which, when they were written, took the form of a collection of aphorisms, spicules of epigram embedded in a protoplasm of commonplace, the whole vivifying a spongy mass which absorbed the ideas of other people rather than originated new ones of its own. There are many writers—for the most part young ones—in the present day to whom this description applies, and publishers look askant upon works which are gems of literary composition rather than of imaginative construction. And Eric's masterpieces: "An Indigo Inspiration by a Blue Bard" (written in a moment of depression); his "Petrifaction of Passion, a Pathological Problem" (written when his vocabulary of eulogy of the Princess had suddenly dried up); and several similarly entitled effusions reposed peacefully in the pigeon-hole that he described as the "Walhalla of Rejected Addresses," and over which he had inscribed on a strip of gummed label, "*Lasciate ogni speranza, voi ch' entrate!*"—"Abandon hope all ye who enter here!"

Still, the ill luck of his manuscripts caused him no pity for himself, only contempt for them. The allowance made to him by his father was an ample one, and any caprices he might have had he might very well have satisfied; but as it was, he had but one thought in life—Daphne! To be by her side, to hold her in his arms and tell her all over again how he loved her—that was all he wanted; and as Daphne was of a practically identical opinion, the studio in Holland Street was certainly one of the happiest places in the world.

Eric Trevanion had perhaps but one thorn in the flesh, and that was Clytemnestra, the coloured woman, who jealously guarded her mistress' lightest actions, and strenuously objected to Eric, not so much on the ground of his being a new master for herself, as on the ground that he stood in quasi-authority over her mistress. Clytie had no moral scruples of any kind, but, with the cunning of her race, with that devotion of self and that selfishness for others that characterizes the darkie, she was convinced that her mission in life was to bring about the marriage of the Princess Daphne and Paul du Peyral, whom, though she had never seen, of course she knew all about.

Clytie had been owned by Victor Préault, his father had owned her father, his grandfather her grandfather; generation after generation of master and slave had looked after one another, and the ideas of freedom, and a vote, and the College of Surgeons were, to Clytie, iconoclastic institutions which she strenuously objected to take in place of the companionship of Daphne, her red bandanna head-gear, and her own mnemonic storehouse of Voodoo pharmaceutical knowledge.

Clytie's mind was a magazine of Creole legendary history and historic legend. As long as she could remember, Daphne had been accustomed to listen almost unconsciously, when Clytie was in the vicinity, to stories of the bayous and swamps of Louisiana, of the early settlers of New Orleans, of D'Iberville, of Bienville, of the Chevalier Le Blond de la Tour, of Indian raids, and of massacres by the Chickasaws, the Choctaws, and the Natchez. Anon her tales would be of the Spanish rule of 1760 to 1770, of the patriot merchants such as Milhet, d'Abbadie, and Préault, of the landing of Don Antonio de Ulloa, and, later, of the Irish Spaniard, Don Alexander O'Reilly, "Cruel O'Reilly" as he was still called in Louisianian folk-lore, of de Unzaga, of de Galvez; in a word, Clytie could have dictated a complete Creole history, correct in its chronology, and fictitious only in its facts. But it was as the chronicler, the *trouvère* of the Préault family, to an ancestor of which an ancestor of hers had been sold in all his picturesque insufficiency of costume, that Clytie came out strong. Clytie fondly imagined that the idol she wore around her neck had originally belonged to this ancestor—it was a shapelessly human affair, which had done duty in turn for correct and lifelike representations of Voodoo, of Obi, of Gitche-Manito, of the Madonna, of Martin Luther, of the Saviour, and of Jefferson Davis—and when she lectured Daphne on her Creole ancestry, she was wont to refer to said idol, whose existence at the time said events did not take place was, to her, conclusive evidence of their historical accuracy; and it was upon one of these family legends, well known among all the branches of the Préault family, that she based her efforts to induce Daphne to reconsider her contemptuous refusal of Paul du Peyral.

Clytie's legend of the Préault and du Peyral families was a remarkable chronicle, based on a good deal of historic fact, and embroidered with a good deal of historic fiction. I prefer, therefore, to tell the story in my own words, shorn of much ornamental eloquence, but enriched with a certain amount of careful research among the archives of the city of New Orleans. In the year 1718, Bienville had succeeded Epinay as Governor of Louisiana, and affairs in the colony were governed principally in conformity to the requirements of John Law's "Mississippi Company"—the South-Sea Bubble that was to explode with such terrific violence two years later. Among the 800 emigrants that landed at Dauphine Island on the 25th of August, 1718, was one Hippolyte du Peyral, an engineer, who formed one of the little band of pioneers who might have been seen in 1720, headed by the Sieur Le Blond de la Tour, "garbed as a knight of St. Louis, modified as might be by the exigencies of the frontier," marking off streets and lots—planning, in a word, the city of New Orleans.

There are doubtless many of my readers to whom New

Orleans would be an undiscovered country were it not for the Abbe Prévost and "Manon Lescaut." I refer to this work because, if the truth must be told, the colony was then in the condition described by Prévost—*i.e.*, in what might be called a state, of troglodytish simplicity as regards its social institutions, and the female society of New Orleans was composed, exception being made in favour of the wives of a few of the officials, and those of the French and Canadian settlers, of ladies who had loved not wisely but too well, if not too promiscuously, in France, and had, after going through a term of probation at the Salpêtrière and St. Lazare, been shipped off by a paternal government to supply the rugged colonists with the gentle influences and reproductive advantages which are the prerogatives of the *beau sexe.* Unless these ladies are traduced by their historian, they appear to have drunk, gambled, and fought on terms of perfect equality with their lords and masters, or, to put it tersely, their proprietors. But among them, a damsel of a finer mould than the generality fell to the lot of Hippolyte du Peyral, and to him was born, within a pistol-shot of the ancient and modern Place d'Armes, a beautiful daughter. This child was some six or seven years old when the gentle Ursuline Sisters established their convent and hospital on what was then called Arsenal Street; and her mother having succumbed to the ravages of the colonial climate and social laxity, du Peyral was glad enough to find there an asylum where the child would be secure from the influences of the almost primeval condition of affairs in the young city, no less than from the periodical raids of Chickasaws and Natchez.

In the winter of 1727–28—I quote from the pages of the Creole historian, G. W. Cable—a crowning benefit was reached. On the Levée, just in front of the Place d'Armes, the motley public of the wild town was gathered to see a goodly sight. A ship had come across the sea and up the river, with the most precious of all possible earthly cargoes.

She had tied up against the grassy, willow-planted bank,

and there were coming ashore, and grouping together in the Place d'Armes, under escort of the Ursuline nuns, a good threescore, not of houseless girls from the streets of Paris, as heretofore, but of maidens from the hearthstones of France, to be disposed of, under the discretion of the nuns, in marriage. And then there were brought ashore, and were set down in the rank grass, many small, stout chests of clothing. There was a trunk for each maiden, and a maiden for each trunk, and both maidens and trunks were the gifts of the king. Similar companies came in subsequent years, and the girls with trunks were long known in the traditions of their colonial descendants by the honourable distinction of the "*filles à la cassette*"—the casket girls.

Hippolyte du Peyral was a substantial citizen, standing high in the good graces of the pious sisters, and he was one of the first to take to his home among the new plantations of Louisiana, a gentle, sweet-tempered helpmate, his lawful wife, a healthy Provençale of some twenty summers. This good couple lived to an equally good old age, and like the worthies of nursery romance, died regretted by all who knew them, leaving a family of stalwart young colonials who founded the du Peyral family, which had accordingly flourished in the state until war, fever, transferrence from one government to another, and other disturbing influences had dwindled the old stock down to concentration in the person of M. Paul du Peyral, the *protégé* and heir of old Préault of Baton Rouge. Thus, after a lapse of a century and a half, the parent stock had been thrown together again by chance; for the nameless daughter of Hippolyte du Peyral, having arrived at years of indiscretion, had run away from the convent and married a handsome, wild pioneer, by name Préault, and had scattered through the state a small but exclusively Creole race of Préaults; a family not, alas! without its place in the scandalous history of Louisiana, for the hereditary taint seemed to be fatally constant, and ever and anon the blood of the girl who had enslaved the fancy of Hippolyte du Peyral would crop out, and produce a woman of gorgeous meridional beauty and dazzling personality, half-tame and half-savage, a type that might be seen in its perfect development in Daphne Préault, the exile, the Princess of the Holland Street colony, in a word, the pure-blooded Bohemian.

Now, the historic outlines and the romantic details of this family history were cherished with true negro persistency by Clytemnestra, the ex-bondwoman; and the dream of her darkie soul was to see the old stock of Hippolyte du Peyral reunited in the persons of Paul and the Princess Daphne, and therefore, when the latter indignantly scorned the condititions of her second cousin's will, in refusing to marry Paul, Clytie held that she was flying in the face of Providence, and valourously invoked the assistance of her multifold deity in jade, to bring about this consummation, to her so devoutly to be wished for.

I have dealt with this family history at some length because it accounts in a great measure for the sympathy—in a way, a tie of blood—that existed between these two strong Creole personalities, separated from one another though they were, by half a hemisphere; a sympathy which led in so large a degree to the *dénouement* of this veracious narrative. It is hardly surprising, therefore, that to Clytie, from whom no secret of her mistress' life was concealed, the position of Eric in the Holland Street *ménage* of the Princess Daphne was a never-failing source of annoyance; an annoyance that she dared not openly show to the principals in this drama, but which made itself felt continually, and especially to Eric, who, early in the game, rechristened Clytie, "Onesima, his thorn in the flesh."

Without risking the reception of a frown from Daphne, which though theoretically less baleful, was practically far more awful to Clytie, than the curse of Obi or the incantation of Voodoo, this antagonism caused itself to be very distinctly perceived on such occasions as she found it necessary in the pursuit of her professional avocations to enter his presence, as, for instance, when she would come in to lay tea at five o'clock; and then a vague feeling of easiness would come over Eric as he sat at his writing-table, from whence he could watch the Princess at her work. Underlying all Daphne's love for him, his super-sensitive nature fancied that there existed a feeling of superiority that only wanted one earthly touch to make it contempt; and this was a sensation he had never been able entirely to get over: it would impress him with a vague feeling of discontent in little scenes such as the following, which were of pretty constant recurrence.

It was five o'clock, and Eric had been enjoying himself vastly, writing an essay—high-flown, satirical, paradoxical—entitled, "The Praise of Publishers, by one of their Victims." The light was nearly gone, and Daphne sat in front of her easel painting somewhat abstractedly, playing, rather, with some of the details of her nearly finished picture. Eric had just concluded his essay with the paraphrase, "He who writes with nought to say, finds his labour thrown away," and, Clytie having set the tea-things with something like aggression of manner, he laid down his pen and looked at the Princess. She was leaning back in her chair, looking lazy and satisfied with her work, now and then making a little dab for some particular point, until the light, as far as painting was concerned, had died out. Then she laid down her palette and brushes, stretched her toes out in front of her, clasped her hands at the back of her head, and rested so, in contemplation of the canvas.

That silence fell which seems to envelop every death, even that of the daylight. No sound disturbs the stillness of the studio till the fire stumbles into a fresh fantasy of fallen cinders, the ashes burst out upon the hearth, and "new-born night begins its little life."

The day has risen and lived its life, it fades and dies, and as it dies there is a moment of stillness that proclaims its death: another life takes its place—"*Le Jour est mort; vive la Nuit!*"

Daphne yawns, stretches her long arms again, and rising,

approaches the fire, where she throws herself into the big lounge as she did on the night that she surrendered herself to Eric, and by degrees settles herself into absolute comfort. Eric has been so quiet that she has almost forgotten his existence, when suddenly he startles her—if so placid a person as the Princess Daphne can ever be said to be startled—by bounding from his seat with an exclamation that partakes of the dual natures of a roar and a snort, and paces up and down the floor, until Daphne, without looking at him, remarks:

"Well! what are you playing at Polar bear in a cage for?"

"I swear!" he exclaims ("Don't!" says she). "I swear," he continues, "I'll never write another line, and I'll burn every paper that I've ever slung ink upon!" and he comes to the fire and takes up his position before her, in the attitude peculiar to and favoured by the Englishman of patriotic instinct.

Hard as steel, and with a little playful sneer, come the words from Daphne's lips:

"Why this sudden philanthropy? Why heap these blessings on the heads of undeserving publishers? Pause! reflect! gracious lord of mine, ere you inflict such privation on helpless humanity—on the world that hungers for the glorious fruit of your transcendent genius, and that has deserved no such salutary punishment at your hands. Let me plead for the world! Oh, write one more Assyrian farce, one more essay 'On the Morals and Pathology of the non-existent races of Central America,' before the fiat goes forth and the doom is sealed!" And she clasps her hands as if in prayer, as, with a fascinating *moue* of mock seriousness, she sinks on her knees from the big lounge, before him.

Eric looked down at her. He made no attempt to hide the pain her levity caused him. She saw it, and her hands fell, as she remained seated on the bear-skin rug, leaning against the sofa behind her.

"I'm blue—unhappy—disappointed," he said; "why do you sneer at instead of encouraging me?"

"Because you live in the nineteenth century and your books are those of the monks of the middle ages. Your standard works might be entitled '*Auctorum ignotorum omnia quæ non supersunt*'—'The forgotten works of unknown authors!' and your romances are simply scholarly epitomes of all that has been said by previous writers on subjects no one cares anything about. There is no boy who has just left college who could not do what you do; you write things that all scholars know as well as you, whilst as for the rest of your readers, you either bore or confuse them. Your writings, *mon cher*, are the apotheosis of the commonplace."

"It seems to me that what you want me to write *is* simply bald commonplace."

"Not at all. I don't see why you must necessarily jump from one extreme to the other. In doing that you admit that you have neither ability to originate nor industry to supply a demand."

"There you go again! You always stand up for the purely meretricious."

"My dear boy, up to a certain point everything is meretricious. Why do you suppose I sold my first pictures? Gabriel Hawleigh's early work was infinitely superior to mine, but mine sold, and his did not. Why? Because I am a beautiful woman, and painted my own portrait indirectly into everything, and with that, I painted subjects which were described as 'daring' by unsuccessful artists disguised as critics. In this way, an interest entirely apart from the work sold my prentice efforts. What you have to do is to prove yourself personally superior—as you undoubtedly are—to mere acquirements."

"In a phrase, you would have me write down to the morbid craving for sensation that characterizes the literary taste of to-day."

"Nonsense! Genius is universal, and requires no dictionary of its own. I tell you to forsake the display of erudition, and cultivate imagination. If I hadn't wit enough to give the public what it wants, and to give it art as well, I should be admitting that I am like every unsuccessful struggler who gives them pure talent—which is a drug in the market. If I could write I *would* make a success, for the reason that I should conceal art so well that those who cannot appreciate it would not find it. A fine lady can wear gingham and homespun, and be called 'chic'; but Clytie couldn't wear my terra-cotta wrapper. Apply this to your erudition. Gild your pill, *tres cher;* gild your pill!"

"Daphne, are you quite sure that you know—that you understand—what you are talking about?"

"Oh! I am absolutely sensible of my own ignorance, but —I live in this nineteenth century of ours, and I desire to live comfortably—luxuriously—and to be 'somebody' into the bargain. My plane is immeasurably below yours, but whilst you cannot look down on me—though you are over my head —I can look up to you and appreciate you. I live on earth, you live in the clouds, and your work is no use there. You haven't yet reached Heaven, so you can't be sure that your works would sell there; and with the present moral obliquity that exists with regard to international copyright, though you might be celebrated, you would probably reap no advantage from your celebrity beyond a pair of first-quality wings and a more than ordinarily curly trumpet."

He turned away almost petulantly.

"What have I done," said he, "that you should talk to me like this? I'm a fool—a sensitive fool—I know; but, by Jupiter, you know exactly where to hit, and you hit hard."

"What have you done? What have you done? You have made me love you, darling, that's all." And she went to him, putting her arms about his neck, and pressing him closer, closer to her heart, until her head sank upon his shoulder, and her voice died away to a whisper in his ear, that she caressed softly with her lips.

Eric was deeply—obstinately—wounded, and he held her in a loose, distracted embrace. He was thinking so much of himself and of his own woes, and it hurt him beyond bearing that she did not worship him blindly—uncritically.

"Suppose," she went on, "you were not rich enough to be independent of your work. Would it be right to throw away the talent you have, on work that is gratifying only to yourself? Be sure, your want of success lies in yourself, not in other people. The cant phrase, 'writing above the heads of the herd,' is all rubbish. Fame is the justification of Talent; strive after it, buy it at any cost. Oh, I know the difference between Fame and Notoriety, and how much easier it is to gain the latter than the former. But to be heard, to be listened to, is the first consideration; make your crowd listen to you, and when you have got them in your grasp, give them what *you* like; but spare no means, however false they may seem to you, to get them there."

"But, sweetheart, you are arguing that Art should acquiesce in its own suppression."

"No—I argue that art should give you the superior force to conquer your tendency to sacrifice everything to it. Don't think I am cruel when I hurt you like this—I am so proud of you, and of your talents. Oh, love, I *must* see you rise above your disappointments. *You* are satisfied to know your own worth; *I* shall never be satisfied until the world acknowledges it. Forgive me, sweetheart, if I seem sordid and mercenary for your sake."

Though Eric adored Daphne, there was always this grain of worldly wisdom in her that jarred upon him; it was indefinable, but intense. But while it was repugnant to him, he was too reasonable not to acknowledge that in much of it she was right. It was almost humiliating to realize that this woman, who was only educated up to the ordinary feminine standpoint, could sound blindly, unthinkingly—with a rush, as it were—the depths of human nature, whilst he, with all his scientific and classic lore, took ten times as long to arrive anywhere near the same point. It came out strongly in her pictures. With all her profound artistic talent, she knew how to leaven the excellence of her work with a something that arrested the eye, with details of human nature which, though admirably executed, he still felt to be essentially meretricious. The word was his nightmare; it was her bank-account.

It was irritating to him to argue with this woman, who, like all self-supporting workers, had a confidence in her own efforts which, being based on practical experience, was unanswerable. He was forced to admit that her instinct was unerring, and that, in spite of her sordid expressions, she was inherently artistic; she could produce with a touch effects that, in others, demanded hours of labor. And above all, she worshipped him, and he knew it; he was her god, and though she strove often to hide the fact, she was mentally on her knees before him, adoring him wildly, and more appreciatively than any milk-and-water maiden who might have flattered him more by listening to and memorizing his incomprehensible poems, effusions which he loved to garb in the jargon of the unintelligible. She was of that type of woman who makes a man what he is. For what? That he may straightway go from her to fling himself at the feet of some pretty specimen of puerile femininity, and in the enjoyment of its inane worship, wonder how he could so long have endured the rather trying criticisms of a woman whose fibre, though passionate and maddening, "was somewhat coarse—of a woman not fit to enter the same room with his Colinette—his Colinette, so pure, so holy, so—" bah! etcetera! etcetera! etcetera!

'Tis a weird world, my masters!

But Eric had not yet found his Colinette. He was enthralled by a personality stronger by far than his own, in all save that she adored him; he was content to live with only one thought in his mind—Daphne! Daphne!—and had anyone told him that the time might come when he would tire of the electric light, and seek the comparative gloom of the unexhausting ozokerit, he would have regarded the prophet with a contemptuous wonder, and would have returned to the dazzling fascinations of the gorgeous Creole with something like pity in his heart for the inexperienced philosopher "who had evidently never *loved*."

Certainly nothing of this could have been foreshadowed by anyone who saw Eric Trevanion take Daphne in his arms, at the end of the conversation I have recorded above, and lose consciousness of the whole world in the thought that this matchless woman was his, and his alone; and as usual, they parted happier than ever in their fool's paradise of varied sensations. It is probable that a man of Trevanion's character would never have been chained as he was, if the course of his love had run perfectly smooth; and it was perhaps Daphne's art of criticising and correcting him that made her tenderness so infinitely more precious to him than it would otherwise have been. An American writer—Edgar Saltus—has said very justly, "The secret of never displeasing is the art of mediocrity;" and certainly one might wander for a lifetime amid the labyrinth of attribute before selecting for Daphne Préault the adjective "mediocre." She was grand, intoxicating, sublime, and infinitely soft; but never "affectionate." The word "affectionate" is too frequently a synonym—an euphemism—for "indifferent"; and Eric was Daphne's very soul, her only thought, her unique religion. And he left her to-day to go to some dinner-party or other, more bound to him, soul to soul, forever; for the instinct of maternity that unconsciously mingles itself with love in every woman's heart told her that this man was destined to be—nay, already was—a thing of her own creation. After dinner she went to his writing-table and spent a couple of hours with his impractical, high-flown manuscripts. He was a Quixote of literature; his essays were gems; not the diamonds, the rubies, the sapphires eagerly bought by the public who understand such things, but the cameos, the avanturines, the labradorites, and chrysoberyls of language, infinitely dearer than diamonds to the collector and connoisseur, but in no wise understood or appreciated by the people.

Whilst she was thus occupied, a thought struck her: she was reading an essay of his on the social customs of the Mayas of Yucatan, as contrasted with those of the people of Atlantis; an ingenious dissertation in which two people perhaps in the whole world—Dr. Le Plongeon and Ignatius Donnelly—would have revelled. She took up Eric's pen and rewrote the entire thing, discarding nothing of his, but adding a quantity of her own, until she had practically produced an essay on the Aztecs of the Parisian Boulevards and the Regent Street and the Piccadilly of the capital of Atlantis; and in its new and almost sacrilegious form, she posted it to the editor of the leading monthly magazine of the English-speaking world. This done, the Princess Daphne, though as yet it was early, went to bed.

Daphne Préault was a physically perfect woman. She had read of heroines of novels who took chloral, and she knew weak-minded women whose prayers for rest, on going to bed, took the practical form of bromide of potassium. To the Princess these things were the romance of the Pharmacopœia. Having wrapped her exquisite body in the clinging silks of her night attire, she was in the habit of falling asleep almost the instant that her head touched the pillow; and with the regularity of clock-work, precisely eight hours afterward, she made one bound from her hardly tumbled bed-clothes into her bath. Thus, at something before six o'clock on the following morning, the Princess surprised Clytie by stepping into the studio, where the spring-morning rays had just acquired sufficient strength to be properly called the light of day.

Swathed in her loose morning-wrapper, she was carefully cleaning and polishing her palette, when suddenly a strange, faint sensation seemed to travel all over her, and a strong shudder shook her from head to foot. She grasped her easel to prevent herself from falling; everything seemed black around her, and when the momentary mist had cleared away, everything seemed changed.

Was it herself or the studio? She touched her hair, and

it seemed as if she were touching the hair of another woman: in an agony of terror, as if to identify herself, she staggered to the looking-glass: yes—there she was—the same hot black hair and Southern eyes; but something seemed altered; another *soul* seemed reflected from the eyes in the mirror, and, looking round, the very furniture seemed unfamiliar, though she recognized it all. Good God! was she going mad? was she still herself? She even went to her writing-table and took up some of the letters that lay thereon. She read, half-aloud, her name and address on one of them, and—oh horrible!—it seemed, in some weird way, strange to her. Then her eyes fell on Eric's table, just as she had left it the night before, and in her agony she cried aloud, "Eric!—Eric!"

"Eric!"

Clytie, hearing the cry, rushed in, to find her mistress lying in a dead faint on the floor of the studio.

It was one o'clock in the morning in New York, and at that instant of time, Paul du Peyral roused Mahmouré di Zulueta from her mesmeric trance.

"Sho, honey! Sho, there! What is it, chile? Tell yo' Clytie what de mattah. You moughty po'ly, fo' shuah; yu's up too early, my pretty"—such were the words of her darkie nurse that rang in her ears as she recovered consciousness, to find the faithful old woman rocking herself to and fro over her prostrate body, and muttering incoherent prayers to her jade idôl for her mistress' recovery.

"Be quiet, Clytie," said she; "I'm quite well, only I've been frightened. I ought to have eaten something before I got to work. Get it me quickly; and mind! don't speak of this to Mr. Trevanion."

"Sho' 'nuff," replied she.

There was little fear of her volunteering her conversation to Eric, whom she in some way connected—she knew not how—with this unprecedented state of her mistress' nerves. And Daphne sat down before the fire, unable for some mysterious reason to rid her mind of thoughts of her early life, of Baton Rouge, and of the would-be husband she had never seen—Paul du Peyral.

By ten o'clock, when Eric arrived, she was herself again, calmly at work, the obsession of her mind having departed as quickly and mysteriously as it had supervened. She had, as a precautionary measure, sent for her doctor as soon as it was fair to rouse him to his day's work, and he had completely restored her equanimity. There was no doubt about it—he was reassuringly positive, as doctors always are on points they know absolutely nothing about—she was quite obviously suffering, said he, from a touch of indigestion. She had eaten something—he could not say what—that had not agreed with her!

That was all.

"By-the-by, Eric," said she, after he had been there some time, "I was reading over some of your stuff last night, so as to secure a good night's rest, and I found that article of yours on Yucatan and Atlantis. I liked it better than ever, and have sent it to the editor of *Smith's Monthly*. Do you mind?"

"Not at all; it is a mere matter of form—he's had it once, and we shall have it back again. I might have saved you the trouble of sending it; but it really doesn't matter, sweetheart. What a good child you are! You're always thinking of me."

"Oh, it's not that—but I *will* make these editors appreciate you."

He came over and kissed her, and went back to his work feeling that the whole world was nothing to him so long as he kept the love of this wonderful woman. Still, was it not strange that she should have suddenly warmed to an appreciation of that article of his?—for he remembered her laughing it to scorn when first he read it to her; but perhaps she was at last acquiring a taste for his work, and he regarded it as a good omen.

Of the curious obsession of her mind that morning neither the Princess nor Clytie whispered a word, and it is probable that, had it never been repeated, he would never have heard anything about it at all; but to Daphne's bewilderment and Clytie's alarm, the symptoms recurred at intervals, generally late at night, and sometimes with such strength that it was hours before Daphne became quite herself again. After such attacks Eric would find her altered in some strange, indefinable way; her manner was hardened, her ideas were more independent and brusque, her whole personality was coarser, as it were, but at the same time touched over with a more languorous sense of luxury, a carelessness that was at the same time more subtle but more pronounced. They had almost ceased to alarm her, for the doctor before mentioned, having been once more consulted, had confirmed his previous opinion on the case: It was impossible to say exactly what the disturbing influence was—probably the home-sick fruit of the Kensington green-grocer; the effect, beyond all doubt, was a certain congestion of the blood-vessels of the cerebellum produced by a disordered state of the stomach. There was nothing to fear in any way. Seven-and-six for the visit—during which he acquired artistic dinner-party conversation for a week—and two of these pills after every attack—too late to prevent the attack—true!—but quite sure to prevent its recurrence—for a time, at least. Er—thank you!

It was one afternoon, about three weeks after her first seizure, that Eric suggested suddenly:

"Daphne, do you remember that night we went to the Parthenon together?"

"Do I remember it? *Cher ami*, do you think I shall ever forget it?"

"Let's go there to-night and see the new piece—for 'auld lang syne,' as it were."

"Certainly, boy; will you dine here, or shall I dine with you?"

"Oh, come down to the Bristol with me, and then we shall not have to hurry so."

And so it was arranged, and six o'clock saw them flying

down Piccadilly again, as on the night when they gave up the world for one another.

They were supremely happy, and they showed it. A brighter spark appeared to gleam in Daphne's eyes as she sat by Eric's side; whilst, for his part, a sensation of utter and absolute contentment seemed to pervade his whole being. He hardly noticed the play, and was only conscious of a lover-like regret that the fall of the curtain chased them once more into the open air. Arrived once more in Holland Street, he was following Daphne into the studio, when suddenly she sprang back, exclaiming,

"Eric! there's somebody there."

"What!" he cried, and strode past her into the studio.

The fire-light threw shadow-shapes, gaunt and monstrous, upon the walls; the imprisoned air seemed heavy with the sensuous perfume of the Princess Daphne's personality; but that was all.

"Bah!" said he, as he struck a match on the sole of his shoe, and lit the gas, "there's no one here. Tell you what it is, Daph; you're getting nervous, and I don't like it. Let me give you something strong; what shall it be?"

She did not answer, and he looked round. Something in her look arrested him as he stepped towards her. She had curled herself up as it were on the hearth-rug among the pillows that had fallen from the lounge, a position, picturesque, passionate, beautiful, but not *hers*. A strange, yearning look was in her eyes, her half-parted lips wore a feverish crimson, and, revealed by the cut of her corsage, he saw her bosom heave as if she suffocated under some strange excitement. It was Daphne, and yet not Daphne; the figure that lay before him was too soft, too sinuous; the position was too undignified, too wild—if such an expression may be applied to a posture—for the calm, cool Princess. He flung himself on his knees by her side, exclaiming,

"Daphne, my darling, what is it?"

For answer she gathered his head in her long white arms, and drew it down to hers, crushing him in an embrace that was almost suffocating, till he could feel the tumultuous beating of her heart as she whispered:

"Oh, Paul, Paul, my darling!"

"Paul!" he exclaimed, as he started from her. "Who's that?"

"What?"

"You said 'Paul.' What do you mean? Come, child, get up, and be sensible."

"Sensible! What do *you* mean? Aren't you Paul? Oh, no; you're Eric. And yet I seem to know a man named Paul. Isn't it you? No. Ah! but what does it matter? Oh, don't look at me like that, dear; put your arms round me, to tell me you are here. Oh! Eric, if you knew how I love you!"

"Yes, yes. But what is the matter with you? You look—you act—so strangely."

"Well, never mind—kiss me!"

"No, you are not yourself; let me get you something.

"Oh, don't trouble yourself," said she, rising suddenly and flinging herself into a chair. "No I'm not myself—I don't care—it pleases me to be someone else for the time. What does it matter? You are not Eric, as far as I can make out—everything seems topsy-turvy—so much the better; it makes a change. Come!"

He stood still, a few paces from her, as if terror-stricken—spell-bound. Was this his grand, graceful Daphne, whose calmness had so often chilled the flame of his love when it blazed highest? Was this the woman who, in the pure devotion of herself to him, had become his, to the nethermost thought of her soul? Good God! the woman who looked at him from the arm-chair through Daphne's eyes was almost coarse—almost animal—in her expression. He turned away and looked into the fire, as if to find there the explanation of the transformation that had taken place before his very eyes. She nudged him with her slippered foot.

"Don't you want to kiss me, darling?"

"Oh, hush, hush!" he murmured, taking a few steps away from her. She sprang to her feet.

"My God! what a fool I am to love you so! I ought to be a sickly, sentimental school-girl, ready to weep with you, laugh with you, dance with you, and sigh all day at your lightest frown. But I'm not. What I am, I am; if you don't like it you needn't take it; there are a hundred men as good as you within as many yards. I must have been mad when I made up my mind that you were the only man in the world. Ah! but the difference between you and Paul!"

That name again! He turned sharply upon her, just in time to see her sway to and fro for an instant, and then to catch her as she fell into his arms.

He laid her on the lounge. Hardly had he done so, when, with a choking sigh, she opened her eyes, and seeing him bending over her, she said, with a half-frightened look, as she saw the hard, cold pain in his eyes,

"Eric, my darling, what is it?"

"You ask *me* what is it. Good heavens! that's what I ask you!"

"What do you mean? Oh, Eric, I feel so strange; just as if I'd had one of those stupid fainting fits of mine. What has happened?"

"Upon my life, I don't know. You seem to have been possessed for the last twenty minutes. Who is 'Paul'?"

"Paul?"

"Yes, Paul. You have been talking—raving—about him, and saying the most awful things to me."

"To you? oh, my love!" Then, after a pause, she covered her face with her hands, and said, in a broken whisper, "My God! am I going mad?"

Eric made no answer.

"I feel," continued she, "as if I had been somebody else, somewhere else, and I thought that you were that horrible man who is in America—Paul du Peyral. Oh, Eric, what does it mean? I can't bear it;" and for the first time since he had known her, she burst into tears.

He knelt by her side and put his arms round her, torn hither and thither by a weird feeling of violent attraction and equally violent repulsion. What was the mystery attaching to this incomprehensible woman?

Little by little she became quieter, calmer—herself again; and when he left her, there was no trace remaining of the manner that had horrified him so, no recollection of the incident which, on his mind at least, had left an impression of uneasiness, if not of positive alarm. He slept but little that night, but determined to learn, without delay, all that he could of this Paul du Peyral, who seemed to cross his path continually, and who seemed to be in some mysterious way entangled in the skein of his existence, and of that of the Princess Daphne.

His opportunity came sooner than he expected it. A couple of days later the Eastons gave a tea-party to the colony, and as their studio was smaller and less picturesque than his, he placed the latter at their disposal, and found himself to a certain extent in the position of host with regard to their guests. If it had not been for this, he would probably have hardly noticed the good-looking vulgarian who was presented to him by Sylvia Easton as "Mr. Charles Sturton-Baker"—the name in full. Mr. Baker had promoted himself from the obscurity of Belsize, N. W., to the dignity of a hyphenated name, and of a manner which he fancied was more suited to the punctuation. Miss Easton, not quite sure of her suburban Adonis when transplanted into Holland Street, exploded a mine in her good-natured endeavour to supply him with a cloak for his personality, by saying sweetly as she presented him,

"Mr. Baker—er—Mr. Sturton-Baker has just returned triumphant from the conquest of social New York."

"This may be my man," thought Eric, as he shook Mr. Baker's hand, and invited him to look at his sherry and bric-a-brac with him.

"So you have been in America, Mr. Baker," said he, by way of opening the conversation; "how did it impress you?"

"Don't you know that thousands of Americans lose their lives yearly by asking that question of foreigners?"

"Indeed! why—how?"

"Because it is the question that one is asked from the moment one lands till the moment one re-embarks, and after a few days, killing the man who asks it of you becomes merely justifiable homicide."

"Indeed! I wasn't aware that I was either transgressing the laws or courting danger when I asked the question. But seriously, it must be a very interesting country. I have always heard that its social institutions are quite unique."

"Well, in what way?"

"Why, that all classes of society are mixed up together inextricably, and you never know whether you have a millionaire driving your horse-car, or a car-driver receiving you in a millionaire's mansion."

"That is to a certain extent true. I have met in my American travels car-drivers and bar-tenders whom I should be proud to call my friends, and millionaires and social magnates whom I should be sorry to have black my boots. Excellent sherry this, Mr. Trevanion!"

"Er—yes. Have some more. I suppose no one ever inquires into his friend's antecedents in the land of the brave and the home of the free."

"Oh, no. A sort of *Fifth-Avenue oblige* keeps them quiet on questions of paternity and grand-paternity. It is only the members of the *haut* Knickerbocker *régime* who discuss their pedigrees; and the descendant of a Dutch adventurer thinks he confers a great honour when he marries the millions of some commercial magnate. The funny part of it all is, that when said descendant of said Dutch rapscallion wants to be particularly insulting to the working-bee in the hive, he describes the latter contemptuously as 'a Dutchman.'"

"And did you come asross the Creole element of society at all?"

"Hardly at all. Few Creoles inhabit the North and East, and when they do, one seldom knows them to be such. Now and then one meets a handsome, stormy-looking man or woman, and hears that it is a Creole—that is all."

"I wonder if you ever came across a Mr. Paul du Peyral?"

The vulgar face became convulsed by an expression that was half astonishment and half leer, as he replied:

"Why, yes—I have come across him; what of him?"

"I know nothing of him, but I should like to."

"Mr. Trevanion, if I read your expression right your feelings toward du Peyral are hardly friendly."

"Well, no; he keeps a dear friend of mine out of a very large fortune, and seems, in more ways than one, to lie across my path—though I have never seen him. You know, it happens so sometimes."

"Then I have the advantage of you, for I have stayed in a country-house with him, and can only say that he was personally very offensive to me."

"Ah! a gentleman, I suppose?"

"Well, yes—I suppose so," replied Baker, on whom the gentle sarcasm was completely lost. "He's one of those affected, half-mystic people who think the world of themselves here, and will want frills on their halos hereafter."

"You evidently don't like him, Mr. Baker—have some more sherry."

"Thanks! No, I don't; in fact, between you and me, old man, he did his best—and failed—to spoil a very pretty little game of mine over there. There is a little girl in New York who thinks herself a second Madame Récamier, but isn't, and who is madly in love with me—all New York rings with it. Now, as she has millions of her own, I have gone in for them, and in a few months you'll see me making her American dollars fly right merrily. Now this du Peyral wanted her for himself, so he abused me to her like mad, and then had to take it all back, as they say over there. Naturally, I should like to get even with him."

"He wants to marry this girl, you say?"

"Well, he wants to marry her money; I don't fancy he is rich himself. Unfortunately, there is an obstacle, I understand—some *liaison* he has formed over there."

"A *liaison*?"

"Yes—see here—I only heard about it by this morning's mail—here's my little girl's letter."

"But, my dear sir, I don't want to read your love letters!"

"Oh, that's all right; go on. Women shouldn't make fools of themselves if they don't want it known. However, if you don't care to know what you ask about, you needn't read it, that's all."

Eric, seeing that the man was in earnest, took the letter, and read as follows:

"My own sweet darling, etc., etc., Charlie! You know that your little girl is unhappy, for when you are away, etc., etc. When you come back—and you *will* come back, won't you, Charlie? etc., etc., etc.—I shall have such lots to tell you that you won't want to hear, etc., etc., etc., naughty boy! etc., etc., etc., darling! etc., etc., etc., married, etc., etc., etc. And I am your own etc., etc., etc., Parthenia. *P. S.*—I had almost forgotten what I wanted to tell you, darling. The other day that loathsome man, du Peyral, called—like his impertinence!—and, oh! my darling, etc., etc., etc., he said the most dreadful things about you. Of course I didn't believe him, because I know in my etc., etc., etc., that you are etc., etc., etc., and I thought no more about it; but he wrote to a gentleman in England named Gabriel Hawleigh, whom I should like to etc., etc., etc., who wrote back the truth about you, which was lovely. And du Peyral was so dreadfully frightened of what you would do to him that he gave me the letter to read, with a perfectly grovelling apology for having slandered you. I hope that, when you come over again, you will etc., etc., etc. The idea of his daring to call at a decent house, when everyone knows that he is somehow connected with that dreadful woman,

Mahmouré di Zulueta, who you know was etc., etc., etc., and is etc., ete., etc." And then, with renewed expressions of admiration, of the domestic servant order, the postscript closed.

"What do you think of that for a letter from a girl with five millions, my boy, eh?" remarked Mr. Baker, as Eric returned him the communication, with an expression of supreme disgust on his face.

"Well, it is hardly a letter that I should think your million-heiress wants hawked round to flatter your vanity; but you certainly seem to have cause to dislike Mr. Paul du Peyral. What are you going to do about it?"

"Ah! that's it. First of all I am going to find out all I can about him and the Zulueta through Murray Hill, an American friend of mine, and then I shall marry my little gold-fish."

"*Je vous souhaite de la chance!*"

"Eh?"

"Good luck to you!"

"Oh! certainly, thanks—great heavens! who is that woman who has just come into the room? What a clipping gal!"

"That is Miss Daphne Préault," said Eric, very stiffly.

"Well, she's A 1, ain't she? Do you know her?"

"Yes."

"I say—introduce her to me, will you?"

"I will present you to her, if she cares about it. I'll ask her, if you like."

"All right, old man; go on. And, I say, do you know—it's a queer coincidence—she's the living image of that man we've been talking about—Paul du Peyral!"

* * * * * * *

"My goodness, Eric," said the Princess, as they entered her studio together an hour later, "why on earth did you introduce that horrid little cad Baker to me?—I believe he was half tipsy."

"He was all you say he is, *chère amie*, but I owed him

some favour, and that was the one he claimed. He had been giving me very useful information about the man who I believe is what the Germans call your *doppelgänger*—Paul du Peyral. He hates him, and if there is anything wrong with Monsieur Paul, he'll find it out through an idiotic but love-lorn American heiress, who is negotiating the purchase of Mr. Baker for her very own, and will, in this manner, save us a good deal of trouble and expense. I've asked him to come and report progress to me. *Il faut souffrir*, you know, *pour être au courant!* One must suffer, to be well-informed."

"Well, it is a devotion on your part which I highly appreciate;" and the conversation drifted on to other subjects.

It was about half-past nine that evening that Eric and Daphne were sitting before the fire, playing *écarté*, when Gabriel sprang into the studio suddenly, pale and out of breath.

"I am going to be hung," he cried, sinking into a chair.

"Good God! Whom have you killed?" exclaimed Eric.

"My picture, I mean—see!" and he produced the notice from the authorities at Burlington House, which told him that its hospitable portals would be thrown open to him on Varnishing day, at the Private View and at the Academy Soirée.

A season of genuine congratulation ensued, which became general a few moments later, when the postman arrived bearing similar intelligence for the Princess Daphne; and as Gabriel rose to leave, having been warmly felicitated by Eric, the Princess took both his hands in hers, and leaning over, kissed his forehead, saying,

"Gabriel, dear friend of ours, I am proud to be the first to salute you on your accession to greatness. A new era has opened for you—and for Maye. May it be eternal, and may we all live long to congratulate ourselves on being the intimate friends of one of the greatest artists of his day."

It was with a tear in each eye that Gabriel rushed from the studio to go on spreading his good news. As he did so, the door slammed violently behind him, and a little mirror that hung by its side fell with a crash, and was shattered into fragments.

"*Absit omen!*" ejaculated Eric. And he rang for Clytemnestra.

CHAPTER VI.

AN ANGLOMANIAC.

In a delicately-furnished male apartment in the hotel which he had come fondly to imagine had been named after himself, sat Mr. Murray Hill, an American gentleman of Spanish appearance and French manners, the aim and object of whose existence was to be taken for an Englishman. With this purpose in view he clothed his symmetrical form entirely in British clothes, was virulent in his abuse of all things American, turned up his trousers in New York when the weather reports announced rain in London, spoke with an amazing drawl, stuck an eye-glass of a perfectly innocuous and supererogatory description in his dexter optic, affected with enthusiasm the society of wandering Englishmen, and was consequently a centre of adulation and imitation in the sacred precincts of the Pantaloon Club, within whose exclusive portals the gilded youth of Manhattan origin strove to hide their honourable Dutch ancestry beneath a varnish of acute anglomania.

From the above description the casual reader might be inclined to write Mr. Murray Hill down an ass, but the casual reader would be vastly mistaken. A better fellow never showed himself at Delmonico's than Mr. Murray Hill; a gentleman in every modern sense of the word, the shady members of the English snobocracy who yearly came to New York for the winter, and who ought to have been proud of his friendship, were seldom fit to be spoken of in the same breath with him; and by those who understood him at his proper value, his little transatlantic idiosyncrasies were readily forgiven, on the principle of "*Nullum magnum ingenium sine mixturâ dementiæ !*"—a great genius is always a trifle mad!

It was unfortunate, however, that his knowledge of Great Britain was not of a kind complete enough to show him what should have been apparent to the merest observer, *viz.*, that Charles Sturton Baker was a cad in the most practical and onomatopoetic sense of the term, for, meeting that person one day at the Sunday menagerie of the Van Baulk'ems, he was led away by his somewhat aggressive personality, and nearly succeeded in launching him in the best society of the modern Gotham. After Baker's return to the land of his obscure birth, he kept up a correspondence with Mr. Murray Hill for his own selfish purposes, a correspondence which he garnished freely with extracts from *Truth*, *The World*, and *Vanity Fair*, on the culinary principle of "flavour to taste, and serve quickly on clean paper."

It was with a lazy tremor of joyful anticipation therefore, that, on the morning of which I speak, Mr. Murray Hill took up the envelope that lay beside his chocolate, and whose postmark, "London," was in no sense—for him—qualified by the letters "N. W." that bespoke its evangelhurst origin; and, breaking the seal, he commenced, with much appreciation, the string of second-hand and original (though imaginary) gossip of the back-stairs and of cheap society journalism. That H. R. H. should have worn in his buttonhole at "The Private View" the entire spike of a double hyacinth bloom was, to say the least of it, thrilling; but it paled into insignificance before the intelligence that a Royal Duke had expressed to Mr. Baker, on the steps of the Marlborough Club, the opinion that, if that sanctuary were conducted more on the lines of the Pantaloon Club in New York, his Brother (with a capital B) would have nothing left to wish for in the world. It was therefore with a new thrill of pleasure that he received Mr. Baker's commission, which was couched in the following terms:

"A few days ago I was talking about you to my bosom friend, Lord Trevanion, and he said to me, 'I wonder whether Mr. Murray Hill could find out for me anything about a man named Paul du Peyral, who lives in New York. He is, I believe, an adventurer of the deepest dye, and should he by any chance be married quietly, it would be a scrap of intelligence that would entitle its author to sincere gratitude in *High Quarters*.'" [Capital H. Q., and underlined.]

Now, Mr. Murray Hill had traversed the world from China to Peru—proceeding in a westerly direction, of course—and consequently Paul du Peyral was not only well known to him, but was also, in the lucid intervals when he was free from anglomania, an object of intelligent admiration to him. But the mania was strong upon him this morning, and he determined, in a social but drastic manner, to enquire into that gentleman's "record," and report accordingly. Mere personal admiration must not be allowed to interfere with patriotic *esprit de corps*, and, posted as he was in matters transatlantic, Mr. Murray Hill had almost come to look upon himself as an Englishman!

His toilet carefully completed, therefore, he sallied forth—that, though hackneyed, is the only expression that ever conveys adequately to my mind the progress of the American dandy down Fifth Avenue—to the Pantaloon Club, in the classic gloom of whose reading-room he found a selection of the gray-headed youth—the *jeunesse argentée*—of New York, and of him who seemed to him the best, or rather, the most promiscuously, informed, he inquired for data concerning that traveller-mystic, Paul du Peyral. The answer was prompt and precise.

"Du Peyral? Oh, yes. A queer chap, but interesting in his way. He was at Mrs. Lexington Park's last night, and he and Eugene Stiggins had rather an interesting discussion on mesmerism. You know, Eugene is awfully good at it, but he confessed himself nowhere in the presence of du Peyral. Why, there was a woman there who humbugged him about it, and said she did not believe in it, and our mystic just looked at her for a minute and then said, 'You can't stir an inch, hand or foot;' and, by gad, sir, she couldn't! I never saw a girl so scared in my life. She began to beg off, and he simply said, 'Hush! you can't speak;' and, by gad, sir, she couldn't! It was wonderful. Then he clapped his hands and said, 'Now you're all right;' and she was. She didn't chaff him any more, but followed him about the room with her eyes all the evening, as if he had bewitched her."

"But who is he, anyhow?"

"I'm not quite sure, but they say he's a Creole by birth. He came here a few years ago, and his ostensible occupation is a study of 'Skeeters and Bluebottles, or something of that kind; but they say that's only a blind—that he performs weird rites in his own rooms with that queer foreign woman, Mahmouré di Zulueta. He'll get his head broken by someone some day, if he performs promiscuously on other people's best girls."

"What's the tie between him and la Zulueta?"

"Well, that is a mystery too, and a rather delicate one. He hasn't known her very long, but they're awful thick—nearly always together, and people say—well—you know! Tom Morrison was catching bass on Lake Ontario some time ago, and saw them together at Niagara, and put them down as a pair of honeymooning turtles."

"Honeymoon?"

"Well—sort of. However, there's no fear of Paul marrying the dazzling Mahmouré, for if he does, all his money goes to the Préaults of New Orleans. Claude Préault was telling me about it the other day. Naturally they wish he'd marry, but du Peyral's too foxy, and doesn't bother about buying the tree when he can always pick an apple."

"Oh!"

Mr. Murray Hill lunched pensively, and then wandered down the mountain side till he reached Paul du Peyral's rooms. He was greeted with effusion, and presented to Mahmouré, who lay in a sort of happy lethargy on a lounge. It was not long before he spoke of the phenomena of the preceding night in terms of admiring interest, and followed an established principle by giving a biassed opinion on a subject he knew nothing about, to the grave amusement of Paul, who itched to give him a practical illustration, but withstood the temptation manfully.

When he was gone, Mahmouré looked after him and said:

"Paul—who's your friend?"

"Male variety of the genus American—sub-order, Dude—class, Anglomaniac. A harmless, gentlemanly fellow, with a lot of good stuff in him, masked by a morbid fear of letting it get out."

"Don't trust him."

"Good gracious, why?"

"Because he is your enemy. Probably he doesn't know why himself, but the way he looked at me and watched you told me that he had some *arrière pensée* in coming to see you. Depend upon it he didn't come here for nothing."

"What an anxious little woman it is! Well—don't be afraid, dear; he can't hurt me, and he's one of the few men I should care to have around. He has seen the world, and it makes him interesting, because he understands it."

"That's the very reason you shouldn't be too thick with him, *cher ami;*" and could Paul have seen Mr. Murray Hill, as he proceeded up-town on a broad grin and a horse-car, he would have been inclined to agree with her. As it was, all he said was:

"Well, the only thing I know against him is, that he was a friend of Charles Sturton Baker's when he was over here."

"That's another name that always frightens me for no earthly reason, when I hear it; depend upon it, Paul, the combination of those two men is bad."

"Well, it doesn't affect *me* if he chooses to keep bad company; you can put it down to a phase of anglomania. But, by Jove! one must have it strong if it blunts one's perception of the moral and social qualities of Baker. But come, let us make an experiment. I wonder whether I could make you 'appear,' as it is called, to Daphne Préault, who seems such a friend of yours over there."

"Oh, not to-day, Paul; you look so tired. It takes too much out of you."

"Nonsense, little one," replied Paul; but his wife was quite right. The rings round his eyes were increasing in circumference and deepening in shade, and sometimes even Paul himself felt uneasy at the lassitude that crept over him. Mahmouré, on the other hand, seemed to be gaining strength every day—her new-found happiness seemed to restore to her the life she had almost relinquished through sheer indifference to it; and sometimes a horrible feeling came over her that, Hermippus-like, she was slowly but surely sapping his vitality, was living with a life drawn in some mysterious manner from his.

"Nonsense, child," repeated Paul; "I am a little tired this morning; that's the result of the mesmerism at Mrs. Lexington Park's last night; but this afternoon or this evening I shall try to make the fair Daphne see a ghost."

"Doesn't it seem a shame," said Mahmouré, pensively, "to worry her in the way we must, when we are living on money that ought to be hers?"

"Good heavens! what do you mean?"

"I don't know. Somehow I seem to have identified myself with her lately, and feel sometimes as if I were ashamed of myself for having been a party to such a dishonesty—for that's what it *is*, Paul, you can say what you like. I can't help looking at it from her point of view; it's the result of our experiments, I suppose—but sometimes it makes me miserable!"

"Don't be ridiculous, girl," replied Paul, almost brutally. "I have a mission to fulfil in the world, and that mission is the perfection of mesmeric science. I could not get money enough by fair means to live in the luxury which is necessary to us for the purpose of our experiments, so having got it by foul, I keep it. I don't care how I get it, so long as I have it."

"Oh, don't talk like that. I'm quite serious—and it makes me feel as if I were a thief."

"Oh, indeed! Why this high moral tone all of a sudden?" said Paul, with a sneer. "I suppose you want me to play the restitution game, and all that!"

"Yes, Paul."

"Great heavens! and it's for *this* that I married you. It's for *this* that I've tried to satisfy for you the scruples that every woman naturally cherishes. Mahmouré, you will oblige me by not mentioning this subject to me again—*never*. You hear?"

"Yes, Paul. There's only one last question I want to ask. If you hadn't this money, should you have enough of your own for us to live on?"

"Yes, I should; but I don't choose to live less comfortably than I do. I don't mind telling you that most of the income of old Préault's money is put aside to provide for you in case I die. But I won't hear any more infernal nonsense about proclaiming myself to the world as a swindler. Now we will change the subject, if you please."

In this little scene all the unscrupulousness of du Peyral's race came out, and it was a kind of poetic justice that Mahmouré should have got such an idea into her head. There is no doubt that it was due to the identification of Mahmouré with Daphne through his own agency. The continual communion of the two souls had made the one woman sympathize with the other, thinking almost with the same mind as she. But neither Paul nor Mahmouré realized this. *He* thought it a sickly sentimentality that must be crushed out; *she* fancied that it was a natural sympathy for the wronged heiress. It was the commencement of a very pretty complication in this history—a complication, in fact, on which the entire history was destined to turn.

If Mr. Murray Hill could have fully realized what was going on in Mahmouré's mind, his task would have been much lightened. As it was he re-arrayed himself in new and more patriotically English garb, and went and called on Miss Parthenia Van Baulk'em.

It happened by good or ill luck that, when he was announced at the Van Baulk'ems' mansion, Miss Parthenia was seated in her boudoir, engaged in transferring the gold stamped band bearing the magic name of Pingat-Laferrière from a ball-dress purchased some years ago in Paris, to the waist of a home-made production of the family dressmaker. Miss Van Baulk'em was about to visit friends at Tuxedo, and felt that this band, carelessly exhibited as the gown hung from its appointed peg, was more calculated to impress her friends than the "unsigned" work of art of her more economical *modiste.* Engaged in this work of indumentary diplomacy, the fair Parthenia was equally busy making confidences on the subject of Mr. Charles Sturton Baker to her "greatest girl-friend"—for the time being—and giving full scope to her venomous little tongue on the subject of M. du Peyral. It was therefore annoying that Mr. Murray Hill should come at that particular moment, but as he was a combination of three things strange among the male adherents of the Van Baulk'em menagerie, to wit, a gentleman, a scholar, and a friend of Mr. Baker's, she deemed it expedient to deviate from the strict path of mendacity, and confess that she was "at home."

Virtue, she felt, was on this occasion its own reward, for Mr. Murray Hill opened the conversation, in terms which were balm to her wounded soul, on the subject of Paul du Peyral, and together they speculated on the possibility of du Peyral having married the beautiful Mahmouré on the quiet. However, the question occurred—what could be his object in doing it?

"Well," said Mr. Murray Hill, in answer to her question, "there could be only one explanation of the thing. In the first place, if report is not, as usual, a liar, la Zulueta is singularly fickle in the bestowing of her favours, and requires chaining; in the second, du Peyral has evidently been infatuated by her; and in the third, he is mad on this mesmeric business, and she is his champion 'subject.' Now, everything seems to point to the fact of his being an utterly unscrupulous adventurer, so, to keep his victim bound to him, and to steal the Préault inheritance into the bargain, it is quite possible that he has married her somewhere without saying anything about it. What we want to get at is evidence of this, circumstantial and documentary. And that is what I propose to do, if I can."

"My heartfelt wishes for your success go with you," responded Parthenia. "If that man isn't what he pretends to be, the sooner he is hounded out of New York with his ballet-dancer—well, actress, if you like—the better. Here he has been, for the last three or four years, swelling about the place as an independent gentleman, making love to all sorts of girls, and marrying none of them, besides creating no end of scandals with married women; so you will be doing a good action to society at large, and a very great favour to me." And the beautiful Parthenia put her hand on Mr. Murray Hill's arm with the coyest little pressure imaginable, and looked with her great brown eyes deep into his.

Mr. Murray Hill was only a man after all, and "Phenie" Van Baulk'em, though vulgar, was very pretty, and when she let him carry her hand unresisting to his lips—for the benefit of "Charlie" of course—he felt that he was indeed a Galahad; and should "Charlie" prove to be a King Arthur, he was perfectly prepared to become a Sir Launcelot to her Guinevere. Mr. Murray Hill was only a man, after all!

That evening Paul du Peyral made his grand experiment of acting through Mahmouré upon Daphne as she slept in Holland Street, Kensington, W., with a measure of success duly to be recorded in the next chapter.

In her mesmeric trance on this occasion Mahmouré retained her own personality, and gave Paul a description of Daphne that astonished him vastly. Was it possible that the Creole heiress resembled him so marvellously in appearance? or was Mahmouré confusing the two personalities, and describing *him* to himself as Daphne Prêault? It was a problem that he reserved to time and himself for solution.

On the following day, as Mahmouré lay curled up among the cushions of the divan, to her amazement Mr. Murray Hill was announced! At first she was going to reply with an indignant "Not at home!" when it occurred to her that if this was an enemy, she might as well cast around him her wiles, to make him declare himself. So he was shown into the snuggery on Forty-first Street which is already familiar to our readers.

"An unexpected pleasure, Mr. Hill," said Mahmouré, as that gentleman seated himself at a respectable distance from the lounge on which she lay curled up as usual.

"A pleasure, Madame di Zulueta," replied he, "that I should have denied myself on the grounds of etiquette, for I know I ought to have asked permission before venturing to call, had it not been that, though I only had the pleasure of making your acquaintance yesterday, my thoughts turned somehow instinctively to you for sympathy as I passed your door."

"For sympathy?"

"Yes, for sympathy with an indignant man; though I have no right to be indignant, for my indignation is on account of other people's business, not of my own."

"But how interesting to find someone so altruistic as to be indignant on someone else's account!"

"Yes, it is, rather, especially as indignation is a very wearing emotion, and produces gray hairs and wrinkles and things."

"Are you not going to tell me its cause? I always thought that you Englishmen never had emotions."

"We *what?*"

"You Englishmen."

"What do you mean?"

"Why, you are English, are you not?" (Oh! the wily Mahmouré!)

Mr. Murray grew pink with pleasure, and as nearly as possible hauled down his colours as he stammered:

"Well, no!—I'm not *quite* an Englishman. Of course my family were English, and that makes me very un-American, thank God!–and I've lived over there a good deal and—"

Mr. Murray Hill would have gone on with his Macaulayesque history of himself, only that Mahmouré, having made her *coup*, didn't care a jot about the fiction she had encouraged, and so merely cut in with:

"But your cause of indignation?"

"Ah, yes," said Mr. Murray Hill, coming back to fact—or rather, abandoning one fiction for another—as he remembered his business: "I have been very much disturbed this afternoon by a very strange case. A young Englishman is over here, slaving at almost menial literary work for a living, compelled to this course by the unscrupulousness of an American blackguard, who, living in England, has contrived to rob him of an inheritance that is justly his."

"Oh, how abominable! can't you suppress the American blackguard over there?"

"Well, blackguard is rather too strong a term. I was led away by my feelings—foolish things to have, are they not? I should have said adventuress, for the swindler over there is a woman."

"A woman? how shameful!" cried Mahmouré, getting interested, and feeling all a woman's vindictiveness against the misdeeds of one of her own sex rising within her as she spoke.

"Yes," said Mr. Murray Hill, reflectively, "it is shameful, for the boy over here ought to be living in elegant independence, as they say, instead of starving to satisfy the low caprice of an utterly unworthy woman over there."

"Caprice? What do you mean?"

"Why, no doubt we should be able to work upon her sense of right and wrong, but she has married over in Europe some hound of a man whom she supports, and therefore there is no chance of inducing her to surrender her ill-gotten wealth."

"Really, Mr. Hill, this is the most abominable story I ever heard. How can a woman be so wicked? and how can a man be so mean?"

"Should you think it any better or any worse if the case were reversed?" said he, rising and walking towards the window. "I mean, suppose a man kept a hard-working woman out of her inheritance to support himself and another woman in luxury?"

This was a stunner! It was her own case exactly, and in the light in which it constantly occurred to her. She looked quickly and keenly at the gentle, courteous creature who was playing with his gloves, at the window, standing so that his back was turned to the light. Was this really a true story he was telling her? or was he, like some modern Machiavelli, touching off a torpedo of truth by firing a fuse of fiction? If he were, not the slightest indication thereof appeared on Mr. Murray Hill's interesting but impassive face, and Mahmouré, lulled into a sense of security, felt a certain relief at having someone to whom she could express her views on her own case, and who would turn a sympathetic ear to the cry of her artificially aroused conscience. Artificially, I say, because had she not become so mysteriously identified with Daphne Préault she would never, in thought, have swerved from her allegiance to Paul and his schemes for his own welfare. So after the first shock of astonishment was over, she replied quite calmly:

"I don't think that theoretically it would make any difference to the morals of the situation, but practically speaking, I think it would make all the difference in the world. For a man can always support himself, and a woman cannot respect a man who lives upon her. If the position were reversed, as you suggest, I am certain that the woman who was supported with someone else's money could be acted upon by sympathy for her fellow-woman, and would herself try and induce the man to make restitution. If he would not do it, and the case were properly presented to her, she would even make restitution herself—supposing, that is, that the man could support himself without the other unfortunate woman's money. And even if he couldn't, I believe the woman would try, even if it came to working for herself. Ah! Mr. Hill, I know we women are awfully hard on one another when we are in independent circumstances, but pity for a really ill-used sister is a very strong factor in many of our actions."

Mr. Murray Hill was very clever, and knew exactly where to stop—he was not like the amateur gardener who stirs up the seed he has sown, with a stick, every day, to see how it is getting on—so he stopped here and proceeded to change the subject. We have remarked above that he was only human after all, and Mahmouré, attractive as she was, even when she was nearest to death, was doubly so now that life was beginning to blaze once more from her beautiful eyes. So Mr. Murray Hill was stricken with the brilliant inspiration of killing two birds with one stone, and replied, coming close to the divan:

"Ah, madam, I thank you from my heart; it is such women as you that make one think better of humanity in general, and of your sex in particular. I bless the day that broke for me when I had the honour of making your acquaintance. A friend of mine used to say that he never knew but one woman who could understand reason, and *she* wouldn't listen to it. You are unique, for you both listen and understand." And he took her hand and carried it to his lips.

Mahmouré drew it away somewhat hastily, and arranged herself more stiffly on the divan.

"Why do you take away your hand?" said Mr. Murray Hill, trying to get hold of it again. "You cannot be so cruel as to refuse my homage—and with such eyes as those that were made to look in love, with such lips as those that were made to smile and kiss."

"Mr. Hill!" exclaimed she, standing up, with a look of terror in the eyes he had insulted.

Mr. Murray Hill believed most of the stories of the "inconsequence" (Balzac again!) of Mahmouré, and fancied that the assumption of dignity was conjured up to spur him to fresh ardour. At that moment Mahmouré heard the click of Paul's latch-key in the outer door of her "apartment," and the look of terror gave place to one of malicious courage. Mr. Murray Hill noted the change, and, misinterpreting it by reason of the inferiority of his ear, flung himself on his knees and tried to clasp her in his arms.

"Mr. Hill! how dare you? Paul! help me!"

Paul had burst into the room, and with one bound had caught the enterprising anglomaniac by the collar. Paul was wiry if not muscular, whilst Mr. Murray Hill was a small man. Calmly, and apparently without effort, he dragged the gay Lothario to the front door, and applying a well-aimed kick to that portion of Mr. Murray Hill's person especially constructed for the purpose by Providence, launched him airily into Forty-first Street, to the delight of a small crowd that was listening to the elevating strains of an itinerant band, and then, returning, took Mr. Murray Hill's hat, gloves, and cane, which he cast after him onto the sidewalk.

"I'm a fool," soliloquized Mr. Murray Hill; "but I have suffered in a good cause. Firstly, it is clear that those two are something more to one another than merely casual lover and mistress; secondly, that being the case, la Zulueta is conscience-stricken over living on the Préault money; and thirdly, I'll break that blackguard du Peyral with all the greater joy for this thrilling episode. My God! let him look out for himself if his record isn't all right!"

Meanwhile Paul, the excitement over and the strain relieved, had sunk exhausted onto Mahmouré's divan. Strange, surely, that a man of such physique should pant so after a trifling exertion like the ejection of Mr. Murray Hill!

"I don't understand it," said he, in answer to Mahmouré's anxious inquiry. "If, like Gautier, I could believe in 'avatar,' I should think my soul were getting, in some mysterious way, separated from my body. I think, if my bodily strength would weaken off with it, the balance would be maintained and my vitality would not be so worn-out, as it were; but it seems to me as if my soul were too weak for my body. I'm not ill; I'm not even tired; but all the same, everything seems an effort to me now."

"Oh, Paul, Paul, are you sure it isn't this mesmerism?"

"No, dear, of course not! or if it is, it is only so in a very slight degree. Something is sapping my vitality, but what it is, and how the change takes place, I cannot hazard a conjecture to explain."

In this respect Paul resembled many a student in psychology. Absorbed in the contemplation of the result, his eyes were blinded to the cause, proximate or ultimate. A less profound student than he would have suggested immediately that the repeated concentration of his whole vital force upon Mahmouré and its transference, through her, to Daphne Préault, was gradually robbing him of his very soul. The effect was visible in his decreased vitality, and in the gradual resuscitation, as it were, of Mahmouré, who, day by day, regained the physique which had been hers before she became, as every one supposed, a chronic invalid. In Daphne Préault, a thousand leagues away, the change was visible in an infinity of almost inappreciable ways. Her Creole nature kept coming out more and more strongly; little coarsenesses, little brutalities, piquant, almost bewitching as they were, would crop out here and there in her language and in her manner of life; and had not the eyes of Eric Trevanion been blinded by his love, he would have noticed a fact that did not escape those of Mrs. Hawleigh, namely that the Princess Daphne was losing dignity.

And Paul? In him the change was the more curious, the more complicated. The loss of his vitality, of his soul-power, as it were, not being the result of any bodily ailment, of any pathological condition, his physique remained identically the same. His figure retained that blended grace and strength which had bewitched Mahmouré, as it had bewitched many a woman—though in vain—before her. His muscular development was unimpaired, but the motor being no longer of a sufficient strength for the machinery, a certain listlessness began to steal over him, which was attributed by his friends to a kind of nervous prostration, by his enemies to discouragement and an evil conscience, and by Mahmouré—and she was perhaps nearest the truth—to exhaustion caused by his unremitting labors of the mind.

It is to this listlessness that may be attributed his indifference to the proceedings of Mr. Murray Hill and Miss Parthenia Van Baulk'em, for though during the next few weeks after the episode above recorded at Mahmouré's, he heard vague rumors of the animosity of that siren and of her henchman, and of enquiries they had set on foot concerning himself and Mahmouré, and their respective antecedents, he did not bother himself to surmise whither those enquiries might lead, but devoted his time, in the privacy of his own apartments, to the tabulation of the notes for his great work on "Psychic Forces, and the influence of Mind upon Matter," which was rapidly approaching completion since he had taken to himself, by chance as it were, so singularly gifted a *collaborateuse* as Mahmouré di Zulueta.

The spring of the year was growing old, and the machinations of Mr. Murray Hill were slowly but surely progressing. Little by little, with the assistance of Mr. Charles Sturton Baker, who, acting in concert with Eric Trevanion, kept him posted on the condition and position of Miss Daphne Préault, he had pieced together the history of Mr. Paul du Peyral, and, this task accomplished, all that remained was to prove the marriage of that individual and Mahmouré di Zulueta. This task he set about with enthusiasm, receiving, by way of advance reward, the approbation of Miss Van Baulk'em, from an interview with whom he one day set forth to find the before-referred-to Tom Morrison, his pulses dancing wildly, his fingers still warm with the pressure of the fair Parthenia's unresisting if not encouraging hand, dazed with the memory of divers blandishments which not even the indiscretion of the novelist can reveal, and which had been lavished upon him by the siren, "for the benefit of Charlie," of course, but in no wise the less fascinating to Mr. Murray Hill on that account. *Entre nous*, dear reader, it had dimly occurred to Mr. Murray Hill that, in the first place, his own income was only sufficient for his own maintenance in elegant leisure; in the second it was a pity that Miss Parthenia's millions should be bestowed upon an alien; and—Miss Parthenia having been more or less successfully chaperoned through a London season by a lady who had hidden most of Parthenia's vulgarity beneath the ægis of her own pure-blooded aristocracy of birth and nature, the said young woman having in turn suppressed her failures and exaggerated her successes with artistic mendacity—in the third, that it would be an excellent scheme to marry that young woman himself, preparatory to carrying her over to London, where, according to her own account, she had a certain apocryphal social position, and where he could gradually cut himself and her free from the associations of her horrible family.

He knew that it would be difficult if not impossible for him to hold, personally, any further communication with Mahmouré; but he bore very minutely in mind the recollection of the way she had received his carefully prepared story of the ill-used Englishman, and felt that, if properly approached, she might become an ally most important in the subversion of Mr. Paul du Peyral; and having occupied a few more weeks in collecting evidence in a manner which is too obvious to need recapitulation here—such as searching the registers at Niagara and so on—Mahmouré was one morning aroused to the contemplation of her matutinal coffee, flanked by an envelope bearing upon its upper left-hand corner the name and address of an eminent legal firm, addressed to her in the alarming legibility of the Remington type-writer.

There is only one thing that alarms a woman more than a mouse or a telegram, and that is an obviously "business" communication. Little wonder therefore that Mahmouré, rousing herself into vivid wakefulness and a sitting position among the pink-silk sheets of her pretty *dortoir*, neglected the ridiculous in favour of the sublime, and forgot her coffee in contemplation of the "lawyer's letter."

If the outside had disturbed her, how much more the inside, which read as follows:

Offices of SELIGMAN, SEARCHER, & CERTIORARI.
No. 195 Nassau St., NEW YORK CITY.

[*Two enclosures.*] *23d May*, 18—

DEAR MADAME:

Information which has recently come to hand prompts us to write to you for corroboration or explanation on a subject which is of the last importance, both to clients of ours and to yourself, and we trust you will answer our communication in the spirit in which it is made, with a view to saving all parties concerned the annoyance and expense of complicated legal proceedings. Without wishing to trouble you with details upon a matter with which you may or may not be already familiar, it is necessary to state that the marriage of Mr. Paul du Peyral entails certain consequences and duties upon the executors and beneficiaries of the estate of the late Casimir Préault of Baton Rouge in Louisiana. From information which has been put into our hands it appears that in the fall of last year you were privately married to this gentleman in the village of Niagara, Ontario, Canada. We shall be glad if you will sign and return to us one of the enclosed documents, to wit, the acknowledgment of that marriage, or its specific denial.

We are, dear Madame,
Yours faithfully,
SELIGMAN, SEARCHER, & CERTIORARI.

TO MADAME DI ZULUETA,
No.— West Forty-First Street, City.

To say that Mahmouré was frightened by this ominous missive is to employ a miserably inadequate term, and one in no sense fitted to the state of the case. Hardly conscious of what she was doing, she dressed herself with lightning rapidity, and flew as fast as an American hansom could take her, over the boulderous moraines known in New York by the euphemism, " streets," and arrived breathless with excitement, at the door of Paul's flat, where she admitted herself with her latch-key. Into the dining-room, lest he should be at breakfast—Paul was not there; into the study, lest he should be already at work—Paul was not there ; through the *portières* of the study, into his bedroom, lest Paul should not yet have risen—and there she found him.

Asleep?—surely not ; for he lay motionless and senseless as she flung herself on her knees by his side. In vain she strove to arouse him from his lethargy; in-vains he implored him to open his eyes, which she covered with kisses. In an agony she tore down the bed-clothes and laid her hand upon his heart ; a feeble, intermittent beat was the only sign which her husband gave her to tell her he was still alive.

Paul du Peyral lay dying.

CHAPTER VII.

CLOUDS.

"WHAT I say is this," remarked Gerome Markham, as he dallied with a muffin and a cigarette in the Eastons' studio, one warm spring afternoon: "morality is a question of geography, and whilst not, perhaps, advocating the same latitude of action as that implied by the motto of the monks of Medenham, '*Fay çe que vouldras*,' still, in the Bohemia of Holland Street, the red, white, and black flag covers a multitude of trifles that would be sins in West Kensington, crimes in the provinces, and eminently good form in St. James's. And on the principle that we have adopted as a precept, 'live and let live,' I don't see what we have to do with Eric Trevanion and the Princess Daphne."

"Well, to a great extent I agree with you, but it does seem strange that Daphne Préault, who has rather gone in for taking a high moral ground, should get herself so very unpleasantly talked about," responded Sylvia Easton. "Give me of your light, for like that of the foolish virgin, my cigarette has gone out!"

"After all, you know," observed Dick Lindsay, who, from a distant corner, beamed through his spectacles on the other three, to wit, Sylvia and Eva Easton and Gerome Markham, "a little scandal—*un tout petit scandalorama*, as Vautrin would say, has the inestimable advantages of an advertisement, and would give an additional value to the Princess' autograph."

"Well, you'd better collect it at once," said Eva Easton, "for Mr. Baker says she's got a grand lawsuit coming on in America, which will probably make her retire into wealthy insignificance. Do you collect autographs, Mr. Lindsay?"

"Not personally; I used to collect them once for a great-aunt from whom I had 'expectations,' but when one day I sent her a slab of plaster, with '*Mene, Mene, Tekel, Upharsin*' scratched on it, and signed '*Belshazzar*,' she left off collecting, as she said it was too great a strain on my inventive faculties. She then proceeded to make a new will and die—I got nothing but her autograph album."

"Well, you ought to be thankful for small mercies."

"Yes, like the man who had gout in both feet and thanked God he wasn't a centipede! But unfortunately I'm not. I'm sure I was meant to live a life of dignified ease, not to drive myself melancholy-mad by writing cast-iron humour from morn till dewy eve, from dewy eve till deuced late. But still, it might be worse. Just fancy being 'something in the city,' like your friend whom you mentioned just now, Mr. Charles Sturton-Baker."

"I'm sure," said Sylvia Easton, "there isn't much the matter with Mr. Baker, except the hyphen in his name—and that's harmless. He makes a great deal of money, which is more than we do!"

"Ah, you'd better get his recipe for us," observed Markham.

"Go to the ant, thou sluggard," said Eva; "consider her ways and be awakened to the error of your own."

"That's just it," returned Lindsay; "I havn't got any aunt—and when I had, I used to wake her up a good deal more than she did me."

"Oh, how dare you? To pun is human; to forgive, divine. However, I'll forgive you," said Sylvia, "and if you're good, I'll get Mr. Baker's recipe for you—or Eric's."

"Well, I don't know that I want either of them, for they seem very similar. Baker is always swaggering about some drivellingly idiotic American heiress or other, that he declares is madly in love with him, poor little thing! And it strikes me that if Travanion *père* knew much about his hopeful son, he'd cut off the supplies; perhaps that's why Eric is so anxious to secure the Princess' fortune for her."

"For shame, Dick!" said Eva. "If you could catch an heiress, you'd do it on the spot, I know."

"Not at all," replied he, shamelessly. "Why, here I am, positively dying of love for *you*, Eva, and we've nothing to live on but bread and cheese, with kisses, whereof the first is not nice in excess, and the second isn't nourishing in *any* quantity."

"Sorry I spoke," remarked Eva, blushing nevertheless a lively crimson, as Dick Lindsay continued to beam on her through the gold-rimmed spectacles.

"Those two will quarrel in a minute," said Sylvia; "they always do. Tell me, Mr. Markham, how are the Hawleighs getting on?"

"Ah! there's a happy family for you, if you like. There's no getting over the fact that 'Sunshine in the Fog' is *the* picture of the year; and now Gabriel floats in golden seas. Dealers and amateurs vie with one another to buy his work, and unless his health gives out, we shall see our dear boy both rich and celebrated in a very short time."

"Ah! and then I suppose he'll marry Maye Trevethick?"

"Oh, *tiens! tiens! tiens!* how indiscreet you are! The idea of a young woman announcing as a fact what we all know—but keep to ourselves. Of course he'll marry Miss Trevethick, and he'll be a jolly lucky fellow; but we shall all be delightedly surprised when it's announced."

"Do you know," said Eva Easton, pensively, as she bent over her work, "I always had an idea that she was in love with Eric."

"I hope not, for all their sakes," returned Gerome Markham. "In the first place, Eric has only one idea in the world, and that's Daphne Préault; in the second, it would break poor Gabriel's heart; and in the third, it would be very ungrateful of her, for without the Hawleighs she'd have been obliged to go out as a governess or companion, or something."

"Pooh!" exclaimed Eva, with a quick glance at Dick Lindsay; "what has gratitude to do with it?"

"Unfortunately nothing," replied Markham, gravely; and he rose to go.

Lindsay followed his example, and the two men left together.

Outside the door Lindsay remarked: "I say, Markham, I don't like the look of things in this street. The Princess is compromising herself badly, and Eric's letting himself drift; one of these days he'll be pulled up short. And I'm afraid there's something in what Eva said about Maye Trevethick caring about him."

"Well," replied Markham, as they parted to go in opposite directions, "all I can say is, I hope not. I should be sorry to see Gabriel and Maye wreck their lives; but I fear Eric is doing that same, even now. 'Who lives will see!' *Au revoir!*"

From the above conversation, which was only one out of many like unto it which the eaves-dropping walls of Holland Street overheard about this time, the reader will have gathered to a certain extent how matters stood with the quartette in whom we are mainly interested. The doors of Burlington House had opened on the first Monday in May to a crowd that were unanimous in their verdict upon Gabriel's picture as "the picture of the year," and Gabriel had the remunerative work of a lustrum on his hands, in the commissions showered upon him by European and American patrons of art. The days of struggle and genteel poverty seemed to have ended for him, and it was with the new light of a great tenderness in his eyes that, nowadays, he would watch Maye at work in her corner of the studio, whilst Mrs. Hawleigh regarded the consummation of her hopes as practically within her reach, and felt that she was amply rewarded for the sacrifices she had made at the altar of her son's genius.

As for Maye, the only change in her was one which was sedulously hidden from the outer world, for she concealed the excitement that an intuitive sense of the approach of a crisis in her life caused her in her heart—her heart, which concealed also the dull, deathly pain that she suffered when she thought, or anyone spoke to her, of Eric. But her home-life seemed even purer and sweeter than heretofore, and filled her often with a dim, soft melancholy, when, at the death of the daylight, she would sit down to the piano in the studio, and Gabriel would follow her into an ecstasy of music with his violin, which was now his one fondly cherished recreation.

Often they would wander among the harmonies of Chopin, of Beethoven, of Kalliwoda, of De Beriot, of Brahms, and of the other masters; but more often Maye would lead off with an improvised theme, and Gabriel, taking it up, would follow her through its variations and modulations, until, trembling all over, he would fall on the lounge in the attitude of the painting in Daphne's studio, and lie silent and happy, whilst Maye resolved the harmonies of the theme as it died away under her fingers.

"Maye," said he, one day, as the music ceased, "how strange it is that you and I should think as it were with one brain when we play! Do you know, dear, it seems to me sometimes almost *eerie* that such a perfect sympathy should exist between us. How is it, do you think?"

"I hardly know, Gabriel," she replied, a strange feeling seizing her heart, and driving the blood, it seemed to her, into her throat. "I suppose it is that we live here in such perfect accord—we three—that the same thoughts occur to us when we play, and express themselves in our music."

"Ah! pray God that you speak the truth, Maye. Sometimes, do you know, the thought comes to me that it may all cease suddenly, and that we might be separated; and the thought is almost more than I can bear. Maye," he continued, earnestly, and coming closer to her, "you have been more than a sister to me since you have been here with us; you know, don't you, dear, that I feel more than a brother to you. For I love you very dearly, sweetheart; you have guessed that, haven't you? I've never told you so, for we've been so poor, though it's been on my lips a thousand times, and in my heart always. But now, thank God, it seems as if a change had come, and even if we are not rich, we shall be quite independent. Can you love me a little in this newer, sweeter way, darling? Heaven knows that the only joy I can find in my life lies in the thought that I can lay it at your feet—will you take it, dear?"

"Oh! Gabriel!"

"Perhaps I ought not to have spoken so soon, but to me it seems as if I had waited, oh! so long, for to-day; but I have an excuse for speaking, dear—I love you so." He sank on his knee by her side, and slipping his arm around her waist, covered the hand that lay in her lap with kisses.

She looked straight before her, with a dry, far away look in her eyes, answering never a word, but clasping the hand that encircled her waist, as if in doubt whether to draw it closer round her, or to fling it away.

"Answer me, darling, won't you?—or shall I wait?" said he at last, trembling for her great silence.

"No, you must not wait any longer, dear; what can I say to you? You and the madre have been so good to me that if I can make you happy in return, I have no right to deny what you ask of me, even though it be my life—myself."

"Oh, no, no, not like that," he cried, springing to his feet; "don't think of gratitude, dear. You know that I shall love you just the same, even if you cannot think me worthy of you as your husband. If you will come to me and be the light of my life, let it be in love, and not in dull, cold gratitude. Oh! tell me that you love me, darling,"

There was a moment's pause as she also rose to her feet, and turning, faced him as he stood, a great half-fearful joy in his eyes. And then she put both her hands on his shoulders, and looking up at him, answered, gravely:

"Yes, Gabriel, I love you very dearly, and I will be your wife if you want me to."

His answer was to clasp her wildly in his arms, and then, as she broke from him and ran out of the studio, he sank once more upon the lounge, almost unconscious with the exquisite joy of the moment that made her his.

And she?

She ran up to her own room, and flinging herself upon her bed, burst into an agony of tears.

She had never realized perhaps till that moment how she loved Eric Trevanion.

* * * * * * *

Meanwhile the days that came and went brought little change to Eric and Daphne, so far as their love for one another was concerned; but already there had crept into it those tiny carelessnesses which seem to be the fate of love after the first flush of its dawn has paled into the broad daylight of custom. This, however, did not affect Eric so much as the terror that sometimes took possession of him—a terror that some horrible change was taking place in the soul of the Princess whom he had elevated to be his Queen.

There is no doubt about it, humiliating as is the confession, that there is something singularly unpleasant to man about maladies of all kinds. If anyone shows symptoms of faintness or other distress, in a party, the men get perfectly miserable with nervousness. Not so the women; they, as it were, gird themselves together and watch, vulture-like, for the moment at which their services will be required. This difference comes out equally in conversation. What is so interesting to the female mind as a discussion of the maladies to which the conversants and their friends are subject, the epidemics of infantile diseases which have attacked such and such families of their acquaintance? Not so the man. Man A. says to man B., "How's C?" "Oh, C! poor devil! something wrong with him, I believe. Had measles and went out riding, got thrown and broke three ribs, got a chill lying on the grass, and the worry of it all gave him brain fever! Come and have a glass of sherry—going to the D.'s this evening?" Now this would have formed the subject of an hour's conversation to *Mrs*. A. and *Mrs*. B., with illustrations of what happened to C., what Dr. E. had said about him, and the remedies exhibited.

From all of which the reader will gather that the nervous and sometimes almost hysterical state into which the Princess Daphne was getting, by consequence of her repeated "mad attacks," as Eric used to playfully say and seriously think, was not so much a cause of pity to him as one of nervous irritation; and when he saw them coming on he would dissemble and fly; and when she described them to him, he used to pay little or no attention, or laugh at her. Therefore the account of her visions fell flat when she told him of them, and he merely put them down to a higher development of her nervous condition, which the doctor who has before been mentioned still ascribed to "a trifling indigestion, a slight derangement of the stomach which this draught will effectually," etc., etc.—"seven-and-six-pence—thank you!"

But Clytie listened with weird-struck ears to the account of how, three times at least, Daphne had been awakened by an indefinable sensation that something was looking at her —of how, on clearing from her eyes the mists of sleep, she had seen before her the figure of a lithe, supple, but withal beautiful woman who looked at her out of great soft brown eyes, which, so far from frightening the Princess, rather attracted and soothed her than otherwise; and Eric felt almost alarmed at the importance she ascribed to these visitations, and almost annoyed at the quasi-affectionate interest she took in what she playfully called "her ghost."

However, a more serious consideration had crept into the politics of the Eric-Daphne *ménage*. We have said that Eric lived in somewhat princely style in the colony, on the liberal allowance made him by his father. Now the elder Trevanion was an individual most easy to get on with so long as he wasn't contradicted; but differ from him on a course to be adopted, and the firmness on which he prided himself, castled in his old Cornish manor, became divided from pigheadedness by a line of demarcation that was fearfully slight. In the earliest days of the love of Eric and Daphne, Trevanion *père* gave an entertainment "to the county," and as was his wont, sent for Eric, as his son and heir, to assist in entertaining the innocuous magnates who (their names beginning, almost to a man, with the ancestral Cornish syllables, Tre, Pol, and Pen) considered that to be a Cornishman was to live, whilst to be anything else was merely to exist—on sufferance. Eric, like an historic prototype, answered that "he could not come," and having nailed his colours—or rather Daphne's colour's, the red, white, and black of Bohemia—to the mast, just didn't. Trevanion *père* was much annoyed, and began to make enquiries into what could possibly keep Eric in London when he wanted him at Trthwwsthpllgg Manor. The result of his enquiries was that his letters to Eric began to hint at a proximate return to Trthwwsthpllgg, and an ultimate marriage and culminating respectability of behaviour, with solemn dinner-parties and grandchildren at recurring intervals. To these suggestions Eric replied at first not at all, then playfully, then sarcastically, then seriously, with a point-blank prayer to the governor not to talk bosh.

As an immediate result, Eric was apprised that if he did not at once return home and marry a Cornish maiden, and give other trifling evidences of submission to parental authority, the supplies would be cut off, and the commissariat would dry up. "There can only be one excuse for you to remain in London," papa Trevanion had said in this letter, "and that is, that you have found idiots sufficiently weak to buy your pictures, or editors sufficiently courageous in their ignorance to buy your articles on the 'Potentiality of the But,' and so on. You therefore can get on without an allowance from me, and from this quarter it ceases."

And so Eric found himself in the exciting condition of having to make his own living—or dying—by his own unaided exertions.

Here was naturally food for thought, and for a couple of days Eric was very thoughtful. At the end of that time, as he sat idle at his desk in Daphne's studio, she came up behind him, and, putting her arms about his neck, laid her cheek against his and said:

"Eric, you are not kind; there's something on your mind that you haven't told me anything about. What is it, old man?"

"Oh, nothing of importance, dear," he had replied, a little wearily.

So she had insisted, using the thousand arguments and persuasions that a woman who knows her power can use with impunity, until at last, taking the letter above referred to from his pocket, he handed it to her without a word. In similar silence she read it through and returned it to him.

"Well?" he said, finding that she made no remark.

"Have you any money of your very own—independently of the governor?"

"Not a penny."

"Good! you will have to make some."

"How?"

"Why, by writing stuff that will sell, of course."

"Well, I've been trying to do that for months," he replied, "and I dont seem to have got the knack of it yet."

"Of course not," returned Daphne, "because you haven't absolutely required to sell your work. *Now* you do, and you must adopt a different style."

"It strikes me I shall have to adopt a different style of existence altogether. I don't see how I am to go on spending a thousand a year on nothing per annum, paid quarterly."

"So much the better for you, Eric. Your days of amateur literature are over; you must descend from the altitude of transcendental essay to the dead level of the pot-boiler. You must write stories for the magazines and articles for the reviews; paragraphs for society papers, and political squibs. You are no longer Samuel Rogers, you are Lucien de Rubempré."

"What's the use, Daph? the editors will 'regret that want of space prevents,' etc., etc., as heretofore. I was never Samuel Rogers, and I wont stoop to copy Balzac's gentle hero. Why, only yesterday I got a letter with the stamp of *Smith's Monthly* on it. I didn't even open it, I knew so well what's in it."

"Where is it?" asked Daphne, a queer look coming into her eyes, as she held out her hand.

"Oh, it's here somewhere—here it is," said he, giving it to her.

"Ah!" said she, opening it; "this was unimportant yesterday or the day before. It isn't so insignificant now. Your article on 'Atlantis and Yucatan' is accepted, and you will get the proofs in a day or two."

"What!" he exclaimed; "why, those people refused it once."

"Well, they've seen the error of their ways, that's all," replied the Princess, with a little laugh. "Now, look here, Eric; you've got to take this matter into your own hands 'right now,' as we say in America. This letter proves that if you will only take my advice, you'll get on all right. In the first place, you have the finest studio in Holland Street. You don't paint, and you don't want it, except to spend money in; you haven't got the money to spend now, so you don't want the studio, and you must give it up. Oh! don't make faces; I know what I'm talking about. Just opposite, there are a couple of rooms both vacant and cheap. You can make them very pretty and comfortable with some of the stuff you've got in your studio, and you must move in at once and set to work in earnest."

"But, Daph, I can't suddenly proclaim myself a pauper."

"That doesn't alter the fact that you *are* one, dear."

"Please, don't."

"But you *are*, Eric."

"Well, if I can't afford to live in the old place, how can I in the new?"

"Why, very easily. In the first place you are going to make money by writing, and until you have made it, I have plenty. Besides, my solicitor, or rather the solicitor to my second cousin's estate, tells me that he thinks that that money will come to me after all, in a short time. I suppose Paul du Peyral has grown tired of bachelorhood at last. We have plenty to live on, in any case."

"Thank you! I don't want it to be said that the moment I got poor I married you for your money."

"Married! Good heavens! who talks of marrying? we're very happy as we are. The only difference will be that when you were rich you spent your money on me, and now you are poor, I spend mine on you. Nobody need know anything about it!"

"Daphne! by Jupiter, you *do* want me to become Lucien de Rubempré in a hurry. Do you imagine that I—*I*, Eric Trevanion, am going to live upon *you?* Hush!—not a word more if you please on the subject; you insult me—unintentionally, I know; but your proposition is an insult all the same. Don't you *want* to marry me?" He had risen and was pacing feverishly up and down the room. At her answer he came to a dead full stop in front of her.

"Not in the least!" she said, calmly; "I prefer to remain as I am!"

"Good God! what am I coming to?" he cried. "Never dare to make such a suggestion to me again—you hear!—never *dare.*"

"Eric—I dare anything. I love you, and I intend to make a great man of you. You have all the possibilities, and if you will take my advice, you are bound to succeed. For the moment, however, you want my help. It is yours to take—and mark me, my mind is made up."

"Well—so is mine. It is useless to prolong this discussion—we shall not agree. I am going home now to think matters over a little. When I come back, don't let me hear any more of this preposterous thing. Perhaps I *am* going to be successful—well, success means independence, and I *will* be independent. *Au revoir.*"

"*Au revoir,*" she said, lazily stretching herself in the divan as he left the studio. And ten minutes after, the

Princess, with a little ironical smile on her lips, had fallen fast asleep!

Later in the afternoon he burst in upon her, pale with anger, and with a roll of proof-slips in his hand.

"What have you been doing with this article of mine?" he exclaimed, by way of greeting.

"Making it salable, *cher ami*," she replied, with a grin.

"Making it vulgar, you mean. How dare you interfere with my work? You can talk as much as you like; fortunately I have sufficient self-respect not to take your advice; but oblige me by leaving my work as I finish it. I shall alter these proofs so as to make them resemble, at any rate, my original manuscript—let this be the first and last performance of this little comedy."

"Do as you like, Eric. If you like to make a fool of yourself, do. Your stuff will only be re-rejected at the last moment."

"Time will show. Now, let us drop the second unpleasant subject that has arisen between us to-day. I wonder you can worry me so, when you know I have so much on my mind!" he concluded, querulously.

"Well, well, darling, I did it for the best, and I hope that in time you will come to look at things as I do; meanwhile we wont talk about it. Oh! don't be angry, dear; I love you so."

But he *was* angry. He returned her caress in a very half-hearted way, and his manner hurt her finer nature, which happened for the moment to be in the ascendant. Presently he broke the silence again by saying:

"I've been thinking over what you said about moving out of the studio, and have been seeing exactly how I stand. By the time all my bills have come in, I shall be pretty hard up, until some of these editors pay me for my work; so it will be better for me to move. I don't see why I should be ashamed of being poor. I'll see about the necessary arrangements at once."

"Good!" she replied, drawing him down by her side on

the lounge. "I am almost glad the governor has cut up rough, do you know, dear; I shall have you more to myself now, and I shall be more a part of your life in future."

It was almost with a sense of discomfort that he listened to her words, and presently he disengaged himself to go over to his own writing-table. And in the long silence which followed, the thoughts of the two were taking an identical direction: both realized that a new era had dawned in their lives, but they looked forward into that future with very different feelings—feelings, however, that they did not express to one another.

In an hour Eric had removed from his article almost every trace of the Princess' handiwork, and had posted his corrected proofs to the editor of *Smith's Monthly*, feeling almost satisfied with himself. She had meant well, he said to himself; she was a good girl, and he was very fond of her. Ah! the world? Ah—yi! Let us remark, *à propos de bottes*, that between "*une femme qu'il aime*" and "*une femme qui l'aime*" there is only the difference of an apostrophe—and what is punctuation in a love story?

And so Eric settled down to a new life. Of course his abandonment of the gorgeous studio next door to the Hawleighs was a theme for great wonderment in the colony, but it became generally understood that Eric had had reverses of some kind, and, being no longer the merry plutocrat of hitherto, had cut down his expenses and had taken to literature in search of a livelihood. This did not in any way impair his position in the colony; on the contrary, they liked him the better for it. There were few, if any, of "the boys" who did not know what it was to be periodically "broke," and that Eric should come to the same complexion seemed to draw him still nearer to them, and went far toward abolishing a certain feeling that had existed in holes and corners, to the effect that the wealthy amateur had no absolute right to share the pleasures and sorrows of the colony, but was admitted rather on sufferance than otherwise.

Eric had, in these first days, but little doubt of his ultimate success as a man of letters, though it struck him as decidedly odd when he got a polite communication from the editor of *Smith's Monthly* to the effect that in its altered form his article was not suited to the requirements of the magazine, and asking should it be inserted as it stood in the duplicate proof sent therewith, or should the article, in its new form, be cancelled? Now, Eric wanted the money somewhat, and the magazine paid well and promptly; should he pocket his pride and accept what he called the Princess' "garblement"? After much consideration he decided so to do, and, to the sorrow of all persons concerned, be it related that this was apparently, for a long while at least, Eric's first and last literary success. From this time forward, so surely as he sent an article or story to any periodical, so surely was it returned to him. Once or twice he posted a many-times-returned manuscript to some third- or fourth-rate magazine of no antecedents and doubtful future, and got it in, but never got paid for it, considering it something gained to have got rid of it at all.

And thus did Eric's literary apprenticeship begin, with all its trials and disappointments. Who is there of us who woo the Muse of Literary Fame, who has not been through it? The stories of young writers who, reduced in circumstances, have made a wild sensation, and sprung to the first rank with a first work, have ever been, to me, purely apocryphal, as they must ever be to anyone who has adopted literature as a profession and not as a recreation, and who has pitched his literary tent, so to speak, day after day in that "Elysium of the Literary Unwashed," the Reading-Room of the British Museum. The dogmatist who laid down the paradoxical axiom that "No man can make a living by letters until he is dead," exaggerated of course—exaggeration is the prerogative of the inculcator of axioms; but it is equally true that, except in a few very rare instances, men who have written standard works for all time, have been men in absolutely independent circumstances, whose works cost them far more to write than they ever brought home to their authors in the form of publisher's cheques. Now and then one hears of a great success made by a writer of fiction who has never before seen the light of day as it shines upon a book-stall. If we only knew his esoteric history, we should find that his book is made up of the few good things that have brightened three or four previous still-born productions; and our opinion in the matter is usually confirmed by the subsequent publication, "on his reputation," of the sweepings of the waste-paper basket to which he had consigned his "Rejected Addresses."

For the man who has the pluck to destroy his rejected manuscripts and start fresh, regarding his futile efforts merely in the light of "practice," I have always reserved my choicest salaam; I have known but few such. And if it is an agony to the wealthy amateur to see his works, like the curses of the proverbialist, come home to roost, can ye imagine, "ye gentlemen of England who live at home in ease," what are the feelings of the young writer who has put off importunate landwomen and tradesmen with a promise of payment "on receipt of a cheque from his publishers," when he arrives home late at night from some Bohemian entertainment or other, and sees on the table in the hall, by the dim light of the frugally lowered gas-jet, an oblong package, with a letter tucked under the string which secures it, and he thinks to himself, as, without looking at it, he carries it up-stairs in the dark, "Which of them is this?" and presently unwraps some pet essay or other, on which he counted with all the fondness of a confiding mother? Ah, sirs! *then* is the moment of tears, not of tears which flow from the lachrymal glands, but from the tear-well in the heart, as one asks one's self the question, "Am I a failure?—shall I ever be able to write for a living?" We of Bohemia know what it is—we have suffered, *nous autres!* and I am not writing these lines for the eyes of the specialists who periodically write an article to order, on their hobbies, or for the public characters whose signature covers a multitude of literary sins that are unpardonable in the scholar, but for the earnest student who has apparently wasted the best years of his youth acquiring an education that seems utterly useless when he tries to earn five pounds with a prostituted pen.

And this was the case of Eric Trevanion, who now for the first time realized that heretofore, to him, apocryphal condition, of being "hard up"; who learnt to climb upon the knife-board of a Kensington omnibus in lieu of waving his umbrella at the passing hansom; to spend hours in the dingy book-shops of Holywell Street, instead of sending a peremptory order to Quaritch or Bumpas; to cast an interested glance at the prices marked on the goods in a grocer's window, instead of sauntering into the antique silver shops in Hanway Passage to see if there was anything he could buy. And Eric felt it all keenly, all the more so when he found himself returning a compulsatory negative to postulants who had always found him hitherto "good for a fiver," under the euphemism of a loan. And with it all he became more and more of a recluse, more irritable with the Princess, when she would suggest subjects to him which he considered beneath his dignity as a scholar to discuss in print, and more sensitive than ever when she would make any remark that seemed tinged with an inquiry on the question of finance.

And Daphne felt it more keenly still. She used to scheme to lighten his worries in a score of ways, whose principal difficulty lay in that of their concealment. Thus, one day she said to him suddenly, "By the way, Eric—what rent do you pay opposite?"

And when he told her, she replied, "That's just like you! you're the most casually extravagant creature I ever knew. Why, So-and-so, who has the corresponding rooms in the next house, only pays a third of that sum. I shall have a talk to your landlady about it."

And Eric, who stood in some awe of the said enchantress, whom he constantly feared he would some day be compelled to ask to wait for her rent, replied grimly:

"Well, don't let me rob that person of the pleasure of a conversation with you."

"And you know," continued the Princess, "the bachelor-man is the natural prey of the London washerwoman. I shall send Clytie over to you for your clothes every week, and you must pay *me*. I will *not* have you robbed all round as you are now."

And to Eric's astonishment, a few days later, his whilome terrible landwoman informed him that, as she heard that he contemplated moving next door, she would be glad to have him stay, and pay the next door rent, which was, in fact, one-third of what he had hitherto been paying. About this time also Daphne grew captious about dining with him in town, preferring vastly to have him come and picnic with her in the studio; or anon she would burst in upon him in his own rooms, carrying the complete outfit of dinner in a basket, and exclaiming:

"Eric! I'm bored, and tired of my old studio; I've come to picnic with you—here's my share; what have you got?" and then she would ransack his cupboard in search of potted comestibles and other trifles which she knew Eric kept "on the farm." And she did it all so charmingly, that Eric never dreamt that she had any motive ulterior to her own amusement, or that "the rent next door" was precisely the same as what he had always paid.

It was on one of these occasions, when she had descended upon him, the bearer of more than ordinarily good cheer, that she said at the conclusion of the meal, when they had drawn their chairs to the fire, which was now almost rendered unnecessary by the advancing spring:

"Do you know, boy, I've got a scheme for you. I was sitting the other day at a dinner-party next to a provincial journalist, and he told me all about an undertaking that made me think at once of you. He is the editor of a big concern in a big midland city, and is starting a magazine to be written by London journalists. They are going to pay very well—two pounds a page—because all the articles are to be strictly anonymous, so anonymous, in fact, that not even the contributors are to know the name of the magazine, or where it's to be published. The articles are to go to him, and he sends a cheque on receipt of the corrected proofs. Well, I offered at once to write for him, and he jumped at the offer. Now, I *can't* write, but you can, and as we're very poor we must pocket our pride. You shall write the articles, and I'll put in a touch here and there. I promise not to alter what you write, and when he sends me the cheques I shall claim twenty-five per cent. for my share of the work, and as negotiation fee. You mustn't ask any questions about it, because I swore I wouldn't betray him—will you go into it with me?"

"My dear girl," answered Eric, "I'll do anything that'll make money. I've come down to that. What do you want for a start?"

"Oh, dish up any of your old impossible stuff a little, and hand it over. I'll see that it gets in all right."

And so Eric set to work again. The Princess was as good as her word, and hardly "garbled" his manuscript at all, and he returned his first set of proofs, feeling that at last the tide had turned a little. For a space the cheques came in with cheerful regularity and liberality, and Eric and the Princess used to laugh together over what he used to call "The Mysterious Magazine," which they used sapiently to agree could never pay its proprietors, so absolutely in advance of the merits of the "copy" was the price they paid for it. And for a couple of months Eric seemed to be in a position to laugh at his former troubles, especially as not only did he make a good thing by writing Daphne's articles for her, but also the editor of a leading weekly had betrayed a disposition to accept, publish, and pay for a few articles of which Eric declared himself heartily ashamed, but which necessity made him sink his personal feelings and write.

At the end of that time he sat one day in the Princess' studio finishing an article for her, and scribbling some letters, when he found that he had not an envelope left in his pigeon-holes. He rose and went over to Daphne's table to find one, and not seeing any in the place where she usually kept them, tried to find, without troubling her, the reserve stock. In pursuance of his quest, he opened a drawer in whose lock the key stood invitingly, and the first thing that met his eye was the whole set of his articles for "The Mysterious Magazine," the corrected proof of each neatly folded up with the manuscript. A horrible, sickening sensation took possession of him as he took them out and verified them, and, white to the lips as the ghastly truth flashed across him, he rose and, presenting them to Daphne as she sat at her easel, which had hidden him from her as he stood at her table, said, in a deadly, quiet voice:

"Daphne, what is the meaning of this?"

Her face was scarcely less white, her eyes scarcely less troubled and dry than his, as she made answer to him:

"Oh, Eric! where did you get those from?"

"I was looking for an envelope; there was none in your case; I opened the top drawer, and the first thing that caught my eye was this packet. Well—answer me—what have you to say?"

She kept silence, looking dumbly at the bundle, and he continued:

"Does the magazine of which you have spoken exist? Did you ever meet such a man as you described the editor to be? In God's name, Daphne, answer me, or I shall go mad!"

She covered her face with her hands, and sobbed forth her answer:

"Oh, Eric, my love, forgive me—forgive me! I can say nothing, only that I loved you, and it made my heart ache to see you so poor—to see you suffer so. I knew that some day, when you had made a name, they would be valuable, and anyone would be only too glad to take them from me for you. I was only buying them in advance—it was an investment, Eric."

For answer he flung the packet at her feet, and strode

from her presence. When he returned twenty minutes later, his eyes flaming with passion, she was sitting in the same position, her brushes lying with the manuscripts at her feet.

"So," he began, "you have lied to me from the beginning, and you have cheated me into living on your charity. I did not ask your alms—I refused them, as I refuse them now. My God! how can I have been so blind? You thought that that wretched woman over the way would keep your secret—well, so she might have done had I not by good luck chanced upon these papers. I trust you are satisfied with the success of your scheme. Egad! it was well contrived—very well contrived. How dared you insult me so?—do you hear me?—how dared you?"

She had sunk upon her knees before him—she, the proud Princess Daphne of a few short months ago—her face hidden in her hands.

"Don't speak to me like that, Eric—I can't bear it—you are killing me. It was for the best—it was for the best—I loved—I love you so! Ah! won't you forgive me, dear?"

"Never!"

She rose slowly to her feet and staggered to the hearth. There her forces left her, and she flung herself on the lounge in an agony of tears. And Eric Trevanion, his face deathly pale, his brows contracted as if with physical pain, stood looking at her.

And as he stood, no sound breaking the silence but her sobs, amid the hideous humiliation of it all there came over him the realization of how great a love was this of hers for him. Few men can withstand tears, if they are genuine, and well from a breaking heart; so at last he drew nearer to her, and kneeling by her side, put his arms about her prostrate body. As she felt them, she turned and flung hers round his neck, burying her head upon his shoulder.

"Come, Daph," he said, at last; "don't be so unhappy about it. I know it was only your true, loving heart that made you do as you did. It is I who should beg for forgiveness, and I beg for it here on my knees. I spoke harshly, cruelly, just now—I had no right to do so. You can understand my feelings a little, can't you? I know yours, and I forgive you the moment's worry you caused me—forgive you from my soul."

And so, little by little, her sobs became more intermittent, and at last ceased entirely, as, lying in his arms, she raised her beautiful eyes to his and he kissed away from them the last tears that trembled on her lashes.

When they were both comparatively themselves again, they fell to talking naturally; and when at last he saw that she had quite recovered from her paroxysm, he rang the bell, and Clytie brought in tea and lit the gas. Her sharp eyes saw that the Princess had been weeping, and she levelled at Eric a look of undisguised hatred, which, however, he scarcely noticed, though, unreasonably, he felt this afternoon more than usually inclined to reciprocate her aversion.

When she was gone, and they had settled themselves comfortably, he said:

"Now, Daph, let's talk business."

"Yes, Eric," she exclaimed, eagerly, "that's what I want you to do. I knew that you'd never consent to accept this money from me—and see—I have kept an exact account of everything I have spent for you. It has been nothing to me, for you know I am quite well off. Very soon you too will be rich and prosperous, and then, never fear"—this with a little laugh—"I'll exact it from you to the uttermost farthing—I promise you I will."

And so they calmly discussed the question and their mutual arrangements for the future. The past was irremediable, the money was spent that she had given him, and with her sweet casuistry he came almost to look upon her future loans as not so shameful after all, for he felt within himself that his present poverty *must* soon come to an end.

They were thus employed when, suddenly, a distant report shook the studio, and some fragments, apparently of glass, fell upon the skylight in the roof.

"Great heavens! what's that?" exclaimed Eric.

"Goodness knows," returned the Princess, anxiously; "what do you think it is?"

"There has been an explosion somewhere—let's hope it's only the boiler of some conservatory or other. I tell you what—I'll run out and see if it was in Holland Street." And he disappeared.

In ten minutes he returned, looking very grave.

"Oh! what is it, Eric?" cried the Princess.

"It was an explosion of gas, dear—and I'm sorry to say it was in Gabriel Hawleigh's studio. It had got turned on somehow, and when he went to light it, it exploded, blowing the whole of the skylight out."

"And Gabriel?"

"I'm afraid he is terribly hurt. Fortunately there was no one else in the studio at the time."

CHAPTER VIII.

TRANSMIGRATION.

Yes! Paul du Peyral lay dying.

So said the doctor for whom, in an agony of terror and grief, the distraught Mahmouré had sent Paul's body-servant. He might live, said the doctor, for hours, or for days, but most probably it would be a question of the former: it was the beginning of the end; and after having made the most thorough examination possible, the medico was forced to admit that he was absolutely and completely baffled by the nature of the disease which showed such alarming symptoms.

Mahmouré, being questioned, gave the fullest possible particulars of Paul's habits of life—which were regularity itself. She told all she knew of his studies, of his scientific and psychological pursuits; and concerning these latter the doctor made especially minute and interested inquiries. At last his examination—during which Paul had lain in a state of semi-consciousness—ended, and the doctor rose and took his leave, saying to Mahmouré as he went:

"The case to which you have summoned me, madam, is one which appears to be unique in my professional experience, and which cannot be dealt with by any form of pathological treatment that is familiar to me. I am not, however, of that class of physicians who will gladly see a patient die rather than yield a point of etiquette, and meet in consultation a doctor of the Eclectic school. If I may be allowed to suggest I would ask you to send for Doctor Schuyler Van Boomkamp, a young practitioner whose *specialité* is psychological complaints, and who has made a profound study of them in Paris, Berlin, and Leyden, from which latter school he is a graduate. If you will beg his attendance here at three o'clock, by that time Mr. du Peyral will most probably have regained consciousness, and I will be here soon after that hour to consult with Dr. Van Boomkamp."

During the day, as the doctor had predicted, Paul recovered consciousness, though his weakness was so great as to be almost paralysis, and noiselessly Mahmouré came and went in his room, ministering to his wants, and rewarded now and then with a few half-articulated words of thanks. The thought of what she had originally come about never once entered her head, nor did it until she was reminded thereof in her conversation, that same afternoon, with Dr. Van Boomkamp. As he is a not altogether unimportant actor in the development and conclusion of this drama, a word about him may not be out of place.

Schuyler Van Boomkamp was a man of thirty-two, tall, but with a pensive stoop in his shoulders, and a grave inclination of the head forward and sideways, that was habitual, a smooth-shaven face, and hair of an uncertain colour that had become slightly touched with white, eyes rather deeply set and of an intense steel-gray, a clearly cut nose and thin lips, his whole personality completed by a pair of icy-cold, long, white hands, with beautifully formed nails, and a pair of equally icy-cold *pince-nez*, from behind whose gold rims the steely eyes literally froze the prevarication ere it gushed from the fountain of the brain. He always dressed exquisitely, but invariably in the fashion of a few years ago; and to-day, when Mahmouré was summoned from Paul's bedroom to speak with him in the study before he saw the patient, she realized, the moment she saw him, as he courteously handed her a chair, and in smiling showed her a set of teeth as fine and white as a woman's, that she was in the presence of a man who, like Paul, was *the* unique specimen of his kind.

After giving him the same general particulars as she had given to Paul's own doctor, Schuyler Van Boomkamp asked her question after question concerning the mesmeric phenomena in which she had been the percipient, investigating them with a minuteness that almost appalled Mahmouré, and examining into causes, agencies, and effects in a manner that might almost have made her fancy he had been present at their *séances*. As he concluded his examination—of which he had taken copious notes—a ring at the bell and a step in the parlour announced the arrival of the senior medico. Mahmouré was about to summon him, when Dr. Van Boomkamp, arresting her with a gesture, said quietly:

"There is one final question that I must ask you, Madame di Zulueta—on what day were you married to Mr. du Peyral?"

"Dr. Van Boomkamp!" She had turned and faced him, her eyes stricken wide with apprehension.

"Do not be distressed, *madame*, I beg of you; and I assure you, though the assurance is hardly necessary, that the information will rest as profoundly confidential as the rest of our conversation. Of course I know that you are legally married to our patient; you have told me so unconsciously fifty times this afternoon; but it is important that I should know the exact date."

"On the 25th of September, last year, in the village of Niagara, Ontario, Canada."

She made the answer almost mechanically, under the spell of those terrible eyes. Schuyler Van Boomkamp made a last note on his *carnet*, and joining his *confrère*, the three entered Paul's bed-room together.

Paul lay propped up by pillows, very weak, hardly able to articulate a word, but yet conscious, and the moment Dr. Schuyler Van Boomkamp entered the room he fixed his eyes upon that gentleman, never letting his gaze wander for a moment. After verifying the diagnosis of his older colleague, Van Boomkamp said to the dying man, in a low but deadly distinct voice:

"I am about to ask you some questions; can you concentrate your mind upon the answers?"

An inarticulate whisper broke from the patient, in which

the words "understand"—"too weak" were alone recognizable.

"Madame di Zulueta," said the doctor, "I must ask you to restore temporarily a portion of the vitality you have unconsciously drawn from our friend here. Kindly take your seat close to the head of the bed here. So—thank you. Now place the tips of your fingers under the patient's head, so that they lie along the spinal column at the point where it leaves the brain. So—good! Kindly make an effort of will to transfer some of your very abundant vitality to him. Mr. du Peyral, you are feeling stronger—can you answer my questions now?"

A flicker of light returned to his dull eyes, an infinitesimal tinge to his hollow cheeks, as he replied in a weak but perfectly distinct voice:

"Certainly, doctor."

The older and more orthodox physician sat petrified with amazement, but watching the proceedings of his young colleague with fascinated interest. Then the examination began.

"Are you in pain?"

"No."

"Do you feel in any way light-headed?"

"No."

"Are you in full possession of all your mental functions?"

"Yes—in a way."

"You mean that your brain works with its usual clearness, but without its wonted rapidity?"

"Exactly."

"Have you ever had an attack of this kind before?"

"Once only."

"And that, I presume, was immediately after some more than ordinarily violent effort to compass some psychological end?"

"Yes."

"What was its nature?"

"I had summoned to my mind a picture of the subject upon whom I have been making my experiments in Europe."

"Ah! and you saw her?"

"That was my impression."

"To return to your present condition: there is apparently no alteration in your physical condition?"

"No."

"No loss of weight?"

"Not an ounce."

"No emaciation—no loss of muscle?"

"None whatever."

"Raise your leg in bed."

"I cannot."

"Raise your arm above your head."

"I cannot."

"Ah! Kindly remove your fingers from his neck, *madame.*" Mahmouré did so.

"Now tell me, what are your sensations?"

A contraction passed over his features, but though his lips moved, no sound came from them.

"Be so good as to replace your hands, *madame.* So—thank you. Now take a deep breath, put your lips to his, and breathe softly, so as to fill his lungs if possible with your own atmosphere."

Mahmouré did so, and a strong shudder shook the dying man.

"Doctor," he said, "do not let her do that again—she cannot bear it. I know that it must be my life or hers; let it be mine—my work is ended. But I know yours, doctor, and I beg you, if you will, to take up mine where I have left it." As he said these words his voice had almost regained its natural strength, and at the conclusion of his sentence the muscles of his face relaxed once more, and he sank still deeper among the pillows that supported him.

"That will do, *madame,*" said Van Boomkamp, rising. "We cannot arrest the end; it must come in a short time now, probably in a few hours. You wish to remain with him, I presume? Pray do so, but do not touch him more than you can help; the excitement will be too great for him. Now, doctor," continued he, turning to the older man, "I shall be glad of a few minutes conversation with you." And he led the way into the study, closing the doors behind them carefully.

"What is your opinion on this case, sir?" he began, when they had seated themselves.

"Dr. Van Boomkamp," returned the other, "when I diagnosed the condition of our patient this morning, I am proud to say that I found that my experience and medical skill were wide enough to tell me that I was completely baffled. As you see yourself, there is no tendency to a diseased condition of the heart, liver, lungs, spine, or brain; it is not nervous fever; it is not hypochondria or lymphomania. If disease is here, it is a disease of the life, of the soul; and at the amphitheatres of anatomy, a life, a soul, has yet to be dissected—we know nothing of it. Though, therefore, the name of Schuyler Van Boomkamp is one that causes the orthodox faculty to look somewhat askant (as you know), your fame as a psychologist has reached me from sources that I respect in Paris and Berlin, and especially from the more esoteric schools of Leyden University. I therefore counselled Madame di Zulueta, who takes an interest in this young man that we can perhaps understand, to consult you, and having assisted at your examination I can only say that I am proud to meet you in consultation on a case which, I frankly confess, is beyond the range of my orthodox and perhaps old-fashioned experience and studies."

At the conclusion of this exordium Schuyler Van Boomkamp bowed respectfully, though without rising, to his senior colleague, and then, removing his glasses, he wiped them thoughtfully and readjusted them. Then he made answer in the slow, measured terms of one who is stating a collection of carefully ascertained and determined facts.

"Sir, I have not been in the habit, as you know, of encountering this frankness in my consultations with the faculty, or rather that branch thereof which you represent. I will answer you with equal frankness, and I hope lucidity, strange as must appear to you my unalterable convictions on the nature of this case.

"We have here a man of very rare and very highly developed psychological powers, whose name is about to be appended to the already almost interminable roll-call of the martyrs to science.

"He is bound by ties, earthly as well as spiritual, to the very highly magnetic woman who is with him at this moment, and through her he has become connected in a manner, mysterious to the ordinary mind, with another woman, who, though a thousand leagues distant from him, is probably also connected with him by some half-forgotten tie of blood, and is certainly connected with him by the bond of a coincidence of personality which strikes even myself as being almost miraculous. Madame di Zulueta is an extraordinarily receptive woman, and when first their *liaison*—let us call it that for the sake of definition—commenced, she was at the lowest ebb of vitality, physically and psychologically. The absolute regularity of his life has left his physical constitution unimpaired, but by dint of continually hypnotizing his companion, he has gradually transferred his vitality to her, and it is practically with his *soul*, with his vital force, that she is living now, has regained her health, her strength, almost her youth. But of this vitality which he has poured into her, only the grosser atoms have remained as fuel for the machine of her life; the more ethereal, the more subtile portion he has transferred, through her, to this woman on the other side of the ocean, by name, it appears, Daphne Préault.

"Your diagnosis of his condition is of course"—and he bowed again—"pathologically, scientifically correct, but the vital condition in which he finds himself at this moment is this. Pray follow me very carefully. His magnificent and unimpaired physique requires a commensurate strength of vitality, of soul, to support it in the condition known to us as

'Life.' That soul he has gradually transferred, until what is left of it is insufficient to maintain the 'life' in so powerful a physical machine. If his body had weakened *with* his soul, he would undoubtedly have continued to live, though upon a lower plane of vitality; but it has not done so, and now the remaining vestiges of soul are about to leave him, and produce, in a perfectly healthy body, the phenomenon known to us as 'Death.' The problem which is about to be solved before our eyes is this: into which of these living personalities will the final transference take place? It may be into that of Madame di Zulueta, but I hope not, for she is not physically strong enough to bear the burden, and it would probably result in some form of mental aberration with her. I am inclined to expect that it will be the body of Miss Daphne Préault that the residue of his soul will seek. You doubtless think that I am expecting a kind of metempsychosis, a kind of reincarnation such as formed the basis of the Pythagorean philosophy—well, in a measure, I am. I have once seen such a phenomenon take place in a little village in Poland; we are about to witness its repetition, and, in the interests of psychology, we may congratulate ourselves on our almost unique experience."

He ceased speaking, and for a few moments the elder man kept silence. At the expiration of those moments he rose and said:

"Dr. Van Boomkamp, the theory you have expounded to me is so unexpected, so marvellous, that I am absolutely unable to give an opinion in exchange for yours. Excepting as an observer—and as a deeply interested one, believe me—I have nothing more to do with this case; I see that I cannot arrest the finger of death, and I leave our patient in your hands, for—though against my will and judgment—I am bound to confess that you have laid before me an aspect of the case which, extraordinary though it be, I am not in a position to controvert. When do you expect that death will supervene?"

"In about four hours."

"You will be here?"

"Certainly—and you?"

"With your permission—yes."

"Good! we will meet here then at about half-past seven."

And, leaving a message to that effect for Mahmouré, the two physicians left the house.

When they returned, at the time agreed upon between them, she was sitting where they had left her, at the foot of the bed where Paul du Peyral lay, also as they had left him, half-conscious, and apparently paralyzed. His pulse was thin, hard, tense, and rapid, and as Schuyler Van Boomkamp replaced his hand upon the bed, he looked significantly at his companion and said:

"It is a matter of minutes."

Mahmouré buried her head in her hands, and for the first time burst into a flood of tears.

The two men took their seats by the bed in silence, the younger making rapid notes in his memorandum-book.

The profound silence of the room was only broken at intervals by a convulsive sob from the woman, and Van Boomkamp shaded the lamp more carefully to make the twilight complete. Suddenly the dying man moved, and all three riveted their attention even more closely upon him.

His lips moved, and a sound escaped them, the purport of which the listeners could not catch. Then, suddenly, half rising into a sitting posture, his eyes opened wide, a flush of colour mounted to his cheeks and as instantaneously died away again, as he stretched his arms before him, and crying, in a grand, ringing voice, "Daphne!—Daphne!"—he fell back upon the bed. They turned in the direction his eyes had taken, and Mahmouré cried out in terror:

"There! there! do you not see her?"

"Who? Where?"

"Daphne—Daphne Préault," she murmured, and then added, as she covered her face once more, "Ah! she is gone."

Van Boomkamp took Paul's wrist for a moment, put his

ear to his mouth, and then placed his hand upon his heart. He glanced at the older physician, and then, laying his hand on Mahmouré's shoulder, he said softly:

"It is over—he is gone."

"Dead!—Oh, God!" she cried, "and his last thoughts were of her. Oh! Paul, Paul!" and she buried her head upon the dead man's breast.

* * * * * * *

During the four days that elapsed between the death of Paul du Peyral and his funeral, Mahmouré never left her husband's body, refusing to see anyone, to be comforted, almost to sustain life, and would not arouse herself from her apathy to gratify the curiosity which the circumstances of Paul's death had excited.

New York rang with it for at least three days. The sudden death of the man who had been such a problem in society, the sudden appearance on the scene of a wife, the stories of the colossal fortune Paul had tortiously enjoyed by concealing the marriage which had taken place, said the gossips, immediately on the death of his *first* wife ten years ago, all were weirdly interesting, and formed the staple subject of conversations at dinner-parties, germans, the opera, in church, and in other places where the School for Scandal of New York meet to paint their neighbours the deepest possible black, in the hope that its own members will look a shade grayer by comparison. Miss Parthenia Van Baulk'em looked upon it as a visitation of Providence, a direct interposition of Divine power in her favour, and almost took to herself the credit of having killed the man who had dared to form a true opinion of her tinsel troubadour. And when Mahmouré du Peyral, as she was now called, refused to place herself on exhibition, and give particulars on the subject of Paul for a small fee, popular indignation reached its zenith; and, from the altitude of Fifth Avenue, descended with full force on her unconscious but beautiful head.

She denied herself peremptorily to all save Schuyler Van Boomkamp and Paul's man of business, and in the settlement of his estate the latter gentleman had his hands full. It was a complicated affair. Paul had saved money, and had bequeathed everything to his wife; but the difficulty lay in separating from the property that was undeniably his, that portion of the proceeds of the Préault estate that had fallen to his lot since his marriage with Mahmouré. Representing, by way of amateur "*amicus curiæ*" or "guardian *ad litem*" in the interests of social justice, Mr. Charles Sturton-Baker, and so, indirectly through Eric, the Princess Daphne, Mr. Murray Hill, with the assistance of Messrs. Seligman, Searcher, & Certiorari, was making himself very officiously offensive; and as his reception by Mahmouré du Peyral was a matter not to be thought of for a moment, he was thrown back on the congenial companionship of Parthenia Van Baulk'em, who was making her arrangements to spend the season in Europe, where she fondly imagined she would find "her young man" in society, and whither Mr. Murray Hill felt anxious that she should go in the capacity of *his fiancée*, though he still kept up the fiction that it was entirely "for her and Mr. Baker" that he had started rolling the nucleus of the snow-ball of worry that was weighing upon the mind of the erstwhile desired Mahmouré.

The last instructions that the solicitors of the Préault estate had received, had been to extract to the last cent from the estate of Paul du Peyral the proportion of income that had been received by him since his marriage with Madame du Peyral; and Mr. Murray Hill, smarting under the memory of Mahmouré's contemptuous rejection of him and of Paul's *argumentum ad caudam*, not to mention the encouragement that twinkled from Miss Parthenia's reddish eyes, had started a wild rumour that Paul had been secretly married before this marriage with Madame du Peyral—indeed, there were people who thought that he went through the marriage ceremony clandestinely with someone about once a week—and filing affidavits, managed to tie up the whole estate for months prospectively, and to put Mahmouré into what was practically, for her, a position of considerable embarrassment.

Through all her troubles she had one staunch and true friend, a friend who had come accidentally to her side, and who had made a complete study of her case, legally, personally, mentally, and physically. That friend was Dr. Schuyler Van Boomkamp.

After the funeral of Paul du Peyral he had come to her and said:

"Madame du Peyral, I have taken the liberty of enquiring somewhat into the circumstances of the case which has been preying on your mind since the sharper anguish of your husband's death has been softened. You will naturally want a friend to represent you in many matters that a woman cannot well manage alone. I offer myself as that friend, at the same time as I offer myself as a physician."

"As a friend, Dr. Van Boomkamp," she had replied, "I accept your offer gladly, and as frankly as it is made, and I know what I have to thank you for when I see the columns and paragraphs about me in the papers; but regarding you as a physician, I hope I can decline your offer, for, now that I am rallying a little, I find myself returning to the health I enjoyed before my husband's death."

"Exactly," replied Van Boomkamp; "but you must be careful. Your health is a very curious problem, even to me; you live practically by means of a transmitted vitality, a vitality that excessive excitement would seriously impair, and that must therefore be very carefully nurtured. You do not allow the newspapers to worry you, I trust; I fear the case of the 'Préault-du Peyral' estate is going to become a *cause célèbre.*"

"Oh! I don't mind them, Dr. Van Boomkamp. You see, I have no friends in New York to speak of. The imaginative efforts of American journalists seldom, I think, worry their objects. They can never be more than weapons in the hands of one's enemies wherewith to annoy one's friends. I have enemies, for some mysterious reason, it seems; but

I have no friends to whom they can send clippings from the morning papers day after day, as is, I believe, the custom over here."

"Well—that's good! I shall look in periodically to see how you are getting along, and whenever I hear anything that in my judgment you should know, you shall know it. At present it seems as if all that has to be done is a subtraction from Mr. du Peyral's residuary estate of the income paid to him since last September, so that in a few weeks you will have nothing more to worry you in any way whatever. What are your plans?"

"I am going home," she said, a far-off look stealing into her great brown eyes.

And then, seeing that the doctor maintained silence, as if waiting for an explanation, she added,

"To Greece, you know; that is where my people originally came from; we have always called it 'home.' My village lies between Pyrgos and Corinth, on the Gulf of Lepanto. I shall buy a villa near the old place, and die forgotten under the same skies that looked down upon the hardy men of Argolis, my forefathers, when they gave up their lives for the freedom of the Peloponnesus."

"Your resolution, madam, is an excellent one," returned Van Boomkamp, gravely; "the climate of the Morea is the one that will give you the completest rest"—he had been about to say "the longest life," but he changed the expression for fear of alarming her.

To the young eclectic physician, Mahmouré was a study of intense interest; living, as she did, at second-hand, as it were, everything depended upon her remaining in a quiet frame of mind. Under those circumstances she might live to be an old woman; but should any unforeseen occurrence make too heavy a draft upon her precarious vitality, he had grave fears for her reason, if not for her life. When, therefore, the new complication arose—the throwing of the whole estate into Chancery, or its American equivalent, for the purpose of making enquiries—and he saw that not only might Mahmouré be put to inconvenience and expense for many months, but she might be even seriously embarrassed by a course of action of whose effects he felt certain that Daphne Préault, the person principally concerned, was in ignorance, he came to Mahmouré one day, and finding her nervous, irritable, worried, he made to her a proposition which was sound on the face of it.

"You can do no good," he said, "by remaining here. The atmosphere of antagonism that surrounds you is bad; besides, the hot weather is at hand, and you must leave the city anyhow. Why not go to Europe?—to London, *en route* for Greece? Your affairs do not in any way require your presence here; you can safely leave them in the hands of your attorney, whom I have ascertained to be a man of absolutely unimpeachable rectitude. By such a course many objects would be served: in the first place, you will obtain the change of air and scene in great need of which you stand at present; in the second, you will see, if you like, Miss Daphne Préault, and doubtless come to some understanding with her which will be to your mutual advantage; in the third, you will be nearer your ultimate destination, and the rest in London will serve the double purpose of shortening a journey that might overtax your strength, and of enabling you to complete many arrangements before you proceed to the Peloponnese. I may add, that I have myself accepted an invitation to proceed at once to Paris to assist Dr. Charcot in certain observations important to mental science which he is making at the Salpêtrière. I shall stay in London for some weeks before crossing the channel, and shall therefore be able to keep an eye on you, on your health, and on your business, with a beneficial result to all three. Think it over."

Mahmouré du Peyral thought it over, with the result that, the next time Schuyler Van Boomkamp called upon her, her mind was made up, and her arrangements were completed; and a fortnight later the passenger-list of the Royal Mail Steamer *Anatolia* contained the names of Schuyler Van

Boomkamp and Madame du Peyral; and a grave, ascetic-looking man with steel-gray eyes and gold *pince-nez* might have been seen pacing her decks as she ploughed across the Atlantic in proper "Cunarder" style, in the company of a woman, small but exquisitely made, with an oval, oriental face, great, soft brown eyes, and a mass of tawny hair, with which the north-west wind seemed to love to play for very wantonness, to display its glossy beauties to the gulls and petrels.

CHAPTER IX.

THE REINCARNATION OF DAPHNE.

"WELL, and what does Critchett say?"

"Hardly anything; he says that by a miracle there might be enough of the optic nerve left on which to form the basis of a hope that, when the inflammation has gone down, sight may be partially restored."

"And are both eyes equally injured?"

"Yes, or apparently so."

"Poor old Gabriel!"

"Yes, it's hard, isn't it? just at the moment he had made a name. However, let's hope for the best."

The speakers were Bernard Rawlinson and Eric Trevanion. They had met just as Eric left the Hawleigh's house at the conclusion of a visit of enquiry, about a fortnight after the explosion in Gabriel's studio. A novelist is not allowed by the Canons of the Cult to sympathize, himself, with his heroes, but it must be conceded that a sadder tale was never told than that of Gabriel Hawleigh's blindness. For an artist to be blinded is certainly a tragedy of the saddest sort; but how much more sad if that artist be at the outset only, of a successful career! Here was Gabriel, however, poor and in love. The moment had arrived when his anxieties seemed to be at an end. Fortune, won at length by his persistent wooing, had smiled upon him and extended her hand, and at the moment that he stepped forth to grasp it, the blow fell that shattered in an instant every hope that he had built up for himself; and, boy as he was, sitting for the most part alone in his darkened room, the first threads of gray began to peep among the strands of light-brown hair that fell in picturesque confusion over his brows.

Mrs. Hawleigh seemed—as well she might—crushed by the blow which had fallen upon them, the culminating point of all these years of struggle against poverty. For the moment, fortunately, money was not lacking, for the great Academy picture having been purchased by a celebrated amateur for what, to Mrs. Hawleigh and Gabriel, seemed a vast sum, the news of his accident spread like wildfire, and it being currently reported that Dr. Critchett had declared his blindness to be incurable, dealers and collectors alike had contended for Gabriel's previous works, which, by the advice of Sir George B——, were sold by auction at Christie's, and brought prices such as Gabriel had never dreamed of in connection with his own work; and—such is the irony of fate—many a canvas that had been rejected by the Institute, the Academy, and the Grosvenor, went for prices even higher than that realized by "Sunshine in the Fog." The fact that Sir George B——bought the first picture in the sale, and "Miss Préault, the eminent lady-artist," the second, may have contributed to this result; at any rate, on the Monday following the sale, Mrs. Hawleigh received a cheque that relieved her mind of any anxiety as regards either the proximate or immediately ultimate future.

The eminent oculist who had taken charge of the case offered but one shadow of hope: as soon as he could be safely removed, and could without danger be exposed to the light of day, Gabriel was to be taken to a little cottage on the borders of Dartmoor, almost on the boundary line which divides Devonshire and Cornwall; and after a few months of this quiet, pure, and invigorating atmosphere, the best or the worst would be known, and Gabriel Hawleigh would know irrevocably whether he might one day look again on the faces and scenes he loved so well, or whether he were doomed to be led through life—blind!

And Maye? Maye Trevethick—what of her? Ah, sirs! who shall pry into the secrets of a woman's heart? How shall I dare to say what were her thoughts as she sat in the dark with her poor blind Gabriel, holding his hand in hers in silence, or talking gently to him of their plans, of the events in the colony, such as she knew them, of the rumours from the world outside Holland Street which came to her and which she memorized in case they might interest the boy whose light had become so great a darkness. In all the unwritten history of faithful women, no story is sadder than hers, no devotion more heroic, no love and duty more sacred: to tend Gabriel, to anticipate his needs and humour his sick-man's fancies, had become her life; and she lived it, showing no trace of aught but a gentle, feminine devotion to the lot that had become hers, whilst—well! who shall pry into the secrets of a woman's heart?

And so the days passed on and grew into weeks.

Of Eric Trevanion in these times some of those who had eyes saw very little, whilst again some who had eyes saw a good deal! He did not mix very much with the colony now; he was poor, and, like every man who from affluence has come to poverty, he felt it almost as a disgrace, and no longer held his head high in the air with a merry word or a proud little laugh for everyone.

The Princess Daphne watched him with a light of deep anxiety in her great grave eyes, as he would sit at his desk, often for hours together, crushed, as it were, beneath the load of disappointment that began to take a tangible form in his increasing penury. Little by little his bric-a-brac, his pictures, his curios, his Eastern carpets had been sold to pay the landwoman, the baker, the grocer, and other people necessary in the scheme of even an artist's existence. And every time the Princess made him accept some small loan, the operation became more and more distasteful to him. He had even begged the elder Trevanion to give him another six months' law, but in vain. "Return here, settle down, and marry a county girl," had responded the Autocrat of Trthwwsthpllgg Manor, "and I'll pay your debts, and you shall be a man of independent means; but I refuse to keep you, as you are living now, in opulence, luxury, and debauchery"—and Eric would look round his little retreat with a bitter smile, and wonder what the governor's ideas of opulence, luxury, and debauchery were.

"Well?" the Princess would query sometimes, after a more than ordinarily protracted pause.

"Nothing—capital and labour don't seem to be hitting it off together in my case, Daph. An author seems to me to be very like a man who has found a well of natural gas on his farm, but hasn't the capital to lay down the pipes which shall conduct it into the houses of the community. The pipe-man is the publisher, and I haven't found one to undertake my gas yet."

"But the gas exists all the same—stop the flow until the capitalist comes along."

"I can't; it's too strong. At present my books are in the limited edition of one manuscript copy, as Alexander the Great used to insist upon Aristotle's works being produced. It won't do *me* much good if three thousand years hence my writings become as popular as his. Even the Chaldean author who cut his work on the wall of a palace at Nineveh had a better 'show,' in the American sense, than I; and the gentle Babylonian who wrote romances on a cylindrical seal, had at least the satisfaction of knowing that a copy of his book reached the world every time the owner sealed a letter. It isn't good to make a living by literature, dear."

"It's better than making it by the means that so many men employ, Eric. The easiest way to make a living, to my mind, is by inheritance, the next is by marriage, and the next is by being a bachelor—all of them nice, easy occupations. Wait a bit, old man, and you'll coin money."

"It seems to me that if I wait a bit I shall have to—and take the chances of being caught at it! I quite agree with the philosopher who said, 'Poverty is no sin, but all the same it's damned uncomfortable.' They talk about the merry Bohemianism of a literary life. Egad, Daph! I feel about as merry as a stuffed bear with corns, put out in the rain as a furrier's advertisement."

"Well, try something else—promote companies like the

Eastons' friend, Baker, and take the chance of imprisonment for fraud—as he does."

"Ah! I think I might get up a good sporting company or two. I had an uncle once—a bishop—who got up a joint-stock concern for bringing about the fulfilment of scripture prophecies. He was great on the law and the prophets, but when the other directors found that he wanted to lay down all the law and take up all the profits, they didn't sink the capital, and consequently (paradoxical as it may seem) the company didn't float. And as for the bishop! Solomon in all his fury was not enraged like one of these."

"Eric, I believe you're descending to the kind of joke which is called a pun. When I said 'do as Mr. Sturton-Baker does,' I meant in finance, not in vulgarity."

"I don't see why you should be so hard on Baker; it's through him and some friend of his in New York, to satisfy some private grudge or other, it would seem, that we got on the track of Mr. Paul du Peyral's marriage, and recovered for you the fortune which is to be yours in the course of a week or two."

"Well, I'm very sorry he had anything to do with it. Couldn't you have got anyone else?"

"Nobody so cheap."

"All right! as you are the person principally concerned in that money that I don't want—I—"

"Daphne! how dare you?" cried Eric, flaming up at once; "how dare you insult me so? True, I have the misfortune to owe you a certain sum of money that you cheated me into taking. That is no reason why you should insult me by suggesting that I have any thoughts for myself in watching your interests in America."

"Then why bother yourself? *I* didn't ask you to."

The old dangerous light was coming into her eyes as she spoke, and finally, starting to her feet, she cried, in a hard, altered voice:

"Good heavens, man! can't you tell the difference between love and egotism? If I'd wanted this money of my cousin's I'd have married Paul du Peyral—sometimes I wish I had. Anyhow, he's man enough to be a good scamp, instead of a desponding, faint-hearted creature who won't raise a finger to help himself except in his own useless way. Bah! I'm tired of your high moral tone!"

Eric rose, and took his hat preparatory to leaving in silence—hurt to the bottom of his soul. As he turned, the Princess Daphne, pressing her hands to her head, fell forward upon the floor.

In a moment he was at her side, had raised her gently and laid her on the lounge. Not a sign of life! not a throb of the heart! Her face was deathly white, her hands were tightly clinched. He had never seen her like this before, and with a strange feeling of terror he sent off post-haste, not for the doctor without an idea beyond indigestion, but for an eminent physician, whose waiting-rooms are the rendezvous of half the queens of London society. As good luck would have it, the great man was at home and alone, and within an hour of the Princess' seizure he arrived in Holland Street.

Daphne had been put to bed by the distraught Clytie, and after making a rapid and silent examination, Doctor P—— joined Eric in the studio.

"Your wife?" queried he, briefly.

"No."

"Ah!" and he took a scrap of paper to write a prescription.

"Has she ever been like this before?"

"Never. She has had curious fainting fits; there have been times when she has apparently suffered from a kind of obsession—but it has never been protracted and profound like this."

"Ah! Who is her regular attendant?"

"Dr. ——; he lives opposite."

"Send for him."

In a few minutes the doctor we already know arrived,

and metaphorically grovelled before his superior, to whom nevertheless he remarked immediately and consequentially:

"It is, I presume, one of Miss Preault's recurrent fainting fits—resulting from a slight stomachic disorder. I have been in the habit of exhibiting—"

"The spectacle of a schoolboy playing at being a doctor," rapped out Dr. P——. "It has nothing to do with faintness of any kind; and as for indigestion—pooh!"

"You think it grave?" said Eric, anxiously.

"Very grave," replied the physician. "The cause is beyond me—the effect is only too apparent."

"And that is?"

"What are you to Miss Préault?" said Dr. P——, taking Eric aside.

"She is dearer to me than anything else in the world."

"Sir, I am sincerely sorry for you—I can give you no hope."

"None whatever?"

"None."

"When will the end come?"

"At about midnight."

Eric turned, burying his head in his hands.

"If, when she recovers consciousness, as she may do, there is any delirium, let her have this prescription," said the physician, on leaving. "I can do no more—I regret to have been able to do so little. Good afternoon." And he left the house, obsequiously attended by the local G. P., whom he indignantly ignored.

At midnight a single lamp burned dimly in the Princess Daphne's room, and Eric, who had been sitting motionless beside her since the moment her death-sentence had been pronounced, rose and bent over her as, with a sigh, she opened her eyes and looked into his—speechless—motionless—but conscious of his presence. Once or twice, in answer to the appeals he made to her in a passionate whisper, her lips moved as if she would fain have answered him, but no sound broke the silence in answer to his prayer, save the gurgling sobs of the black woman, who crouched upon her knees in a corner, alternately choking and muttering incomprehensible invocations to her poly-personal deity in jade.

This continued until a quarter to one; then, on the night air, there was borne to his ears the last swell of some chaunt that died in the Carmelite church near by. Roused by this, a dog howled behind the house, a fretful, unhappy howl, broken by little yaps before it settled into its lugubrious breve and descending semibreve. The Princess moved and seemed to say something, but if so, her whisper was drowned by a burst of drunken laughter that rose from some band of revellers who had taken Holland Street on their way home.

When all was still, a faint flush came into Daphne's cheek, and Eric, his heart bursting with grief, laid his head close to hers, lifting her beautiful arms and circling them around his neck as he enfolded her body in a last distracted embrace. Clytie had risen and was standing at the foot of the bed.

"Eric—my love—" whispered the Princess Daphne, royal still, though in the arms of death, "I am going—remember—I loved you, and none but you—you were my life—my religion—I had no thought that was not yours. Good-bye—keep the old place where we've been so happy. I can't see you, darling—but I know you are there. Good-night!"

The head fell back as he held her in his arms—he could feel her dying as he held her. The already cold body grew colder, the *live* feeling seemed to die out of it, the eyes opened and then half closed, the lips parted a little, and a sigh escaped them which Eric caught in a wild, agonized kiss. The body was heavy. The arms had fallen from about his neck. The Princess Daphne was dead!

* * * * * * *

As he held her in his arms, her head lying back upon his

hand, the silence of the death-scene was broken by a shrill cry from Clytie:

"Oh, Gord! Mars' Eric—look dar!"

Her white eyes shone in the darkness, as she pointed with a withered black finger to the side of the bed opposite to Eric.

Nothing!

"What do you mean, woman?" said Eric, angry through his grief at the interruption.

"Yaas, dar—yaas, dar!—oh, Mars' Eric—don' yo see 'um?—dar, now he touch my honey chile—oh, Missy Daph!"

Eric had turned his head to where the black woman's finger had indicated a figure invisible to him. Now he turned again to Daphne. Good God! was he mad? A spark lit the great eyes, which had opened a little farther; the lips gave utterance to a little gasp, as the woman swallowed and sighed; a single strong beat announced the reawakened heart, as Daphne Préault gave a wild look in the direction of Clytie's unseen Thing, and exclaiming, in almost her strongest voice:

"*Paul!*" fell back upon the bed insensible, but alive.

Alive! Eric rose to his feet, an icy-cold sensation of terror seizing in its grip every fibre of his body. What had happened? He hardly dared to think. Clytie was once more crouched in her original corner, no longer sobbing, but praying volubly to the idol—returning thanks doubtless for his recent performance.

Eric seated himself and wrote on a leaf of his note-book: "*Crisis over—she is alive—must see you—can you come at once?*"

"Clytie," said he, "you love your mistress; if you want to save her life, take this to Hanover Square at once. Don't lose a second—find a cab at the church;" and with a nimbleness that Clytie would never have confessed to being capable of, the darkie idolater was gone.

In half an hour she was back with another slip of paper. "*Am in bed—very sleepy—will come in the morning—a miracle has happened—she will live—give my prescription if necessary.*" That was all—and somehow Eric felt that it was enough.

The Princess was breathing peacefully—her unconsciousness seemed to have given place to sleep. And she slept till morning. She was restored to him from the dead. Restored, did I say? Well, hardly! "The Princess" had reached that undiscovered country from whose bourne no traveller returns. Daphne Préault came to life! She was never "The Princess Daphne" again.

* * * * * * *

The traces of fire faded slowly from Gabriel Hawleigh's face. The agony of inflammation had left his cicatrized eye-balls, and, with carefully shaded eyes, the happy young artist of a month before felt his way timidly about the house and studio he knew so well. With trembling hands he would lightly touch the furniture and hangings, and a sharp contraction of pain would come over his features when his hands met his paint-box or palette, or other artistic paraphernalia. The absence of the pictures which had lain about seemed to hurt him, and they kept him as much as possible out of the studio, whilst "the boys" would come in and sit and talk with him, avoiding with all the tact of which they were capable, the subject of his affliction. Sometimes unconsciously someone would bring his mind back to it by accident, and then a sharp spasm of grief used to shake him, whilst Maye or Mrs. Hawleigh dexterously turned the subject.

The doctor whose fiat had gone forth that Gabriel was to be removed as soon as possible to the moors, was not one of those immortalized medicós who

> "come in haste,
> To suit their physic to the patient's taste;"

for the thought of leaving Holland Street, which he knew so well, for a place that he might possibly never see, was a perfect nightmare to the blind man. But Dr. Richardson was inexorable on the point: setting aside the benefit that he hoped might be derived from the pure, heath-scented atmosphere of Dartmoor, the continual brooding over familiar surroundings that he could only feel, even in the weeks which preceded his departure, began to have a perceptible influence on Gabriel's mind—he was becoming irritable, fretful, impatient, as blind men are apt to do when ill-health is added to their infirmity; and therefore, as soon as it was possible to move him, they started for the cottage that they had found with the assistance of Eric Trevanion's knowledge of the neighbourhood, for it was comparatively—for Dartmoor—close to Trthwwsthpllgg Manor.

No better description of their retreat could be given than that contained in Mrs. Hawleigh's first letter to Daphne Préault. "Here we are," she wrote, "on the borders of Dartmoor, three hours' drive from the nearest town, and a Sabbath day's journey from London. I do think Dr. Richardson might have sent us to some more civilized corner of the world. I feel as if I were banished forever from everyone I have ever known in my life; but I don't complain, as it is for my poor boy's sake. Miles of moor all round us! and I fancy the nearest civilized habitation is the convict prison—if one can call that civilized. For my part I live in constant dread of a sudden invasion of escaped convicts, in horrid, unbecoming striped stockings, and with things like bluebottles, supposed to represent broad arrows, all over them. But the air is lovely, and already Gabriel seems less fretful than he was in Holland Street."

And so, for a time at least, the Hawleighs seemed to have gone out of the life of the Holland-Street colony, and Eric, for one, had perhaps realized what a loss they had sustained in the departure of the genial matron and the grave-eyed maid who raised the little house from a studio to the sweet dignity of a home. Yes—he missed them, for since the recovery of Daphne, an indefinable and almost weird change had taken place in her personality.

Even to Eric the change was inexplicable. Daphne Préault was, if possible, even more beautiful than she had been before her illness, but it was a different kind of beauty.

Her carriage had lost dignity and had acquired grace; her great, dark eyes were matchless as of yore, but their look was no longer calm and imperious, as it had been when she raised them to his, at the conclusion of her song on the night of Gabriel Hawleigh's Bohemian *soirée;* the lovely curves of her mouth had lost much of their firmness and had acquired a certain soft, flickering smile that was inviting in its subtle mockery, but no longer benign and pitying as it had been when first she smiled upon Eric Trevanion; and in her attitudes, as she lounged about the studio, there was a languor which she had not possessed before. In her music there was a quaint, sensuous harmony that had not characterized it when she was "The Princess Daphne"; in her speech, a word here, a glance or a smile there, betrayed a lower standard of intelligence; and in her painting the detail of Meissonier had given place to the morbid minutia of Van Beers and of the latest French school. She would devote hours to painting some demi-mondaine, sleeping carelessly the sleep of exhaustion in an absolutely "esoteric" attitude; and at the conclusion of her work she would draw a brush full of bright vermillion across the canvas, and tell Eric that it was a painting in his school—"An Impression of Humanity in Primary Colours." Into her caresses there crept a *je ne sais quoi* of inexplicable earthliness, that almost repelled whilst it intoxicated him. The change she had announced as possible in her had taken place. The savage side of her nature seemed to have got the upper hand.

She was less womanly, and more female.

These were dark days for Eric. His poverty told upon his spirits; he no longer cared to go into society, as heretofore, and it was only at rare intervals that he could be tempted forth into the world of men. Another factor which conduced to his distaste for society was that Daphne betrayed a tendency to cross-question and catechise his going-out and coming-in; she would chaff him about the women he met at dinner-parties, and almost make him "scenes" about them—in a word, he was beginning to feel a little friction of the chain that bound him to Daphne Préault. It is a horrible thought for a man that he is bound to a woman by ties of financial dependence, even when the accord between them is perfect; but when a certain uneasiness has sprung up between them, it becomes frightful; and Eric began to experience a horrible feeling of revulsion when Daphne began to claim as a right the little services he had felt himself so honoured by her accepting as favours. Of one acquaintance of his she was especially jealous: this was the eminent Doctor P——, who had apparently taken a fancy to this grave young man, and had asked him to call upon him in Hanover Square, an invitation of which he had eagerly taken advantage. One day Dr. P—— had called, semi-professionally, he said, upon Miss Préault, and after he had gone, she had said:

"I never want to see that man again—I don't trust him; he seems to be watching us all the time he talks; he'd like to separate us if he could—and I'll take good care he doesn't. Mind that, Eric!"

The speech had jarred upon him, more in its tone than in the words she used, and the next time he called upon Dr. P——, he said nothing about it to her. It was the first action of his life, since he had known her, that he had not told her all about.

One day she was lying on the lounge, reading a newspaper, one shapely foot trailing on the floor, the other lying on a cushion at the foot of the lounge, when suddenly she looked up and said, "Eric, we must see this new play at the Prince's Theatre; let's go on Wednesday."

"Very sorry, *chérie*," he had replied, "but I can't."

"Oh, that's all right," returned she; "*I'll* get the tickets; it wont cost you anything."

He turned very pale, and then very red, as he answered: "It's not that, dear; I have an engagement."

"Oh—indeed! you didn't tell me—what is it?"

"A dinner-party at Dr. P——'s in Hanover Square."

"Ah!" returned Daphne, "I don't wonder you said noth-

13

ing about it: you're always with that odious man, it seems to me—he interferes with everything."

"You can hardly say that, Daphne; it's only the second time I've dined there. Surely you don't mind my going; one meets interesting people at his house, and this dinner is in honour of a celebrated American doctor who has just arrived."

"Come and sit down here."

He sank on the lounge by her side, a little nervously, and she put her arms round his neck and drew his head close down to hers.

"Don't go, darling," she whispered; "stay here with me—I'll give up the play, if you'll give up the dinner—I don't want you to go—that doctor doesn't like me, and I know he'll separate us if he can."

"But, my dear girl—I *must* go. I've accepted, and I can't put off a man like Dr. P—— at the last moment."

"You are determined?"

"Well—yes, dear."

"Oh, very well, then! go to your horrid dinner-party. Anything to get away from me, and go about flirting with other women. I wonder you don't give in to your dear father and go and marry 'a county girl,' in Cornwall—it would about suit you. You'd probably suit *her*, now I've made a man of you, and you've got tired of me."

She pushed his head roughly away from her, and turned her face into the cushions of the lounge, pretending to go to sleep. Eric sighed deeply as he returned to his writing-table. But his mind was made up—he would dine at Dr. P——'s on the following Wednesday.

Until the evening in question nothing more was said, on either side, on the subject. When seven o'clock on Wednesday evening arrived, however, and Eric was just leaving the house to go home and dress for his party, as he passed the dining-room he saw, through the open door, the table rather coquettishly laid for two—just as in the first days of their love. His first impulse was to return to the studio and ask for an explanation; his second was to do nothing of the kind, and with a little proud toss of his head he passed on and across the street. Whilst he dressed, however, the one thought that surged through his brain was, "Whom does she expect?—whom does she expect?"

He had almost lulled his mind to rest by the artificially-produced conviction that Daphne, having been stricken with a horror of being alone, had sent for Sylvia or Eva Easton to dine with her. But why had she not told him? This was a question which solved itself as he stood at the looking-glass in his window tying his cravat. It was just half past seven, when a cab drove up to Miss Préault's door, and Mr. Charles Sturton-Baker, springing out, disappeared into the house. It was with a queer, strained sensation, like a nasty taste in his mouth which he could not get rid of, that Eric Trevanion took an omnibus at St. Mary Abbot's and proceeded, by way of Bond Street, to Hanover Square; and though the dinner was interesting, and the American doctor was in every respect a remarkable man, his soul was in Holland Street all the time, and as soon as the first lady gave the signal for departure at eleven o'clock, he also made his escape to regain Holland Street on foot, in the fresh air of the cool summer night.

Miss Daphne Préault's house was quite dark, and he stood on the pavement in front, deliberating whether to go in as usual, or not, for some minutes, his latch-key in his hand, his heart beating with that strong, measured thud that the coolest of us have experienced in moments of agitation, however impassive and unconscious we may outwardly appear to be.

At last he persuaded himself that to refrain from going in would be, in the first place, cowardly in him, and in the second, an insult to Daphne, so he turned the key and stepped through the house into the studio, which he could see from the hall-door was illuminated. As he walked down the little passage, how he prayed that he might find her alone! and, such is the contradictory nature of man's feelings, the moment he stepped into the studio he felt he would have given worlds to have found Mr. Baker still there.

The ex-Princess Daphne was lying asleep on the lounge in an attitude of the most delicious lassitude. She was wrapped in one of her softest and most easy *négligés*, her head thrown back on her hands, which were clasped behind it. She did not wake as he stood on the hearth-rug, his back to the empty fireplace, looking at her, just as he had stood on that other night that seemed already so long, long ago; and as he looked at her, a feeling of horrible, undefinable dread stealing over him, he went back in his mind over all the short past he had trodden with her, and which had seemed so exquisite to him. Was it all over—was it irrevocably ended, to-night? A voice deep within his heart—so deep that he could not reach it to stifle it—told him that it was so indeed; and then a great, profound pity surged up in his mind, and his eyes filled with tears. He knelt softly by the sleeping woman, and, bending over her, touched her lips with his. Without opening her eyes, and with a little sigh, she returned his kiss—ah! so sweetly, that he was about to fling his arms round her, when she raised the lids from the grand brown eyes he had so often closed with his lips, and, seeing him, uttered a little exclamation of surprise, in which he detected a ring of mingled disappointment and alarm, as, turning her head away so as to avoid him, she said:

"Oh! it's *you!*"

He sprang to his feet with a strangled gasp of pain and rage, and stood staring down at her as she slowly turned her head and looked him defiantly in the eyes.

Not a word was said for a few moments.

* * * * * *

It was Daphne who first broke the silence:

"Well," she said, "did you enjoy your dinner-party?"

"No."

"No?—Why?"

"Because, strange though it may appear to you, I would

sooner have killed myself, or have been struck blind like poor Gabriel Hawleigh, than have seen that man enter your house this evening."

"Ah! you spy upon me?—Well—I presume I am at liberty to ask whomever I like to my own house when you are away amusing yourself elsewhere."

"Oh! of course—My God!—has it come to this?"

"Why, certainly, *mon cher*, why not? Why can't you live and let live."

"I don't live—this is worse than death to me. Since when has that man been coming here in my absence?"

"Since you have made it a recurring practice to be absent—how selfish you are! He has my interests at heart, and comes to consult with me on my American affairs. You know he is in some way interested in them himself, and you surely have not forgotten that it is through him that I have obtained, or shall obtain, the fortune Paul du Peyral cheated me out of."

"I congratulate you," said Eric, bitterly, "on the means whereby you have obtained his skilled coöperation. Good God, Daphne, how changed you are! I have felt it ever since your illness—it needed but this to convince me. I could almost believe that *you* are the subject of a marvellous story that was told us to-night by the American doctor who arrived in this country only yesterday."

"Ah! a story? What was it?"

"I am not in a mood to tell stories."

"But I am in a mood to hear them. Tell me this one."

"He told us of a man whose death-bed he attended in New York—a man who was the incarnation of all that was unprincipled; who had by some supernatural means projected his soul—his vitality—into some woman over here, by means of his mistress, over whom he had obtained a marvellous mesmeric power. I could almost believe, looking at you as I see you now, that you are the woman."

"I am."

"What do you mean? Daphne! do you want to drive me mad?"

"Not at all, my dear boy. Your American doctor's name was Schuyler Van Boomkamp, was it not?"

"Yes—how did you know?"

"Inductively, through Mr. Baker. The man over there was Paul du Peyral; his mistress was in fact his wife, Mahmouré du Peyral, *née* di Zulueta; and I am Miss Daphne Préault of New Orleans, his blood relation and, by a coincidence, apparently his double, at your service."

Eric stood looking at her in horrified amazement for a few moments longer, and then, without a word, turned and left the house. Daphne Préault rose from the lounge and spent an hour with her thoughts before going to bed.

The whole thing, from Eric's entrance, seemed to be a twisted version of that other night in the preceding autumn.

* * * * * *

On the following morning Eric did not make his appearance as was his wont. The hours crept by, filled for Daphne with idleness; lunch-time came, and still no Eric.

"Well," thought Daphne, "he's in a huff about something or other. Really, that man becomes wearisome—*assommant*. Heaven defend me in the future from a rich man who's grown poor!—they're the worst kind of paupers, because they're so impracticable. Heigho! I hope kind fate will send me some visitors—I'm bored with myself."

As if in answer to her prayer Clytie entered the studio at this moment, bearing a card. With a feeling of genuine relief Daphne stretched out her hand to take it, hoping that it was a man, or at the least an interesting woman, with whom to while away the hours of afternoon; she did not feel inclined to go out; she would far rather sit and chat lazily at home.

As she looked at the card, a sudden grip of pain seemed to seize her, and a flush rose to her brow which as quickly gave place to a white, hard, stern look that augured ill for the reception of the visitor.

The name on the card, printed in tiny block letters, was "Madame du Peyral."

We have none of us heard or thought much of anyone without making to ourselves a strongly defined mental picture of their personalities, a picture, as a rule, so widely differing from the truth that the difference, when we see how great it is, strikes us as a keen disappointment, if not as an insult to our intelligence. Since the news of Paul's marriage to an actress had reached her, Daphne had conjured up an unvarying picture of Mahmouré. She expected to see a rather loud-looking woman—tall, voluptuously formed, with a handsome, bold, foreign face—a face to suit the name, Mahmouré di Zulueta. She had seen the type in all its glory at Nice, at Monte Carlo, at Ems, at Aix: they are usually called "Mme. la Princesse de Quelquechose," and are generally to be seen dashing up and down the most frequented *allées*, in wildly luxurious landaus or victorias, whose panels bear highly emblazoned coats of arms, and the cockades of whose coachmen's hats are decorated with little scraps of divers-colored ribbon. They are also usually attended by quiet, dignified men, all of them built alike—that is to say: complexion ivory white, hair and moustache white and trimmed *en brosse*, perfectly dressed, patent-leather boots, light gloves, tightly buttoned in drab-coloured frock coats, white hats, canes with gold heads, the air of "Diplomacy" stamped indescribably but unmistakably upon them, the whole arrangement identified with and known by some noble Russian name. The type pays little attention to the woman by its side, whom one catches one's sèlf wondering vaguely about—whether it be his wife, sister, or *chère amie*.

This was the kind of woman whom Daphne Préault prepared herself to snub, as a gentle frou-frou of skirts heralded the entrance of Mahmouré. The door closed and the two women, animated by such different feelings, faced each other; but instead of advancing, by a singular and simultaneous impulse each stopped as if transfixed.

Perhaps no one ever belied a name as did Mahmouré, dressed to go into the world. She had essentially that undefinable pose which only the true gentlewoman can possess, whilst so many gently-bred women lack it altogether. Always dressed in an absolutely original arrangement of the very last fashion, she would have been remarked anywhere, but not, as is usually the case, in consequence of her gown *per se*, for she had the art of subduing and rendering harmonious the most bizarre "creation," and for "form" would have been singled out from any crowd. Where this little foreigner got her manner from was a marvel to the envious; it seemed in no sense acquired, but instinctive.

Daphne's hand which held the card dropped mechanically to her side, and the pasteboard fluttered to the floor. Her eyes were fixed on Mahmouré's face in questioning wonder —where had she seen this stranger before? The face seemed perfectly familiar, yet unknown; and it was attractive to her with an attraction beyond the power of words to describe. She remembered nothing of her indignation; the thoughts of resentment she had felt due to Mahmouré faded away. She felt as if a new era had sprung up in her feelings since the moment her eyes first rested on the small sable-clad figure that stood motionless before her, the pale face, framed in its burnished bronze hair, standing out weirdly from the dark surroundings.

This strange sympathy that took possession of Daphne was the more absorbing from the fact that it was quite new to her—for she was not given to what is called "gushing" over women. Though she liked them very well, she never made nor needed "greatest girl-friends." The affection which seems to be such a necessity, such an all-absorbing *lien*, between some women had always been a matter for wonder to her. In her school days, when some girl or other had sought her in friendship, and had drifted into adoration, as girls *will* drift, Daphne had never been able to understand why she should be expected to waste her time in promiscuous osculation. She would submit in a gracious manner to being kissed; it seemed to please the other girl, and didn't hurt her—but why?—but *why?*—she would question. After she had grown up, and after she had begun her Bohemian life among "the boys," women betrayed a tendency to like, to admire, and to adore her—her magnetism seemed to reach them to an extraordinary degree. Their liking may have been due to the fact that, fascinatingly beautiful as she was, sensuously and a trifle masculinely formed, she had admitted no man before Eric to her close friendship. However it was, certain it is, that in society she was run after by all the women whose names were most quoted as associating at ultra-fashionable functions; and the tributes to her talent which reached her in the form of letters and bouquets, each year, after the opening of the Academy, were almost invariably addressed in the fashionable female hand, and scented *au point de délire.* She sometimes wondered at it, for she never strove for their patronage or friendship. At last she accepted it unquestioningly, thanking her feminine admirers for the many charming afternoons they gave her, and passively permitting herself to be loved, as is always the *rôle* of one principal in a great friendship.

Therefore was she the more amazed to find herself drawn irresistibly to this little woman, whose big eyes were fixed on her with a strange, far-off look. Her prejudice faded, her fancied anger fled—all were merged in an uncontrollable desire to comfort and welcome the sad, sweet-faced woman before her. She roused herself and advanced a little, stretching out both hands so as to take Mahmouré almost in her arms as she said:

"You must let me welcome you to England," and for the first time in her life offered her lips to be kissed by a woman, impelled by a fascination which was stronger than herself, and which was wholly due to the strange magnetism of her visitor's personality.

And Mahmouré, who had remained meanwhile as one in a dream? As she gazed, an almost supernatural look flamed from her eyes—at first it was one of questioning, then by degrees the questioning turned to recognition. It was the woman she had seen at Paul's bedside at the moment of his death! Her eyes became moist, and lit up vividly; the pupils dilated till the colour of the iris seemed blotted out; a weird, sullen darkness filled them, heavy and soft; and then, as Daphne's lips touched hers, a flash illumined them before they closed, as she leaned upon the other woman, murmuring in a sigh as she threw back her head, almost unconscious, "Paul!"

Instantly both women recovered themselves. Of what inscrutable influence had they been the sport? Both were confused, but Mahmouré, whose momentary aberration was the more easily understood and explained, was the first to regain her ordinary equilibrium.

"This is a strange meeting, Miss Préault," she said, "and I fear I frighten you; pray forgive me. I don't know quite why I should lose my head on meeting you. I came to talk severely business. If I tried to explain why you affect me so strangely, you would laugh at me."

"Oh, no! Believe me, I am as astonished as you—but somehow I seem to know you, madam."

"And I, you," replied Mahmouré. "The instant I saw you all recollection of time, place, and circumstance seemed to leave me. I seemed to be in a dream, for I saw in you the man whose name is so familiar to you, and who was so dear to me, Paul du Peyral! I should feel bitterly ashamed of my folly were I not sure that you will forgive and forget the weakness of an invalid."

"But I am not angry at all," returned Daphne. "Come, let us sit on the lounge here, and you shall tell me all about yourself. As you can imagine, I have been anxious—not to say curious—to see you in the flesh, for—I too have a confession to make that will seem foolish and hysterical to you. I seem to have seen you before—in a dream, or somehow—so we are not strangers—what does it mean?"

"I don't know how I can explain it, Miss Préault—"

"Call me Daphne—won't you—Mahmouré? Yours is

such a beautiful name that I should love to call you by it in exchange."

"Please, do. Well, to continue: I think the sympathy between us rests on our having both been influenced by the same man—who resembled *you* as if he were your twin—and who was *my* husband. It is of that I came to speak to you—I have wronged you deeply—can you forgive me?"

"There is nothing to forgive; we shall be great friends, I know."

"Ah! how good you are!" exclaimed Mahmouré; and she kissed the hand that Daphne extended to her.

They were seated close together on the lounge, and though an ordinary observer would not have seen anything strange in the appearance of the two women, one of them at least had by no means recovered her self-possession. It was Daphne who could not reconcile her own conflicting sensations—she could find no reason for the intense, soft satisfaction that she felt under the influence of Mahmouré's presence, of her touch, of her gaze, of her kiss.

It seemed like a new obsession, and it troubled her; but at last she explained it to her own dissatisfaction as being natural magnetism—or madness. But she thought that if Mahmouré was mad, she was a singularly interesting maniac; and as the low, tender voice spoke on, the desire to befriend her and to love her grew stronger and stronger, till at last she gave herself up to the moment, and she and Mahmouré plunged, confidentially, into stories of their past lives, of the events that had established such a sympathy between them, and had finally brought them together.

The afternoon was drawing to a close with tea and chatter. Daphne had denied herself to every visitor, and the two women, completely at their ease, sat, or rather lounged on the divan, exchanging confidences as the hours sped by.

"Very well, then," said Daphne, as if concluding an arrangement; "that is settled; so long as you are in England you must spend much of your time here with me. The questions of business that exist between us can be disposed of in a morning, and we must see all that we can of one another whilst we can. You cannot think how strangely happy I am that chance should have thrown us together like this. Our friendship, though sudden, must be lasting; promise me, Mahmouré, that it shall be."

And Mahmouré, lying among the cushions, looked up into Daphne's beautiful eyes and said:

"I promise you!"

For answer Daphne bent and kissed the beautiful lips that had framed the words, as if to thank them. A sudden noise made her raise her head suddenly, and Mahmouré also started up into a less "easy" position.

Eric Trevanion stood before them.

Daphne blushed scarlet, for no earthly reason that she could give herself, as she rose, and, going to the tea-table, said:

"Madame du Peyral, this is my great friend and ally, Mr. Eric Trevanion. Eric, this is Mme. Paul du Peyral."

Eric bowed profoundly and raised his eyes to Mahmouré's, What was the intense feeling of antipathy that surged over him as he met her steady gaze? He could not tell. But he grew pale as he took his tea-cup from Daphne, and he felt that, whatever might be the character of this beautiful little Oriental woman, she was an enemy to him, a barrier to be, between himself and Daphne.

He could not reason it out, but as he put Mahmouré into her hansom when she took her departure, and she leant upon his hand in getting in, the same electric thrill of intense antagonism shot through him, and he turned back into the house.

CHAPTER X.

THE AUTOCRAT OF TRTHWWSTHPLLGG.

On the few occasions when I have time to think at all, I have often thought it strange that so few Englishmen know anything of one of the most glorious districts of their native land, save from the pages of "Lorna Doone" and the writings of Baring-Gould. The Amateur Pedestrian is a strongly English institution, but the proportion of pedestrians who explore the beauties of Dartmoor is ridicuously small by comparison with the army of knapsack-fiends who yearly invade the lake district of Cumberland, the Peak scenery of Derbyshire, and Scotland generally. I am not going to challenge comparison with Blackmore in a description of Dartmoor. Had Gabriel Hawleigh been able to see the beauties that were bathed in the exquisite heather-scented atmosphere that day by day brought back the colour to his wan cheeks, he would have made many a study of landscape from the neighborhood of the little cottage in which the Hawleigh household found itself installed just beyond the borders of Cornwall. But Gabriel was blind, and it was in vain that Mrs. Hawleigh endeavoured to discover any sign that the veil that hid the life around him from his eyes showed any tendency to lift, and give back to her son the glorious gift of sight.

The cottage that they had found was little short of an artist's paradise. A little house of one story, shut out from the lonely moor-road by a privet hedge, and sheltered from the winds by high elms and poplars, which bowed their heads in sage appreciation of the secrets whispered to one another by their intermingling branches, when the moor winds woke them to murmur.

Their lives were as quiet and uneventful as lives can be. Maye and Gabriel made music together a good deal. Fortunately, Gabriel, virtuoso as he had laughingly declared himself to be, had the faculty of playing by ear, and from memory, highly developed. Now that the faculty had become a necessity, it had increased wonderfully, and they spent long, happy mornings together, lost in the clouds of harmony with which they filled the little cottage, playing over all Gabriel's old repertoire, learning new masterpieces, which Maye would play on the piano for Gabriel to pick up on the violin, and yet more often breaking into the wild, passionate improvisations that had been the delight of the favoured few in the Holland Street colony who had been permitted to hear them.

In the afternoon, the two would go out for walks on the moor, arm-in-arm, chattering gayly over the points of landscape which Maye described, as minutely as she could, to her poor blind boy. And when, as sometimes happened, Gabriel had a return of his old listlessness and disappointment, and wanted to be left alone with his mother or with his thoughts, Maye would wander forth alone, and explore the country for new spots to which she might lead Gabriel when next they took the air together. It was on one of these solitary excursions that she made an accidental discovery that was the beginning of the end of my story.

She had been practising with Gabriel all the morning, and in the afternoon he had felt tired, and had gone to his room instead of taking his customary stroll on the moor, and Maye, feeling hipped and cramped in the little house, had shod herself with the uncompromising boots which she reserved for such excursions, had armed herself with the ground-ash sapling that was her constant escort in her country walks, and had started out alone, along a new road, which led she knew not whither.

As she walked, the girl's mind was busy revolving the changes that had come into her life, analyzing her feelings with a calm introspection that would have done credit to the Princess Daphne herself. She loved Gabriel Hawleigh with all her soul—but did she yield her heart to him? Though she was as steadfast as ever in her purpose to marry him and strive to make his life lighter for him in his blindness, yet a vague questioning mood would sometimes come over her, which frightened her, though she took it in hand, and never let it interfere with her course along the path of what she considered to be her duty. Were I writing a romance—telling of things that never happened—I should have caused my ideal maiden, Maye Trevethick, to love her betrothed husband all the more wildly, all the more devotedly, for his blindness, but I am speaking of a real, living woman—a good, pure, English maid, with all the real feelings of her age and sex strong in her healthy young soul. Maye was not a girl to idealize, or to hide her feelings from herself. She was nineteen, and full of life and of wonder at the world; she had all the curiosity, the enthusiasm, of her age; and she had bestowed her fair young self, a tribute of gratitude, upon the boy whose life she was, whose light she was to be in every sense of the word, whose mother had been a mother to her, and to whom she was bound by every tie of recognition. Yes! My ideal maiden should have loved the boy the more dearly, the more devotedly, for his affliction; but Maye, though strong in her single-hearted purpose to marry Gabriel whenever he should wish it, realized that her life was doomed to be blotted out, to be devoted to the care of an invalid whose only knowledge of her fresh young beauty must be the memory of the face he had so often fixed upon his canvas—the face that went laughing by in the darkness, in his picture "Sunshine in the Fog," whilst the blind man made music for her laughter that it joyed him to hear, but whose smile he would never see.

"Oh! Gabriel—Gabriel!" she cried out sometimes in her great loneliness; "if only I could give you my eyes, and my life with them, my poor blind love! You will never see me again—and after we are married it will be the same—darkness—darkness—always—always. Oh, God! I am a wretch to feel it like this, to think of it even for an instant; but the thought is sometimes terrible—terrible. If only I could think of nothing but his faithful love, his strong, true-hearted devotion to me before he became a great man—and blind; but I can't—I can't. What use is it that I am young, and that people tell me that I am fair?—he can never see me now. What use will it be to make our home beautiful around him? Oh! why has my love changed so? I do not love him less—ah, no!—not less; but the love is not the same. Would that I could be his servant instead of his wife?—but that cannot be. Even when we were in town Eric Trevanion was more useful to him than I; and now he constantly wishes that Eric was here with us. Pray God he may not come—but no, he cannot—he has only one thought, and that thought—Daphne! Ah! why do I not hate her?—but I can't—she loves Eric so dearly—and I? —well, well, I felt like a fiend before I left London, when I wished that *I* were blind that he might lead *me* about and read for me, as he did for Gabriel. Oh, Gabriel, Gabriel, why is my love for you changing?—for I can feel it changing, here at my heart; and the thought is killing me."

And, wondering thus, she walked along the Cornish roads, buried in thought, and not noticing whither her wandering feet were leading her. She was roused suddenly from her reverie to see the sun slanting to the west, and knew that it was time she returned home. Returned home! Yes, certainly; but where was she? She appeared to have reached the borders of the moor, and not a human habitation was in sight, not a human being of whom she could ask her way.

After considering the matter profoundly for a while, at a place where three roads met, she decided at last to follow one of them, in the hope of meeting someone who could put her right, and started off, feeling a little bit frightened, and, to tell the truth, a little bit tired. But she dared not acknowledge this to herself, for she knew that she had a long way to walk home, even after she got the direction, and that she must not increase her worry by the confession, even to herself, that she was weary.

She had walked along the road she had chosen for upwards of a mile without seeing any sign of human occupation of the county, and was beginning to feel a singular tendency to cry—for Maye was only a woman, after all—when, the road taking a sudden turn, she found herself confronted by a high gate leading apparently into a park. There was no lodge, but the private road inside the gate showed such signs of cultivation that she concluded that it must lead to a house, and so, mustering all her courage, she opened the gate, which was fortunately not locked, and went in.

Where *was* that house? The drive, for drive it appeared to be, seemed interminable. Tired as she was, it seemed as if she had walked for hours between the high and carefully trimmed hedges of rhododendron and laurestinus, and she was just preparing to give up in despair and retrace her footsteps, when suddenly the hedges stopped, opened, and the road dipped. I say dipped, because she found herself standing on the summit of a steep declivity, where the road suddenly plunged into a great hollow, at the bottom of which lay what seemed to Maye to be the most beautiful old house she had ever seen in her life. The precipitation of the incline was modified for wayfarers by the road curving round it to reach the bottom by an easier slope; and it stopped at a moat, a veritable moat, the mediæval appearance of which was only modernized by its being crossed by a comparatively new stone bridge, which seemed to be carefully gravelled.

On the moat itself a few swans and innumerable ducks sailed hither and thither, leaving broad fan-like wakes behind them on the mirror-smooth surface of the water; and, apparently surrounded by the moat and standing in a sweet, soft lawn that resembled green plush as she looked down upon it, there rose a lovely old house, built half of gray stone and half of grand old ruddy brick, with here and there an excrescence in the form of a wing of a more modern style of architecture. The whole seemed softened and tender, as if its angles had been rounded off by the gentle, continuous kiss of Time, which had spread over the crevices of the masonry an embroidery of soft lichens, with here and there a tuft of saxifrage or a golden ball of stone-crop. Into the deathly stillness of the summer afternoon a perpendicular column of blue smoke rose here and there from the clustered chimney-stacks, and gave a touch of life to this old-time manor-house; and as she stood stricken motionless by the beauty of the place, she espied a gardener driving a mowing-machine over a far angle of the inner lawn. A gentle whirr rose into the air from the machine, and then she saw, dotted here and there on the slopes that surrounded the house, lying lazily under the oaks and elms that protected this elysium from the winds of the moor, a few great black oxen, which gave no sign of life save an occasional sway of the head as they reached for some hitherto unnoticed tuft of clover.

A feeling of intense repose stole over her weary senses as she prepared to descend into the hollow and ask the man who was mowing, where she was, when suddenly her purpose was checked by the sound of wheels behind her. Whatever it was that approached, humanity, in some form or other, must accompany it, so she waited until the vehicle should reach the spot where she stood as if enchanted. The sound of the wheels drew nearer, and at last a dog-cart turned the corner, driven by a man. Maye's first feminine spasm of apprehension was banished as, on a second inspection, the man appeared to possess the requisite number of years to allay her sexual alarm. It was an *old* man, and the dog-cart perceptibly slackened its speed as its occupant caught sight of the girl standing there, looking at him.

As he saw that she was about to speak, the driver stopped his horse, and the trim servant who clung to the back seat jumped down and posted himself, tigerwise, at the animal's head, as the old gentleman, with an awkward movement, jerked off his hat and threw it on again.

"I have lost my way," began Miss Trevethick, quailing a little under his questioning look, "and I came up this drive hoping to find someone who could direct me. Can you tell me how to get back to the village of Arthisham-by-Dartmoor?"

"Arthisham-by-Dartmoor! Do you wish to walk back there this evening, young lady?" said the old gentleman, with a look of astonishment.

"Yes—if you please—is it far?"

"It's nine miles."

"Nine miles!—oh dear! what shall I do?—they will be so anxious about me."

"They?"

"My aunt and my cousin. I live with them about a mile beyond Arthisham. I came out for a walk, and missed the road home—oh! how can I get back?—will you please direct me?"

"But, my dear young lady, it will be nearly dark before you get back; you will miss the road again. Dear, dear, dear—what an unfortunate occurrence!"

"I think, sir," said poor Maye, striving hard not to burst into tears, "that if you could send a servant a little way with me, to see me on the right road, I can find my way back. I am accustomed to going about alone."

"But you should have brought your cousin with you; pardon me, has it not been a little imprudent of you?"

"My cousin is blind."

"Oh!—Forgive me, pray;" and the old gentleman's face was crossed by a look of perplexity as he glanced from the young girl, looking so pretty and so piteous before him, to his steaming horse.

"I tell you what, young lady; I hardly know what to say to you; but if you will jump up here, we will go down to the house, and whilst my man harnesses another horse to a phaeton, my housekeeper will give you some tea—you must want it—and then my man here will drive you home. No, I will take no excuse; I haven't any daughter of my own, but

I should be very sorry, if I had one, to let her walk twenty miles."

And so Maye got up, her weariness almost dazing her, a feeling of infinite comfort and safety stealing over her as she took her place at the old gentleman's side, and reached the front door of the old house across the moat.

"What a lovely old place—" she began, but her admiration was cut short by the appearance of an eminently respectable housekeeper, who, after giving her a searching glance of strong disapproval, took her in charge and carried her off, after a few words of explanation from her master, to perform the mysterious rites of the brush and comb.

When she came down again to the great hall, whose polished floor was strewn with fine old English rugs, her unexpected host was ready to do, bachelorwise, the honours of the tea-table, and whilst she chatted with him about her adventures of the afternoon and the old-time pleasance in which she found herself by such a lucky chance, she was almost sorry when a most modern and comfortable phaeton drove up to the door, and a pair of strawberry roans pawed the gravel as if impatient to carry her away from this Eveless paradise.

Maye rose, and thanking her host, prepared to go.

"If you will not be bored by an old man's company, my dear, will you let me drive you home? I shall be able to reassure your aunt—er?"

"Mrs. Hawleigh."

"Exactly—your aunt, Mrs. Hawleigh, on the subject of your long absence. She must indeed be uneasy about you."

"I shall be delighted, I am sure," said Maye, a feeling coming over her that she liked this gruffly courteous old Cornishman very much indeed.

And so they got into the phaeton, and her elderly Galahad took the reins.

"I am quite gratified at the accident that has procured for me the pleasure of your acquaintance, Miss Hawleigh," said he, as they reached the top of the hollow and began rolling swiftly down the drive she had walked up with such very different feelings half an hour before.

"My name is not Hawleigh," corrected she; "Mrs. Hawleigh is my aunt. My name is Trevethick, Maye Trevethick."

"Trevethick! why, that's a Cornish name," replied her escort.

"Yes—my father was a Cornishman."

"*Was* a Cornishman?"

"Yes—my father died in India five years ago."

"God bless my soul!—you are not going to tell me that you are the daughter of Claude Trevethick, of the Indian Civil Service."

"Yes—did you know him?"

"Know him! Why, yes, very well—and his wife too—she—?"

"I am an orphan."

"Dear, dear, dear! poor child! But I'm right glad to have met you, my dear, and am more than ever thankful that you lost your way this afternoon. Dear, dear, dear! I wonder if you ever heard your father speak of Eric Trevanion of Trthwwsthpllgg Manor?"

* * * * * * *

Eric Trevanion! Eric Trevanion! She was driving home with Eric's father—"the Autocrat of Trthwwsthpllgg Manor," as she had so often heard Eric laughingly call him.

Her feelings at the strangeness of the situation—the varied emotions that it roused in her soul, combined with the weariness that was beginning to take effect on her poor, tired little body—caused her almost a feeling of faintness, and she sank into a reverie which Mr. Trevanion, taking it for natural exhaustion, forebore to disturb with any attempt at protracted conversation. So they drove along almost in silence—the old gentleman periodically ejaculating:

"Dear, dear, dear! what a little world it is!—just think of it!—how strange!—who would have dreamt of it? Egad!

it's like a novel. So you are Claude's child?—dear, dear, dear!"

And so they reached the cottage, where they found Mrs. Hawleigh and Gabriel in an agony of apprehension, which changed into a chorus of gratitude and satisfaction as Maye disappeared, thanking "her preserver" once more for his charity to her.

Mr. Trevanion remained but a few minutes, but before he left he had heard the latest news of his son, whom he was astounded to find was a friend of the family; and he took his departure, promising to return next day to inquire after the maiden whom he had rescued so fortunately, and in whom he expressed an interest that was more than paternal.

On the following day, true to his promise, and on many days following, Mr. Trevanion came over to see the Hawleighs and Maye, till at last Gabriel laughingly declared that he was getting quite jealous of Eric Trevanion, senior, and should send for Eric Trevanion, junior, to keep his father in order. It was a hard trial sometimes for Maye when old Trevanion would pour forth his solitary woes to Mrs. Hawleigh, in the little cottage parlour, on the text of his son's absence.

"He has a comfortable home waiting for him here, my dear madam; why doesn't he return to it? Starving! I've no doubt he is; he was never made to get his own living, and never will. I don't ask much of him—only that he should come down here and live with me, part of the year, at any rate; and then, it's high time he married—we Trevanions have always married young, and never out of the county. I don't know who that Miss Préault is, that he seems to be so fond of, but I wont have my boy marrying an American adventuress."

"Miss Préault is hardly an adventuress," mildly expostulated Mrs. Hawleigh. "She comes of a very fine old American family of the South—she is certainly very beautiful, and very fond of Eric," concluded she, guardedly.

"That is all very well—that is as it may be, of course—

but a Trevanion must marry a Cornish girl. Trthwwsthpllgg Manor has never been shared by a foreigner, and, please God, it never will. Tell me—did my son know your niece before she became betrothed to your son?"

"Oh! yes, Mr. Trevanion. We have known Eric ever since he came to London."

"Is it possible?—is it possible?"

Maye rose and joined Gabriel on the veranda, where he loved to sit for hours at a time, listening, he said, to the world-sounds, differentiating, with all the super-sensitive keenness of a blind man's ear, between the innumerable murmurs that filled the quiet summer air.

Left alone with Mrs. Hawleigh, Mr. Trevanion returned to the charge.

"Tell me, my dear Mrs. Hawleigh," said he; "what truth is there in the stories they tell of my boy and this Miss Daphne Préault? What is the meaning of this infatuation of his?"

"Really, Mr. Trevanion," was the still guarded answer, "I cannot tell you more than you already know. They are great friends and constant companions, and Eric seems very anxious to marry her."

"Good heavens! when he might have married your niece! I tell you, my dear madam—"

"Hush!" exclaimed Mrs. Hawleigh, in an undertone; "Gabriel will hear you; his ears catch almost every sound now; it is his keenest sense."

"Well, well!" returned Eric's father, in a lower tone, "it's no use crying over spilt milk in that direction, and I should be very sorry to see my boy rob another man of his sweetheart; but I confess to you that I'm very uneasy and anxious about Eric. We are not children, my dear madam; my boy says nothing about marriage with this woman, and there is only one interpretation to be put upon it. I know he must be very poor, and sometimes I have a horrible dread that he is indebted to her for material assistance. Will you not help me? I'm hasty and bad-tempered—a little too authoritative with him, perhaps; can you not soften my methods by supplementing them with yours?—can you not help me to get him down here?"

"I will try, Mr. Trevanion."

"And then I want you all to come over and live at Trthwwsthpllgg until your son's sight is restored, or sufficiently so to enable him to return home. You are cramped and lonely here; at Trthwwsthpllgg there are distractions of all kinds, even for a blind man. Ah! do not say no, my dear madam; it is an old fellow's whim, and it is for my son's sake that I ask it of you."

So Trevanion *père* wrote another and more urgent prayer to his son, to leave his modern Circe, or Helen, or whatever she was to him; and Mrs. Hawleigh wrote him a long letter full of entreaties from Gabriel, who longed to have him come and read to him, and talk to him as he had done in the last days in Holland Street. But Eric was enthralled by his own morbid sensitiveness, and had not the moral courage to break the chain that was beginning to gall him so fearfully.

> His honour, rooted in dishonour stood,
> And faith unfaithful kept him falsely true!"

Well, well, he was not so very much to blame—he was only a man, after all, and I never knew a man who was morally as strong as the weakest woman I ever met. This is a fact which has been remarked by far profounder observers than I, and the explanation has yet to be found for it. I suppose that it is the compensation that is given to woman for her physical inferiorities and infirmities; perhaps it is in consequence of this physical inferiority that she is always more or less on the defensive, and has realized the advantages of delay and patience. At any rate the man has yet to be born who can scheme towards an end, can wait behind his defences, can act with the pitiless directness, and if necessary bear the mental and physical agony that every woman can bear—*not* in consequence of her education or determination, but simply because she is a woman! Woman always acts on her convictions, unless she is in love; and she is nearly always right to do so. This is doubtless why women always ask for a reason, and never listen to one. This is, however, by the way; let us return to our story.

One of Mr. Trevanion's greatest delights was to come or send over for Mrs. Hawleigh, Gabriel, and Maye, and keep them at Trthwwsthpllgg Manor all day, sending them back the last thing at night; and Gabriel seemed to revel in the quiet that filled the hollow round the old manor-house. His host had fitted up, for the special purpose of receiving the family, a boudoir that had belonged to Mrs Trevanion,—who had died when Eric was quite a child,—a little room situated in an angle of the house, with a conservatory leading out of it; and in this conservatory he had arranged a lounge shrouded by ferns and high plants, where Gabriel could lie when he felt weary, revelling in the moist, soft perfume which filled the place. There he would remain for hours, as he did on the verandah at the cottage, whilst Mrs. Hawleigh and Maye explored the hidden treasures of the grand old building, from haunted garret to subterranean passage leading nowhere, below the moat. The whole place was a perfect paradise to Maye, who was always discovering new nooks and beauties in it, and in her frankly expressed appreciation, came nearer and nearer to the old man's heart as the days collected into weeks. Even the old housekeeper got over her suspicion of this new face about the house and Mr. Trevanion used laughingly to call her "the fair Chatelaine of Trthwwsthpllgg." It may also be mentioned that Maye had given further evidence of her Cornish origin by being the only person about the place, with the exception of Mr. Trevanion, who could say "Trthwwsthpllgg" quickly, without premeditation, and without immediately suffering from paralysis of the tongue.

"I envy you your children," said their host to Mrs. Hawleigh; "upon my soul, I envy you. I wish my boy were more like yours, and I wish Maye Trevethick were going to be my daughter-in-law instead of yours."

And Mrs. Hawleigh would laugh it off, though sometimes she threw an anxious glance in the direction of the pair as they walked round the moat arm-in-arm, Maye chattering gayly and describing it all to Gabriel; he with his blind brown eyes fixed on the darkness before him, whilst he smiled at his conductress and played with the fingers of the hand that held his own.

They had been living happy in this new phase of their exile for about three weeks when an anxious day dawned for Mrs. Hawleigh. Dr. Richardson, Gabriel's London physician, had determined to come down to Dartmoor to report on the progress of his patient towards recovery. It had been almost impossible to say, before the Hawleighs left town, what Gabriel's chances really were. His health was so impaired by the shock that a perfect diagnosis was almost impossible, and Dr. Richardson had promised to come down, when the grand air of the moor should have had its effect upon Gabriel's bodily health, to make a new examination of his eyes. The long-looked-for visit was now expected, and it had been arranged that Maye should spend the day at Trthwwsthpllgg Manor, returning only after the departure of Dr. Richardson in the evening for London. He could not stay over until the following morning.

Accordingly, "the Autocrat of Trthwwsthpllgg" had driven over early and carried her off, taking her for a long drive round the neighborhood before they arrived at the manor-house for lunch.

In the early afternoon the old gentleman and the young girl were sitting together on the lawn within the moat, when suddenly he startled her by saying:

"Have you any definite notion when you are going to be married, my dear?"

"No," she had replied, suddenly awakened from a delicious reverie about nothing at all.

"Supposing this blindness of Gabriel Hawleigh's should prove to be really incurable after all?"

"Well?"

"In that case would you still become his wife?"

"Oh, yes! Mr. Trevanion. How could you doubt it for a moment?"

"And what would you live upon, my dear?"

"I—I—don't know," faltered Maye, helplessly. "I never think about it."

"But surely you *must* think about it, my child. Do not think me inquisitive or impertinent, but I think I understood Mrs. Hawleigh to say that the only means you have consist of her annuity and what Gabriel made by his painting."

"Yes—that is true."

"And if Gabriel can never paint again? Supposing (which heaven forbid!) Mrs. Hawleigh should die? What would you young people do?"

"I—I don't know," answered the girl. "I can paint a little, and I can play the piano. I could teach—and—and —I suppose we should get along somehow," she concluded, vaguely.

A long pause ensued, which was broken at last by Mr. Trevanion saying, as if to himself:

"What an affliction! what an affliction!—for an artist of all men, too! Just as he had planted his foot on the first rung of the ladder of fame—to be blinded, with only his art as a means of support! Well—well! how capricious Fortune is! There is my son Eric; he might be rich and prosperous, and can see as well as you and I can; whilst poor Gabriel, who depends on his eyes for a living, is blinded at what is practically the very commencement of his career."

"Oh! do not speak of it, I beg of you, Mr. Trevanion—it is all so sad—so sad—and so hopeless."

"Well—there! I won't say any more about it. But—Maye, my dear child—forgive me if I say that if you could have loved my boy, and he had been worthy of you, I should have been the happiest man in Cornwall—nay, in the world! If only you could have loved him!"

If only she could have loved him! Ah—yi!

And deep in her heart Maye knew that the love of her whole life had been given, long ago, to the son of the man who sat by her side pleading for his boy—who had never known—and asking nothing better than to end his days in his beautiful old manor-house, whilst the woman by his side laid her touch upon everything there to brighten it, and the old oak-panelled corridors echoed with the laughter of his grandchildren.

* * * * * * *

The drive back was accomplished almost in silence. Mr. Trevanion left her at the garden gate, promising to drive over in the morning to hear the news about Gabriel.

The news about Gabriel! Dr. Richardson had come and gone; had gone away looking very grave, and leaving with Mrs. Hawleigh only a very slender remnant of the hope she had brought with her from Holland Street. He was to hold another consultation with the eminent oculist in London, and in a week or ten days, at most, was to write Mrs. Hawleigh his final opinion and verdict on the case of Gabriel, her son.

This was the news which the laird of Trthwwsthpllgg heard next morning when he came over to the cottage—news which he received with genuine expressions of grief. Only Gabriel seemed unaffected by his lot—he wandered about the house quietly as heretofore, now and then playing a few bars on his violin, which lay ever ready to his hand in the little parlour, or strolling out into the garden among the flowers, which he had come to know by their perfume and touch.

Before he left, Mr. Trevanion said:

"By-the-by, in my concern at receiving your news I almost forgot to give you mine. Eric, my boy, has at last yielded to our prayers—he is coming down to Trthwwsthpllgg. I am going to meet him at the station on my way home."

CHAPTER XI.

ATTRACTION AND REPULSION.

"It is a long lane that has no turning," said a philosopher whose name is, I believe, lost to the posterity by which he is quoted. The critically-disposed may say that the turning is of little use to the traveller if he does not reach it before he falls from very weariness. Another proverbial philosopher has said that, "When things are at their worst, they are sure to mend." This dogmatist had more reason than the other, and if he thought of it at all before he said it, he had probably observed that things mend when they are at their worst, because it is then and not until then, that, throwing everything aside, and sacrificing our feelings to the instinct of self-preservation, we are forced to make the supreme effort which, made earlier in the game, would have obviated the progression of "things" to their possible worst. It must not be supposed that I recommend the utilization of the supreme effort one moment before it becomes absolutely necessary; on the contrary, *nec deus intersit, dignus ni vindice nodus*, as the Classic says. Never—despite the axiom—do to-day what can possibly be put off till to-morrow. Procrastination, as I have before remarked in these pages, is the soul of business, notwithstanding the oratorical assertion of the copy-book to the contrary.

Things were not yet at their very worst for Eric Trevanion. It was fortunate for him and for my story that he did not know this. Had he imagined that it was possible for him to be more supremely wretched than he was when we left him last, he would assuredly have killed himself. His feeling for Daphne Préault was only one of the profoundest pity—a pity that was reflected upon himself.

Eric Trevanion was pitiably poor: he had rebelled against receiving assistance from Daphne, and was living, miserably, on what he could make by his pen. His pride being crushed, he no longer wrote in the high-flown, debonair style of the scholar and man of the world: he had turned his talent to baser uses, and had made it pay him, inadequately to his bare needs, but still it paid him. His poems, which were sicklied o'er with the stupidity and incomprehensibility of the decennium in which he lived, came home to him like curses, send them where he would: at length he had made a holocaust of them, and in sheer cynicism had scribbled off a set of rhymes of social small-talk, with a slang refrain. These he sent to a society paper, which accepted them, paid for them at once, and asked him to write more. An idyllic story which his soul had loved more and more every time a magazine editor returned it to him, he had ruthlessly cut to pieces, interpolating a series of incidents that turned it into a glaring advertisement of a patent medicine. He sent the MS. to the proprietors of said specific, and received by return of post a cheque which cleared his landwoman's scorbutic physiognomy of the scowl it had worn for a month past. With the exception of his lodging-bill he kept out of debt, and for the most pertinent of all reasons—he could not get into it. Things got bad by degrees and beautifully worse, and Eric became a literary hack. The position had one advantage: the occupation of his days, spent among his kind in the Reading-room of the British Museum, took him far from Daphne, who idled away her life in Holland Street in practically no companionship save that of Mahmouré du Peyral, with whom she had struck up an intimacy that caused Eric a mingled feeling of fear, jealousy, and disgust. It seemed to him that in the society of the penniless horde of scribblers who practically lived in the Museum, he breathed a purer atmosphere than that which filled the perfumed studio in Holland Street.

It was at this period of his history that I first got to know him well, for I also was one of the gang that day after day breathed that invigorating atmosphere of book-dust, penury, and ink. We adopted Eric as one of us, for he was as poor as the poorest of the crew, and to-day, when we are most of us respectable members of society, we often talk together of what Théophile Gautier called, with perfect truth, "those happy days when we were so miserable!"

And our misery *was* happy. What a merry crowd we were! There are men whom I meet to-day, rich, respected, and celebrated, who were then poor, disreputable, and obscure. I remember one day in particular, when a man who now commands whatever price he likes to ask, for anything he writes, came down to the Museum, his haggard face irradiated with a smile of triumph—he had not tasted food for forty-eight hours, and I don't believe that the lot of us possessed a pound between us. We crowded round him to hear the news. He had a commission to write a special article for a leading review. He had received five pounds on account, and was to receive fifteen on delivery of the manuscript—and the manuscript was to be delivered next day. He was an incorrigible idler, and we banded together to make him knock off the article, inviting ourselves to dine with him on the following night. Then we left him alone, and in the afternoon I went to his seat to find out how he had got on. He was entrenched behind a fortification of reference-books and authorities; and the article—well! not a line was written; he had spent the day in writing a Latin ode in exquisite elegiacs, which I still possess (it hangs, framed, on the wall of my study), on the contrast between the colour of the Superintendent's hair and Fitzgerald Molloy's neck-tie. He went home that evening without having approached the subject of his article, and we were in despair. He owed me five shillings, and hope had been telling me a flattering tale all day, to the effect that I was going to get it back. Next evening, at six o'clock, he took down to the office of the —— *Review* a positive masterpiece, which practically laid the foundation of his present fame; and "the gang" dined with him at Rampazzi's in Soho, and adjourned for an all-night sitting at his rooms in Great Ormond Street, Bloomsbury. That is how we lived, and Eric Trevanion with us.

We soon "licked him into shape," and gradually he sank with us from literature to journalism, as a preliminary towards rising from journalism to literature by the ladder of advertisement. He was not quite a stranger among us, for I had met him in Holland Street, and Bernard Rawlinson was intermittently one of the crew. It was through him that Eric joined us, and it was to that versatile genius that he owed his first lesson in practical journalism. Eric had been sitting idle at his seat all the morning, when Rawlinson came and asked him why he didn't write, instead of gazing on vacancy in search of inspiration.

"I have nothing to write about that anybody wants to read," replied he, dolefully.

"Well, what of it?" replied the Bohemian; "write about nothing."

"What bosh!" exclaimed Trevanion. "I defy anybody to write about nothing."

"Defy anybody, if you like," was the answer, "but don't defy me;" and, so saying, he sat down and wrote the following, which, short and fabricless, was completely to the point, and sold for one pound ten!

"NOTHING!"

"A Study of Modern Journalistic Art."

"A boy whom I left in a little country town, beloved of parents who were quite unparentally charming, wrote to me a few months ago, and asked my advice as to whether he should give up his obscure and uninteresting, but comparatively lucrative position on a stool in a provincial bank, to embrace the profession of letters, to matriculate in journalism and graduate as a literary man. I sent him at once Balzac's 'Bible of the Journalist,' to wit, the two volumes of the 'Illusions Perdues' and 'Splendeurs et Misères des

Courtisanes,' accompanying this gift with two grains of pure aconitine in a gelatine capsule. I instructed him to read the first, and then, if he still felt himself endowed with a constitution, mental and physical, that warranted him in living or dying on what he could get out of letters, to find a spot where it was not untidy to die, to lie down, and swallow the alkaloid.

"He wrote back shortly afterwards, returning me the poison and announcing that he had decided to follow the fortunes of Lucien de Rubempré, rather than be warned by the fate of Balzac's hero. In vain I pointed out to him the fact that nowadays Coralies and Mlle. de Grandlieus are scarce, if not an extinct race; he abandoned his regular hours and salary, and began to starve on the potential proceeds of precariously launched articles that interested no one, and that editors betrayed a tendency to refuse consistently to buy. Nay more; so badly was he bitten, so profoundly did he develop the hydrophobia of literature, that, realizing his small possessions, he came up to London, like a modern Lucien, and proceeded to starve in the great metropolis.

"Proud as Lucifer, he confided his penury to no one; it had no outward and visible sign save in the poverty of his lodgings, to which he admitted never a soul; and he died in my arms a fortnight ago, of combined starvation and nervous prostration.

"Why? Ah! that is the point. He died because he had nothing to write about, and yet could not write about it. He died—of starvation, here in Bloomsbury—because he could not write unless he had a subject to write upon.

"The man who cannot write about nothing at a moment's notice cannot make a living as a journalist.

"Priggish societies with ridiculous names have met and discussed learnedly—if chaotically—'The Nothingness of Everything': a literary *coterie* that will establish the 'Everythingness of Nothing' has yet to rise, Phœnix-like, from the ashes of unsuccessful journalists. It is a solemn and an undeniable *fact*, that unless one can write a column on Nothing at all, and do it more or less attractively, one has no right to attach one's self to the permanent staff of a journal—in point of fact, one can't get there.

"It is the age of journalistic commonplace; one must idealize commonplace trifles, or one cannot expect to be understood. This state of things arises from the *blasé* condition of the modern reader's faculties. The literary exaltation of Nothing is the only pabulum which the debilitated intellects of a large class of readers to-day are capable of assimilating. Therefore let us establish schools for the development and study of mental anæmia, that a new generation of writers may arise in our midst, whose works shall be 'easily understanded of the people,' because their end is the glorification of Nothing at All.

"[Signed] BERNARD RAWLINSON."

"There," said the picturesque Bernard, as he handed over the manuscript with a smile, "that is how to write about Nothing. Go, thou, and do likewise."

But Eric found it very hard to "go and do likewise." He went through the whole gamut of literary insuccess. Often editors—cultivated men—would be charmed by the epigrammatic way in which he would present the most uninteresting matter, and, on the spur of the moment, would accept his manuscripts; but he scanned their journals in vain in the hope of seeing himself in print, and finally, when he called upon them or wrote on the subject, they would return him his work with something like shame, "regretting that want of space prevented them from utilizing his articles, for the offer of which, however, they thanked him, and remained faithfully his," etc., etc., etc.; and at the conclusion of his day's contemplative quietude in the Museum, he would return to Holland Street, almost dreading to enter the studio which had become associated in his mind with so many sweet and bitter thoughts.

One evening, when he arrived at Daphne Préault's, a surprise awaited him. He had divested himself of his impedimenta in the hall, and penetrated to the studio. As he did so, a man who was sitting chatting with Daphne and Mahmouré rose and held out his hand.

"What!" he exclaimed; "Dr. Van Boomkamp! this is indeed an unexpected pleasure."

"I was waiting for you," returned the psychologist, scrutinizing him keenly through his gold *pince-nez*. "Miss Préault and Madame du Peyral are deep in business matters. I have hoped to meet you again, and to-night my hope is realized. Will you do me the pleasure of taking dinner with me at my hotel, and we can continue the conversation that we began at Dr. P——'s?"

Eric looked at Daphne, and she answered his look by saying: "Yes, Eric. Madame du Peyral and I have some important business to discuss, and some correspondence to go through. We shall be glad to have you out of the way, *tres cher*."

"In that case," said Eric, "I am quite at your service, Dr. Van Boomkamp;" and so it was arranged.

Towards seven o'clock the two men took their departure, and left the two women together.

It was not until they found themselves seated comfortably after dinner in Dr. Van Boomkamp's room at the Hotel Metropole, that they approached the subject which was of the deepest interest to both of them. It was the American who opened the conversation by saying:

"Miss Préault and Madame du Peyral seem to have taken a great fancy to one another, do they not?"

"Yes—it is a very strange sympathy, and one that I cannot understand," replied Trevanion. "As you know, doubtless, without my telling you, Miss Préault and I have been, and I trust are still, very great friends. I know her life very well for the last four years. Until now no woman has ever been her intimate friend; this Madame du Peyral seems to possess a strange fascination over her."

"Strange—yes—to the casual observer, but to the psychologist not so strange. You are, I know, the intimate friend of Miss Préault. Owing to circumstances into which it is not necessary to enter, I know a great deal concerning Madame du Peyral, and their friendship interests whilst it fails to astonish me. It is of this that I wish to speak to you."

"You knew Paul du Peyral?"

"I saw him die."

"Ah!"

"You doubtless remember my recounting a curious psychological case at Dr. P——'s on the occasion of our first meeting?"

"Yes."

"The man and woman in New York, to whom I alluded, were Paul and Madame du Peyral."

"And the woman in Europe?—"

"Was Miss Daphne Préault."

"Good God! She said something to this effect herself, when I repeated your story."

"In all my experience with the workings of mental science I have never encountered a stranger case. Accident has gathered all the threads into my hands, and I have postponed my visit to Paris for the purpose of watching the *dénouement* of the drama, for drama it is, in every acceptation of the term."

"What do you want of me?"

"Well, it is needless to say that whatever you will be good enough to say to me, will remain under the seal of a professional confidence. I want you to tell me all you know of Miss Préault—of her life from the moment you became—er—connected; of her mental state, of her physical illness—everything."

"So be it."

And Eric gave to the American doctor, who listened intently, every now and then making an entry in his note-book or asking for a date, a complete account of the circumstances which had puzzled, had frightened him, with regard to the woman who, before her most serious attack, had been "The Princess Daphne."

At the conclusion of his recital, he said :

"Now, Dr. Van Boomkamp, I have been eminently explicit with you ; may I ask for an exchange of confidence ? What is your explanation of these phenomena ?"

Schuyler Van Boomkamp rose and paced the room in silence for a few moments. Finally, re-seating himself, he spoke as follows :

"The case turns upon a strange coincidence of personality existing between Miss Préault and Paul du Peyral. She was almost what the Germans call his *doppelgänger*, and on his death his personality became merged in hers."

"Then—?"

"Miss Daphne Préault is Paul du Peyral."

"For heaven's sake, explain yourself!"

"Psychological science, founded as it is upon neurology, despite the labours of Georgèt, of Charcot, of Bell, of Bain, of Kollmann, and a host of others, is practically in its infancy. Mesmerism is a phenomenon which the conditions of its existence render very difficult to examine scientifically. Here we have two people, who, though separated by half a hemisphere, were practically identical with one another, speaking psychologically. Through the medium of this strange foreign woman their souls found one another, and little by little Paul du Peyral transferred his psychic force to Miss Daphne Préault. The completeness with which this was done was due to the fact that, springing from a common ancestry, they have, by a freak of heredity, "thrown back," as it were. The exact physical process it is impossible to describe—the result has been apparent in what we will call, for the sake of definition, Miss Préault's fits of obsession. These occurred coincidentally with Paul du Peyral's experiments. The culminating phenomenon occurred with the death of du Peyral : his illness was answered, as it were, by Miss Préault's, and at the moment that he died he fancied that he *saw* her; at the moment of her apparent death his soul seems to have sought hers, and was seen, or apparently seen, by the black woman Clytemnestra, who has always been closely allied with her. His wife, by reason of his repeated experiments with her, has become strongly identified with him, but his *soul* sought that of his *alter ego*—Miss Préault. He was a man of little or no principle; in Miss Préault the good and the bad seem to have been about equally divided ; the good was dying out in her when its place was taken by the salient features of his personality. She lived again with his soul, but the strain has been too great, she is overburdened by a vitality from which she cannot escape, and which she cannot bear; his wife sapped his physical attributes, Miss Préault his mental ones. They are both disordered, ill-regulated, mentally diseased in consequence; Miss Préault is, and has been, in a state of physical and mental hysteria ever since this transference took place; Madame du Peyral, robbed, to use a nautical simile, of her steering apparatus, her guiding principle, has been vainly seeking for it ever since. She has found it; she—though she hardly realizes it herself—fancies that Miss Préault is—well, she recognizes in her new friend the vitality, the attributes, the *personality* of her dead husband."

"Explain yourself! What do you mean?"

"I mean that the position requires the most careful supervision, for though they neither of them know it, and though orthodox doctors would be at a loss to admit it, both these women, when in the presence of one another, are *mad!*"

"My God—how awful!"

"Not awful, but deeply interesting."

"They must be separated, of course."

"No—for that would probably either kill them, or drive them dangerously insane in the ordinary sense of the term."

"What then?"

"They must quarrel, and part naturally."

"But how can that be brought about?"

"It will bring itself about in the ordinary course of events. They will probably quarrel over *you*. When that takes place, Madame du Peyral will pursue her journey to Greece, which has been interrupted by this meeting, and I hope that Miss Préault will regain her health and ordinary mental equilibrium."

It was close upon midnight when the two men parted, and Eric trudged home—save the mark!—to Holland Street.

Seeing a light burning in Miss Préault's vestibule, he went in, and passed through to the studio, where he supposed he should find her alone.

The Creole was not alone. As Eric stood motionless in the doorway of the studio he saw Daphne lying in a lazy, languorous attitude upon the lounge, whilst Mahmouré du Peyral sat by her side, her arms twined round her, looking into her eyes. Daphne was playing lazily with the masses of Mahmouré's hair, which she had unbound, and which were floating in tawny billows all over her as she lay among the cushions. Neither woman spoke, but the silence was far more eloquent than words—and Eric, as he stood looking at them, felt his heart swell with a dull, impotent rage against this Greek who had come and thrust herself between him and the woman he had loved. The slight sound he made in entering was unnoticed by Mahmouré, who had her back turned to the door, but Daphne opened a little wider her half-closed eyes and said:

"Ah! Eric. Is that you? I didn't suppose you would come in again to-night."

At the sound of her voice and her words Mahmouré started away, but Daphne, restraining her by winding her arms about the supple little figure, said:

"Don't go away, dear. He isn't going to stay. Eric, *mon cher*, come in the morning, will you? Madame du Peyral is staying here with me to-night. We did not get through our work till it was too late for her to think of going home alone."

Eric turned and left the studio. He had not spoken a word since he entered. Mahmouré du Peyral had not turned her head in his direction. He was glad of it.

Arrived at his own rooms he spent an hour feverishly pacing up and down, reviewing the position and criticising himself, nothing extenuating, nothing hiding. Week by week, month by month, he lived over again the period of his *liaison* with the fascinating Creole. It had begun with her song at Gabriel Hawleigh's Bohemian soirée; it had ended —ended?—with Dr. Schuyler Van Boomkamp's *précis* of the case of the Princess Daphne, and its corroboration before his very eyes half an hour ago. Hardly more than half a year, but in that time what multifold experiences had been his! Every month seemed an age as he looked back upon the time: he had passed through every phase of worldly condition and every *nuance* of the thing called "love." And what had he now? From affluence he had fallen to poverty —sordid, grinding poverty—and from passionate adoration to a feeling very near akin to profound disgust. Daphne Préault had declined from her altitude as queen of his soul, to a weird, monstrous, unnatural problem; and as he thought of the interview next day great beads of perspiration started to his forehead. What would the morrow bring forth? He felt that, before another sun would set, his future course would be definitively shaped—and in what direction? He could not tell—he dared not surmise.

He passed a restless night, and next morning waited, watching the door of the cottage opposite for Madame du Peyral's departure. At length it came, and ten minutes later he confronted Daphne Préault in her studio.

"I am glad you are alone," he began; "I have been watching for that woman to leave you. I have something serious to discuss with you."

"Have you?" replied she, her womanly scent giving her premonition of a "scene," and drawing herself into a position of aggressive attention. "If you have a great deal to say you had better begin at once, for she will be back here very soon."

"Back here?"

"Yes—I have persuaded her to come and stay with me for a few days—perhaps till she leaves England."

"Oh! indeed! then that makes my way clear before me."

Daphne Préault had selected a cigarette from her case, and, lighting it, had settled herself in the lounge, like some beautiful wild animal, crouching on the defensive, whilst Eric stood looking down at her.

"Daphne," he began, his voice growing stronger and his manner more determined as he went on, "you and I must distinctly understand one another. Our love for one another is not, alas! what it was, and sooner or later we must speak plainly—better to-day than to-morrow!"

"Certainly, my dear Eric—go on."

"You have made life very beautiful for me all these months, and from the bottom of my soul I am grateful, dear; but there should be no question of gratitude between us. A love such as ours has been must live upon itself alone—by itself, and of itself; it cannot decrease, it can only change; and once changed—God help us!—it is extinguished. I have asked you to be my wife. I love you still, in spite of the troubles that have come between us; if you love me in return, I ask you again to share my life with me, and proclaim ourselves one before all men."

"My dear boy—why should I?"

"For every reason in the world—for your purity, for my honour, for our happiness."

"But, my dear Eric, I am quite content to remain as I am—free—unrestrained—Bohemian. Love is for me an ecstasy—I will never make it a bondage."

"Then the love you offer me is not the love I ask of you! It is not love at all—it is mere passion."

"Call it what you will," replied the woman; "it suits me as it is."

"And you would insult the name of love by giving it to an emotion that is capable of no sacrifice?"

"Sacrifice!—have I made no sacrifice already? What would you have of me now?"

"First and foremost that you should give up the friendship of this du Peyral woman. It is infamous, disgraceful, unworthy of you. Then that you should come with me as my wife somewhere, anywhere, to your own America, if you will—but to a spot where no one shall be able to whisper about us as they do here."

"Really, Eric—I think it is as well to be as frank with you as you are with me. Your programme does not suit me. I like you—I am rich enough to indulge my likes or dislikes—you shall share my home, my fortune, if you will—but I will not be bound down by any laws. And mark me—I will not be dictated to. As for Madame du Peyral—or 'the du Peyral woman,' as you contemptuously call her—she attracts and she pleases me. I shall keep up my acquaintance with her in any form I please."

"Very well, then," rejoined Eric, turning a trifle paler and looking yet more determined; "you will have to choose between her and me."

"Exactly!"

"And your choice is—?"

"*Mon cher ami*—she has all the charm of novelty!"

"Novelty!—Good God!"

"Yes—novelty. If you must know the truth, you weary me with your sermons on honour, your tirades upon virtue and all that. You took me as I am."

"No—as you were!"

"Well, then," exclaimed Daphne, her eyes flaming at last, "I am changed—you are changed—we are changed—we are tired of one another—let us part! I prefer this woman to you—there!—you wanted the truth—you have it!"

"Great heavens! is it possible?"

"Not only possible, but existent. Let this be an end of it—let us square our accounts and part."

"Our accounts?" Eric turned a vivid crimson, and then became deathly pale. He thought that she referred to the material issues between them, and as he turned away, he added, in a broken voice, "True, I owe you money as well as gratitude—you are right to remind me of it; though I never forget it, night or day."

It was an insult; an accidental one, it is true, for she had not dreamt that he would so construe her expression. Under its sting, she turned upon him and exclaimed:

"Very well, then—since you reduce it to that level, so be it. Give in to your father; he will welcome his prodigal son, and sell his fatted calf to pay your debts. This is the end of everything between us—I despise you, Eric Trevanion!"

"You do well to despise me, Miss Préault," he returned, bitterly—"I am a despicable object, and you have a right to tell me of it."

What she would have replied to this taunt he never knew, for at that moment Clytie appeared at the door of the studio announcing "Madame du Peyral."

It was the culminating point of the scene. Eric recovered his composure as he bowed to Mahmouré, and, taking his hat, turned to Daphne, who was greeting the new-comer as if they had been parted for years. He said:

"I will say good-bye now, Miss Préault; I will send you over a note during the afternoon;" and so saying he bowed and left the studio.

Mahmouré turned after him an enquiring look.

"*Tiens!*" said she; "there has been an unpleasantness?"

"Yes."

"You have quarrelled?"

"Yes."

"About?"

"You."

"*Chérie!*"

A couple of hours later Daphne received a note from Eric Trevanion: it was short, and read as follows:

"I write merely to say good-bye—the scene of this morning leaves no other course open to me—to us. I leave for Cornwall to-morrow. We have a few little matters to settle; I think that I have them clearly stated; you shall hear from me from home in a day or two. I thank you from the bottom of my heart for all your kindness to me, and should you ever want a friend you can count upon me. In any other capacity—good-bye.—ERIC TREVANION."

With a little laugh Daphne handed the note to Mahmouré.

"Ah!" said the latter, "now I am really happy. Do you know, *chère amie*, I loathed that man from the first moment I set eyes upon him."

CHAPTER XII.

"SPLENDIDE MENDAX!"

THE return of Eric to Trthwwsthpllgg was an occasion of profound rejoicing to two people, and of anxiety which bordered on misery to two others. The former were his father and Gabriel; the latter were Mrs. Hawleigh and Maye. Poor Eric, broken in spirit, and bereft of all his old careless merriment, saw only the pleasure that his presence gave to Trevanion *père* and the blind boy. He was too recently arrived from the scenes of the deepest agony he had ever suffered, to take note of the care with which Maye avoided being alone with him, a care that was almost frustrated by Mrs. Hawleigh in her endeavours to the same end. The time for which the cottage had been taken had elapsed, and it had been impossible to resist Mr. Trevanion's prayer that its inmates should move over *en masse* to Trthwwsthpllgg. Mrs. Hawleigh and Maye were strongly opposed to the change, but poor Gabriel—poor, blind Gabriel—received the invitation with the first transport of joy he had known since the accident in the studio. To Mrs. Hawleigh's mild arguments against the advisability of such a step, he had querulously replied :

" *Why*, mother, why not ? I'm tired of this pokey little cottage ; every time I walk two yards, I run up against something—it's narrow, cramped, *étriqué;* and besides, we see so much of the Trevanions that we might just as well be with them altogether. I don't want to go back to London—not until I can see again. I *shall* be able to see again some day—I know it—and I want to look at Dartmoor before I leave it. We must leave the cottage anyhow—why not go to Trevanion's place with the unpronounceable name ?—they really want us to. It must be an awful tax upon them, bringing them over all this way every time. Besides, I *want* to go there—I adore that old place—it's lovely to wander about in, even for me, and *I* cannot see it. Do accept, mother—do accept."

There was no refusing him, and so it was settled, though Mrs. Hawleigh's heart sank within her, and Maye's soul was filled with a vague terror of she knew not what. Only, during the last days before they moved she devoted herself more assiduously than ever to her poor, blind lover. Did he appreciate her devotion?—who knows?—he had become accustomed to being attended to, waited on, to have his lightest wish anticipated. Accustomed—ah!—there it is. Accustomed!

And so they went to Trthwwsthpllgg, and found themselves at home at once. In the little boudoir Mrs. Hawleigh would sit with Mr. Trevanion, whilst Gabriel lay on the lounge in the conservatory, and Maye sat talking to him; or more often she would sit with Maye, whilst Eric and Gabriel went for strolls round the place, or for long drives into the country, from which he would return radiant, and full of Eric's descriptions of the scenery through which they had passed.

"Really, do you know," he used to say, enthusiastically, "Eric ought to have been a real artist instead of a toy one. If his picture-painting equalled his word-painting he'd be famous in no time. He has been describing the landscape to me. There has been such a lovely sunset; a gorgeous blaze of crimson and gold, melting out of the blue heaven into the purple and browns of the moor—the most beautiful thing I ever saw," he would continue, forgetting himself, his affliction, everything, in his artist's enthusiasm; "and the very next picture I paint—Ah! what am I saying?—what am I saying?" And a tear would gather in his sightless eyes as he turned sadly away, to fling himself upon the lounge, or to play a mournful bar or two upon his violin.

Constantly this would happen: happy in the companionship of Eric he would lose all memory of his blindness, to be suddenly reminded of it and stabbed to the heart by the recollection; then he would become fretful, and Maye would soothe him into peace again. Sometimes on these occasions Eric would look at her with something like startled wonder in his eyes at the spectacle of this fair young girl devoting her life to a blind man's care; and if Maye caught his look she would turn a shade paler, and her heart would give a strong, convulsive throb as she turned to hide her face from him.

What is love but contrast? The adored one is different from all the women one has ever met. What a difference there was between Daphne Préault and this sweet, pure maiden who stood before him in all the majestic solemnity of her matchless self-sacrifice! He looked at her, and his look was that of the Catholic to the crucified Christ; and she returned him a look that seemed, in deprecating his adoration, to beg for mercy at his hands. It was the Prince-god Siddartha and the maiden Yasodhara once more:

"*So their eyes mixed, and from the look sprang love!*"

And the days passed by, and with them weeks, but more slowly. Eric would absent himself for longer at a time, and Mrs. Hawleigh's heart was filled with a vague terror. Mr. Trevanion was as blissfully ignorant of the struggle that was proceeding beneath his roof as the blind boy himself, and quite innocently strove to throw his son and Maye together, that he might appreciate the difference between this pure English girl and the delirious Creole he had fled from in London. Of Daphne, Eric had heard nothing. With something like a fear that he was insulting her he had repaid to her the loans which he doubted whether she regarded as such, and she had answered never a word. Only he received a line or two from Schuyler Van Boomkamp, who still lingered in London, and who told him he had done eminently right in leaving Holland Street; that the intimacy of

Daphne and Mahmouré du Peyral showed little or no signs of abatement; and that he began to entertain grave fears of how it might end.

And Maye?—Ah, sirs! who shall pry into the secrets of a woman's heart? If ever she allowed herself to think, it was only to add a new incentive to her imagination in devising new duties for herself that should draw her nearer, should make her more necessary, to Gabriel; and the love that was growing in Eric's heart would probably never have found an answer in that which lay deep and stifled in her own, had it not been that one day Mrs. Hawleigh brought it before her in all its truth.

Maye was sitting alone in the little boudoir, reading a little volume of verse which Eric had brought from London. She had just read a poem which had shaken her to the soul, had terrified her, so close did its possible application seem to her own case, when Mrs. Hawleigh entered the room, and, seeing her sitting—the open book in her lap—looking straight before her, apparently plunged in a reverie so profound that her entrance did not disturb it, broke the silence by saying:

"Where are Gabriel—and—and Eric?"

"Oh—out in the woods and gardens, as usual," replied Maye; "I heard them go laughing over the bridge more than an hour ago."

"I don't know what we should do without Eric: it is really wonderful the way he manages and takes care of Gabriel, reading to him and telling him stories by the hour, and never minding when he grows irritable, poor boy! Curious, is it not, that he should forsake his shooting, and his house-parties all over the county, to stay here and take care of a blind man and amuse his companions? Very creditable, of course, but strange in such a fashionable and rich young man."

"Very," replied Maye, faintly, as she felt her aunt's eyes riveted on her face.

"I hope—for his sake"—continued Mrs. Hawleigh, coming close to her, and laying her hand gently on her shoulder—"and ours, my dear child, that there is no *other* attraction that keeps him here."

"Oh, auntie, of course not," returned Maye, very hurriedly, and growing deathly pale as she continued, with a visible effort; "how could you suggest such a thing? I respect Eric Trevanion for his devotion to Gabriel, and like all men, it pleases—it flatters him, to be respected by a woman. It flatters his vanity. And being such a friend of Gabriel's, he likes me almost as a brother would. But beyond that—nothing—oh, nothing!"

And the girl rose and left the room to run out into the grounds, where she might be alone with the soft, black cattle, and her heart-agony.

Left by herself, Mrs. Hawleigh stood for a moment at the window, and saw Maye run out across the bridge. As she settled to her work, she said to herself:

"Well, I hope Eric is not falling in love at last with Maye. What a calamity it would be!—and yet—poor child!—perhaps—well, well, Eric told me that, when Dr. Richardson's final report came, he would accept some of his country-house invitations, and go away from here, so that Gabriel might get accustomed to perpetual darkness, or that he might grow gradually well under Maye's gentle care. But it struck me that he didn't talk of leaving them together with much enthusiasm. Oh! why doesn't Dr. Richardson write?—his letter is *days* overdue, and the suspense is terrible."

The end was nearer than she supposed. It came on the following afternoon.

Day after day Mrs. Hawleigh waited and watched for the arrival of the post. Daily, from the post-office in the little village, a decrepid courier, known as "the post boy," started on his weary round, bringing in the letters for Trthwwsthpllgg soon after lunch; and often, the minute the meal was finished, Maye or Eric would start for the village, and get the letters before the post-boy had consigned them to his sack, for delivery in their proper turn.

To-day Maye had undertaken this duty at Mrs. Hawleigh's earnest request, and her aunt anxiously awaited her return. And as she waited she soliloquised:

"Dr. Richardson must write to-day, and then we shall know. Poor Gabriel! I hope I shall get as reconciled to his affliction some day as he is now; but at present there is hardly a moment of the day that I can banish the thought of it from my mind, and when I think of it a pang shoots through my heart which is almost more than I can bear. Poor little Maye, too!—poor child!—poor child! How long Gabriel was in love before he asked her to be his wife!—and then that dreadful gas-explosion in the studio which blinded him! Dear, faithful little nurse!—she has shown us since then what a good, true girl she is; what should we have done without her? Still, it seems hard that she should be condemned for the rest of her fair young life to taking care of a poor, blind man, and looking after his helplessness. Besides, what will they live upon if this blindness proves really incurable? Thank God! I can just support him and myself; but she has nothing, and he is no richer than she. I see nothing but starvation in front of them."

At this point her soliloquy was interrupted by the entrance of Maye.

"Well," exclaimed she, as the girl took off her hat, "have you got the letters? the post has not been here."

"No," replied Maye, "I just missed them. That poor old man they call the post-boy had just started on his round in the opposite direction, but I thought he would have been here by now, for I walked slowly, and have been doing a little gardening since I came in. Ah, there! he has just appeared at the top of the slope. I'll run and save him the walk down and up again."

Five minutes later she returned, exclaiming, "Here you are, auntie! Two letters for you, and one big one for Eric. Heigho! there has never been anybody to write to me but Gabriel, and now I write his letters for him. I can't very well write love-letters to myself. Poor Gabriel!—"

"Ah," interrupted Mrs. Hawleigh, "here is Dr. Richardson's letter. This will put us out of our suspense about him. Dear child, I can hardly hold it in my hands, I am so nervous. Do you read it to me. Oh, heaven! if I could only know, without opening it—the best—or the worst!"

She had given the envelope to Maye, and Maye, opening it, had run her eyes over the first lines of the letter. Her face, as she did so, became deathly white, and she said softly:

"You must sit down, auntie darling; I'm afraid the news is not going to be good. Shall I begin now?—yes? Very well."

And she read as follows:

"MY DEAR MRS. HAWLEIGH:—I have had a long and final consultation with Dr. Critchett since I saw your son at Dartmoor, and I regret to say that I fear I must destroy even the small hope which I was able to give you then. There is no longer any doubt that the nerves of both eyes are destroyed, and, this being the case, it would be dealing unkindly with you were I to hint at the possibility of an ultimate recovery. You were good enough to make me the recipient of your confidence, and to tell me of your son's approaching marriage when this accident befell him."—The reader's voice died out for a moment, and then she resumed: "I feel that this must be a terrible blow to his intended bride, for he will never be able to see her again, and I can fully realize what it will be to you to break this news to her. Please accept my sincere sympathy with this sad affliction which has fallen upon you, and believe me to be, with kind regards,

Always very faithfully yours,

E. CLIFFORD RICHARDSON.

As she finished reading, she rose, and, moving to the window leading into the conservatory, she leant against it, struggling to suppress her emotion. Mrs. Hawleigh, who had burst into tears, came to her, and, winding her arms about her, kissed her silently. Then, taking the letter from her, she left the room.

Maye returned to the seat she had occupied before, and sat, dry-eyed—tearless—gazing into the future.

Blind!—hope was extinguished—Gabriel was incurably blind!

And whilst she sat, the twilight deepening over her soul, she heard a burst of laughter in the conservatory, and Eric and Gabriel stood on the threshold. The former, seeing the girl sitting there, a wild, white look in her eyes, started forward a step, forgetful of the blind man's hand upon his arm.

"Why, what's the matter, old man?" exclaimed Gabriel; "I'll trouble you not to stumble when your two eyes have to direct four legs. Is anybody here?"

Maye tried to speak, but her parched tongue refused to articulate immediately. Seeing the struggle, Eric answered:

"Yes—yes—Miss Trevethick is here."

"Then why don't you answer, Maye?" said Gabriel, irritably. "I wish you wouldn't play with me as if I were Caleb Deecie in 'The Two Roses.' Ah! I *saw* 'The Two Roses.' Well," he continued, recovering himself, "you've missed such a treat; you should have come out with us. Eric has been reading me some lovely poems out of a new little book called 'Tares.' They are beautiful—he must read some to you. And we have had another exquisite sunset. You ought to have seen it." And he took up his violin, which lay as usual on the piano, and began playing to himself, "Told in the Twilight," the refrain of the song, "Close to the Threshold."

"Poor fellow!" said Eric, in an undertone to Maye; "it's hard to believe sometimes that he doesn't really see the things he describes to one. Do you know, Miss Trevethick, sometimes he describes you to me so perfectly that I actually see you before me—he delights in doing it. Really, if you heard him you would be both interested and flattered, believe me."

"And believe *me*, Mr. Trevanion," returned Maye, with a wild effort at merriment, as she made him a courtesy, "I *am*. But seriously, how can we ever thank you for your kindness to him and to us? It is only with you that he forgets that he is blind. What would I not give to be able to be to him what you are!"

What Eric would have answered I know not; what he thought was: "And what would I not give to be to her what he is! I wish that I were blind when I see them together." It was her own thought repeated.

They were interrupted by Gabriel suddenly laying down his violin and saying:

"Now, then, what are you two conspiring about? Don't you know that it's very rude to whisper before third parties? I suppose you imagine that I don't count—ah, no, I don't mean that," added he, as Maye went quickly to his side and touched him; "I was only chaffing. Come! what have you been doing since lunch?—and where's the mother?"

"Oh," replied Maye, turning cold and confused at the thought of the imminent explanation, "I walked down to the village because auntie wanted to get the letters quickly, but the post had started, so I came home and tied up those creepers which hang down and annoy you when you come in at the conservatory door—and then the post came in—here's a letter for you, Mr. Trevanion—and then the mother left me alone and went to her room—I think. How far did you walk?" concluded she, desperately changing the subject.

"Tell me," said Gabriel, not heeding her question, "was mother's letter from Richardson?"

"I—I think it was."

"Did mother tell you what was in the letter?" pursued the blind man, with a strong effort to appear calm. "Richardson was to write and say how soon I shall be able to see again."

"No," replied Maye, with forced prevarication, "*she* did not tell *me* what was in the letter."

"I must go to her at once—take me to her, Maye;" and the two disappeared.

Left alone, Eric drew his letter from his pocket. It was directed in Schuyler Van Boomkamp's characteristic fist, and was a bulky letter enclosed in a foolscap envelope. It was with a vague, sickening feeling of apprehension that he tore it open and brought to light a closely written manuscript, headed "*The Narrative of the Coloured Woman Clytemnestra*," and a letter from Schuyler Van Boomkamp. The latter was short, and to the point. It read as follows:

"My Dear Trevanion:—Miss Daphne Préault is dead. The circumstances attending her death constitute, I fear, a horrible tragedy, of which the details are contained in the narrative I have compiled for you, from the account given by the coloured woman who attended upon Miss Préault and witnessed her death. To that narrative I have nothing to add, save that I was able to certify that death ensued from naturally-produced asphyxia, in which certificate a singularly ignorant practitioner, who announced himself to me as Miss Préault's regular medical attendant, concurred, knowing nothing of the case. I am making arrangements for the return of Clytemnestra to New Orleans; she is amply provided for under the will of Miss Préault, the bulk of whose property is bequeathed to you. Finally, as regards Madame du Peyral, if it became necessary at any future time, I could certify that she was mentally deranged, and not responsible for her actions; in any case, under the circumstances, the death of Miss Préault—certainly unpremeditated—might have been accidental. Madame du Peyral left England the same night as the tragedy occurred. I forbore to enquire whither she was bound—possibly to her original destination in Greece. I do not think it will be necessary for us to ascertain; she will certainly not return. I leave, myself, for Paris this evening. Should you wish to communicate with me, a letter addressed, care of His Excellency, the American Minister, will reach me safely.

A word in conclusion, in case we should never meet

again. You and I have been the witnesses of, and to a certain extent actors in, one of the most startling, nay terrific, psychological dramas that it has ever been my fate to encounter in all my experience in mental science. I shall prepare a report thereon, which I shall send you for signature; any details that you can add will be valuable. I think we had better keep our own counsel in the matter, closely and completely, until the story of Daphne Préault and Paul du Peyral shall have become a chapter of forgotten history. I wish you health and prosperity, and shall remain always, my dear Trevanion,

Very faithfully yours,

SCHUYLER VAN BOOMKAMP.

White to the lips, Eric Trevanion looked from the letter he held in his hand to the manuscript, which had fallen to the floor. He picked it up and hastily glanced through the sheets until he reached the last page. Then his eyes dilated with horror, his pallor increased, and he felt as though he would have fainted, had he not fled forth into the air. There his senses seemed to return to him. Composing himself with a violent effort, he returned into the house, and, going to his own room, he locked away carefully Schuyler Van Boomkamp's letter and manuscript in his dispatch-box.

And then a great sense of misery and loneliness came over him, and flinging himself onto a sofa, he cried aloud in the agony of his soul: "Oh, God! and is this the end? Is my life utterly wasted?—utterly spoilt? Blind—blind fool that I have been!—Had I but known where my happiness lay—had I not been stupefied by my ghastly folly—you might have loved me—Maye, my darling, my pure, beautiful love! And now—what is left for me? Ashes—ashes! I am not fit to enter your presence—and yet—I have fancied—but no, she is pledged to Gabriel—God forbid that I should break his heart—should wreck his life more completely than it is wrecked already! I will go to her—perhaps the sight of her sweet, true face will chase this nightmare from my brain —may save me, after all, in spite of myself." And then the lines recurred to him—this time with a new hope in every word:

> *"I hold it truth, with him who sings*
> *To one clear harp in divers tones,*
> *That men may rise on stepping-stones*
> *Of their dead selves to higher things!"*

And so Eric Trevanion sought once more the little boudoir, where he found Maye alone in the twilight, standing at the window looking out into the deepening shadows across the moat.

As he entered the room she turned quickly. The evening light slanted across his drawn, white face, and she exclaimed:

"Mr. Trevanion—Eric—you have had bad news!"

"Bad news!—bad news?—I wonder whether it be bad. Terrible news—yes! but bad!—I wonder—?"

"Oh, what is it?"

"Daphne Préault is dead."

"Dead!"

"Yes."

"How dreadful!—how did she die?—tell me about it."

"She died in one of her curious fainting-fits. She had had many of them in the past year, and since her serious illness a short while ago she has never been her old self."

"I am so sorry—Eric."

"Nay, do not be sorry for her, or for me, Miss Trevethick. Perhaps it is better thus."

"But—you loved her so."

"Loved her?—did I love her?—no; I think—God help me!—that I was bewitched, possessed—mad!"

"But surely—"

"Do not let us speak of it—I beg of you. It is all too sudden, too ghastly. Let us speak of something else."

There was a moment of deathly stillness, and then Maye, womanlike, recovering herself the first, said:

"What are these poems that Gabriel speaks about, that you have been reading to him?"

"A little volume by a young author," answered he, drawing it from his pocket as he spoke. "They are light, of course; but some of them are very pretty. It has been lying about; have you not read them?"

"No—I took it up yesterday, but I was interrupted. Will you not read me one, as Gabriel suggested?"

"Certainly, if you wish it. No, do not ring: there is light enough here at the window. What sort of poem shall I read you?"

"Had you not better go on where you left off?"

"Very well. I was just going to read this one, when it struck me it was getting chilly for Gabriel, and we got up to come home. It is called "*Nachtstuck*," and runs thus:

"*I will lie still, here in the shadow, and turn my face to the wall;*
Mine eyes shall behold no other since they may not mirror you,
Since I may not hear your voice mine ears shall be sealed too,
And my lips are mute to all!

"*But you—oh, my fair, sweet love, you must walk far afield, in the light,*
Not quite forgetting my soul that aches in the darkness here,
Though Time's soft, dead hand puts me from you, each day less dear
Grow the tender mem'ries of night.

"*And that shall be well!—I—am only a wraith from the past,*
No more may my glad arms cradle your drooped gold head,
To you—and because to you, to all—am I henceforth dead.
[*And you knew not that kiss was our last!*]

"*And that is well too!—to the last was our summer sweet,*
To the very end no pale cloud obscured our exquisite days,
Our sun, for the last time, set in a warm, wild blaze,
Making earth and heaven meet!

"*False? Ah, no! hardly that—dear heart, you are not to blame;*
[*Who carps at the sun, or the transient rain, or the fleeting ev'ning dew?*]
And I cavil not at your fair young soul that would fain, but could not be true,
And I love you, aye, the same.

"That you do not ask it, I know, and I would not, alas! but must
Lie here chained and tortured by mem'ry forever; but you, dear, are free:
And the welcomest gift that this wide, blank universe holds for me
Is a little handful of dust!"

As he read, his voice grew lower and more tender. Every word ate into her soul. It seemed as if Gabriel himself was speaking, and it was more than she could bear. The spell of the words lay over Eric too, and he realized every word and its meaning. Had it not been for this they would have heard the slight noise that Gabriel had made as he raised himself on one elbow, to listen as he lay upon the couch in the conservatory. He had come in from the garden just as Eric entered the room—they had not heard him—and now, with a blind man's acuteness of ear, not a word that they had said had escaped him.

Even now he might have made his presence known to them, but that, as Eric's voice ceased, Maye buried her head in her hands, and moaning, "Oh! Gabriel!" burst into an agony of tears. Gabriel waited and listened—hardly daring to breathe in the gloom of the conservatory.

It was Eric who spoke first within the room:

"Ah, Miss Trevethick," he exclaimed, "I have pained you, Maye! This poem has touched you—then it speaks to you as it speaks to me. Poor Gabriel!—of us three I do not know whom I should pity most. You do not answer. Alas! that I should speak so, when every prompting of honour urges me to keep silent. I have no right to speak, as my heart bids me, to the affianced wife of my best friend—least of all when he is afflicted, helpless, as poor Gabriel is, but—I am going away now, and I cannot go without a word."

"Oh, Mr. Trevanion—I beg of you—"

"Ah! don't stop me now—I am leaving you, perhaps forever. Every day that I have been here I have been drawing nearer and nearer to the truth, that I love you—aye! love you more than words can say—than eyes can speak;

and that when I leave you—as leave you I *must*—poor Gabriel's blindness will have fallen on my soul. God help me, for I am utterly helpless myself."

"My duty—my duty—" began the girl, but he interrupted her:

"Yes, your duty and mine; but when I think of your fair young life tied to his in one ceaseless continuance of care for his infirmity, even as you have tended him hitherto; when I think that his eyes can never see you, that you must be chained for all your life to the side of a man whose only knowledge of you is—memory—the remembrance of your beauty, which cannot give brilliancy, for one moment, to the darkness before his eyes, my heart is ready to burst. Ah!" he continued, desperately, losing himself in the torrent of his words, "let me go to him and implore his forgiveness for myself, for *us*. Why should we wreck three lives—as wrecked they must be—without doing any good by the sacrifice? I cannot believe that I have been mistaken—that you care nothing for me—oh! come to me, and be the light of my life."

He had fallen on his knees by her side, burying his head in his hands in the agony of his despair—and she laid her hand gently on his shoulder, as she answered him in a cold, miserable voice:

"Hush, Eric! hush! I can never be the light of your life, if, indeed, that might be, for I have promised to be the light of his. You have spoken truly—he will never see me—you—any of us, again; the letter from Dr. Richardson has destroyed our last hope—Gabriel is incurably blind, and this, if nothing else, makes my path clear before me."

He raised his eyes to hers, and stayed there, on his knees, gazing into her soul, as she pronounced the death-sentence of their love.

"We must not misunderstand one another, dear friend," continued she, "but I would gladly have spared both myself and you this full knowledge of the truth. I am, as you know, without relations, without friends, save for Mrs. Hawleigh and Gabriel; without means of subsistence save what I can gain by my own work. Auntie rescued me five years ago from absolute penury, and whilst I lived with her, Gabriel loved me in silence—during all that weary time. It was only when he became famous and was becoming rich that he asked me to link my life with his; and I consented. What else could I do?—besides—I loved him very dearly—though not as I *could* love. Hush! do not speak! His accident, as you know, has destroyed all his prospects; would you have me desert him now? No, no! We must go away from here—for I own to you, Eric, that you have stirred a deeper feeling within my heart than I knew existed there. Ah! why should I pretend ignorance of my own weakness?—it *is* love! But you are his friend *and mine*—are you not? Help me, then, by your example, to do my duty to our poor, blind Gabriel."

She ceased speaking, and Eric, rising to his feet, took her hand and kissed it as he would have done homage to a saint. Then he said, controlling his voice with a violent effort:

"Then—it is all over. Thank you for this grand lesson you have taught me, and may you be as happy in your new life as you deserve. Forgive me for what is past, dear, and forget, if you can, that I ever asked you to be untrue to your promise to Gabriel. I leave here to-morrow. Think of me kindly, if you can, sometimes. For myself I cannot regret this trial, for it will make my life better, purer, to have loved you as I have come to do. See—I will tear this poem from this little book; and he—must never know! Perhaps we shall never meet again. In that case—good-bye—God in heaven bless you, Maye Trevethick."

He kissed her hand once more, and the next moment he was gone. The silence that he left behind him was broken by a tiny noise in the conservatory. Maye's heart gave a violent bound, and for an instant she seemed to stifle; then she went into the conservatory—it was empty—and flinging herself upon Gabriel's lounge, she sobbed as if her heart would break.

The dinner at Trthwwsthpllgg that night was a silent meal—save that Gabriel made a superhuman effort to appear gay as usual. He and Eric kept up a cross-fire of conversation, in which Maye alone detected the false note. When it was ended, and the Trevanions, father and son, and Gabriel had joined Mrs. Hawleigh and Maye in the little boudoir, Gabriel said:

"Are we all here?—yes? That is good—I have something very serious to say to you all. Yes, mother," he said to Mrs. Hawleigh, who came and laid her hand on his arm, "it must be said sooner or later, as I told you. Sit down and keep silence, all of you, please, till I have done. Maye!—mother has been reading to me Dr. Richardson's letter, and it has decided me to say what I have been on the verge of saying to you—for many weeks—for many weeks. You now know that I can never recover my sight, that I can never again see the landscapes in which I have revelled, the flowers and animals which I have loved; can never again see *you*, save as the beautiful model whose features I fixed upon my canvas and my brain last, before my light became a great darkness. I am poor—very poor—and blind. That, I know, makes no difference to you—but, alas! this physical infirmity has altered my whole being—in a moment, as it were—in a moment—and I should be doing you a grievous wrong were I to conceal my altered feelings from you and marry you notwithstanding. Hush! do not speak—I beg of you. Only forgive me. I *cannot* marry you to make your fair young life one of slavery, even if I *would* do so; and you must not think me fickle or untrue; it is my infirmity—my infirmity, that has altered my whole life."

Maye flung herself on her knees by his side, and put her arms about him:

"I cannot leave you like this, Gabriel—I cannot leave you!" she said.

"I know—I know, dear," he replied; "but it must be so. Eric—your voice, when you have spoken to me of Maye, has told me far more than your words have said—we blind men have keen intuitions and infallible instincts, you know; will you guide for me this child-friend of mine through her pure, sweet life?—and the knowledge of your happiness will be a light to my life which has become so dark."

Eric Trevanion rose in his turn:

"Gabriel—dear old man," he said, "you must not make this sacrifice—we cannot bear it."

"Yes, old friend," he replied, "it must be—it is better so. Mother, dear—we shall not be separated, after all, you and I. We will go back to the old studio, to our old life and my music, and Eric and Maye will come sometimes to tell me of the world they—*see*—around them."

Splendide mendax!

Many years have passed since the day that the story told in the foregoing pages was closed with Gabriel Hawleigh's magnificent lie. The Hawleighs, mother and son, are both dead. Gabriel Hawleigh died in Naples—or more accurately speaking, at Sorrento, whither he had fled in search of quiet, and recovery from a malarial fever caught in Rome—but not before his fame as a musician had rung from one end of Europe to the other, as would have rung his fame as a painter, had not his career been cut short by his accident. There lingers probably in the memory of many of my readers the fame of a violinist who stirred the heart-strings of his audiences as no one has stirred them since Paganini and Sainton stayed their magic fingers under the grasp of death. He was a miracle—for he was blind. And under the *nom d'artiste* which he adopted and inscribed indelibly upon the roll-call of glory, only a few people in England recognized Gabriel Hawleigh the painter.

His mother was with him to the last, but she did not long survive her son. She died in the old studio-house in Holland Street—shall I say of a broken heart? Now-a-days I fear to say it, for, now-a-days, hearts do not break.

Dick Lindsay married Eva Easton, but Sylvia never married anybody: she lives on the Schiavoni in Venice, and paints pictures that are eagerly sought for in the index of the Academy catalogue. Bernard Rawlinson is a great actor now, and never paints at all; Gerome Markham still individualizes the pages of a leading comic paper, and dresses five times a day—he does not look an hour older than he did the day on which I first saw him; and Mr. Charles Sturton-Baker has disappeared. There was a little difficulty about the prospectus of a joint-stock company, which brought about his enforced seclusion for a few years at the expense of Her Majesty's government. When he had served his term he sought fresh fields for his peculiar industry in the United States, exchanging them subsequently, owing to circumstances over which unfortunately he had control, for the pleasant security of Canada.

He did not marry Parthenia Van Baulk'em.

That young lady came over to England to inspect Mr. Charles Sturton-Baker's position "on the ground"—so to speak, and finding that the swain had given to an airy nothing, a local habitation and a name, returned to Fifth Avenue the betrothed of Mr. Murray Hill. They were married in the spring following—and people say that he beats her.

It was only last summer that I went down to Cornwall, to rest at Trthwwsthpllgg Manor, at the conclusion of a more than ordinarily hard spell of work, and gave that terrible polymonosyllable to my publishers as my address for a couple of months. The Autocrat of Trthwwsthpllgg is a grand old gentleman, autocrat now only in name, for the reins of government have fallen to Eric, who is the typical young country squire, very proud of his place and his horses, and on his knees to his wife, who has not aged an hour—I swear!—since I first met her in Holland Street. And in the early morning I used to be awakened by a chorus of shrill shouts from the lawn beneath my windows, proceeding from the throats of Eric's children, to wit, his daughter Dorothy, a young woman of decided and advanced opinions, and her twin brothers, Eric and Gabriel, whom she rules with a rod of iron. They are her juniors by a couple of years, and it is an understood thing that Dorothy is to make haste and catch me up, and then we are to be married!

One evening I was sitting alone with Eric in his armoury, dignified by the name of "study," when our conversation turned upon the old colony in Holland Street, on the Hawleighs, and on "the Princess Daphne." The old wound had long healed over, so I knew that I could approach the subject with impunity.

"By-the-bye," I said, "what a dreadfully sudden thing Daphne Préault's death was!—did you ever hear any of the details?"

"Yes—all of them."

"How did she die?"

"My dear fellow," said Eric, very gravely, "the death of Daphne Préault was one of the most horrible tragedies that the world has ever witnessed. Fortunately for everybody concerned she had been attended by Schuyler Van Boomkamp, the American psychologist, and he arranged matters."

"Why, what do you mean?" I exclaimed; "I never thought there was any mystery. I always understood that Miss Préault was subject to fits of some kind, and that in one of them she had died."

"If you like," said Eric Trevanion, not answering my remark, "I will place in your hands a complete account of her death. It reached me and I read it the day that I proposed to Maye, my wife. From that day to this it has lain undisturbed."

So saying, he turned to a dispatch-box that lay on the table, and, unlocking it, he took thence a few sheets of paper, folded up, and getting yellow with age. These he placed into my hands. I unfolded them and read as follows:

THE NARRATIVE OF THE COLOURED WOMAN CLYTEMNESTRA: GATHERED FROM HER LIPS BY SCHUYLER VAN BOOMKAMP, M.D., LEYDEN, PARIS, AND N. Y.

I was born in the service of the late Victor Préault of New Orleans, on the Belles Fontaines plantation, Louisiana, U. S. A. After his death I came to England with Miss Daphne Préault, and have been with her all the time she has been in this country. Madame du Peyral began coming to the house early in this summer, and she and Miss Préault seemed very much attached to one another. Whenever Mr. Trevanion was not here, Madame du Peyral used to come and remain with Miss Préault. One day Madame du Peyral brought her things and came to stay in the house. The next day Mr. Trevanion left London. I have not seen him since.

Madame du Peyral was here about three weeks; she occupied the room adjoining Miss Préault's on the first floor, and connected with it by a door. They used generally to sit up talking late into the night in one room or the other, and in the morning, at nine o'clock, I used to carry up the breakfast. Often Madame du Peyral would be in Miss Préault's room, and then I used to carry the chocolate in there for both. A few days after Mr. Trevanion had left, a letter came from him, and I took it up to Miss Daphne on her tray. Madame du Peyral was there, sitting on the edge of the bed talking, and the moment she saw the letter she tried to snatch it. Miss Daphne was too quick for her, and she did not get it. I often heard them speak of it afterwards, Madame du Peyral always wanting to see it, and Miss Daphne never showing it to her.

The last morning before Madame du Peyral left the house I took up the chocolate as usual, and as I went into the room I thought I heard their voices raised as if in anger, and when I got in, Miss Daphne was lying in bed looking very pale, and I was afraid she was going to have one of the fainting-fits she used to have. Madame du Peyral was sitting on the bed by her side, looking at her—her face was red, and she had a dangerous look in her eyes that frightened me. The bed-clothes were disarranged, and the two looked as if they had been struggling. Neither spoke whilst I was in the room, and instead of going out again by the door onto the landing, I went into Madame du Peyral's room, intending to arrange it a little, and to be within call. In a moment, however, I heard footsteps, and Madame du Peyral, coming in by the connecting door, said:

"You need not arrange my room yet—wait till I am dressed."

I went out, but came back as soon as I heard them talking together again, and listened at the door, which had been left ajar between the two rooms. Madame du Peyral was saying:

"Why won't you let me see it? I am sure there can be nothing to conceal. I know Mr. Trevanion dislikes me, and that if he mentioned me at all, it was unpleasantly."

"But he didn't mention you at all, Mahmouré—what a child you are!" said Miss Daphne.

"Not such a child," she said, "as to be deceived in that ridiculous way. I know what was in the letter—he wants to make peace with you, and he wants you to give me up. Well, it is very simple for you to choose. You are tired of me."

"Don't be so silly," was the answer; "there isn't a word of truth in what you say!"

Then I peeped through the door-crack, and saw Miss Préault take Madame in her arms. The latter struggled away, exclaiming:

"No—you are tired of me."

"I am not."

"Then give me the letter."

"I can't."

And then Madame du Peyral began to cry.

"Come, Mahmouré," said Miss Daphne, "you excite yourself too much. You are overtaxing your strength. We carry our gossip too late into the night. Even *I* am not so strong as I was. Every night I determine to send you to bed, and not let you sit here and chatter; but then we forget all about the time. I have been feeling unlike myself for days, and this morning I have a dreadful headache. Come, stroke my temples for me, dear."

Madame du Peyral's face was turned in my direction, and as she leaned over Miss Daphne, the same horrible, frightening look came into it. I could see that Miss Préault's eyes were shut. Then the other got up and, creeping across the room, pulled down the blind, and came back to the bed, where she lay down and began passing her fingers across Miss Préault's forehead and through her hair.

Miss Daphne did not move, and gradually Madame du Peyral drew herself into a crouching, sitting position, watching, watching, watching, as she played with the other woman's hair. Suddenly Miss Daphne gave a gasp and struggled a little. Madame, seeing her move, flung herself suddenly upon her, and gripped her round the throat—I did not dare to stir—I was frozen with terror.

Then she began to mutter rapidly and incoherently in a harsh, forced voice.

"No, no!" she said, "you shall not die—I will keep your life in you; it shall not escape;" and she still held Miss Daphne's throat.

The latter moved a little, then a little more. Then her movements grew weaker again, and at last she lay quite still. Then Madame du Peyral stooped lower and began kissing her. I went into the room. As I entered, she looked up like a wild animal just going to spring, and cried, "Go away!—how dare you come in here?"

I was terrified, and put on my things and ran for the American doctor who has been here sometimes. When he came he told me Miss Daphne was dead.

I say that Madame du Peyral killed her.

Her
CLYTEM X NESTRA.
Mark

At this point the manuscript was signed with the mark of Clytemnestra, witnessed by Schuyler Van Boomkamp. A few words were added by the doctor to the effect that Miss Daphne Préault had died of a sudden cerebral congestion produced by over-excitement, and the narrative closed with his signature and the date.

THE END.

POPULAR BOOKS

SELECTED FROM THE CATALOGUE OF

BELFORD, CLARKE & CO.,

CHICAGO AND NEW YORK.

Memories of the Men Who Saved the Union,

Lincoln, Stanton, Chase, Seward, Gen. Thomas, etc., with new portraits. By Donn Piatt. 12mo, cloth, gilt top, illustrated $1 50
Paper covers.. 25

"This is one of the ablest books on the war, and will create a sensation."—*Times.*

"Very few men had the opportunity of knowing the inside history of the war as well as Mr. Piatt."—*Courier, New Haven.*

"Every word of the volume is thoroughly readable, and no one who begins it will lay it aside without going to the end."—*The American, Baltimore.*

Henry Ward Beecher,

Christian Philosopher, Pulpit Orator, Patriot and Philanthropist. A volume of representative selections from the Sermons, Lectures, Prayers and Letters of Henry Ward Beecher, with a biographical sketch by Thomas W. Handford. Illustrated by True Williams. Copious index, 12mo, cloth.......................... $1 25

This volume contains carefully classified selections of Mr. Beecher's views on Religion; Social and Political Affairs; His Remarkable Utterances on Evolution; Selections from his Prayers and from the Plymouth Hymn Book; Communion Sabbath at Plymouth Church; Great Speech in London; Sermon on Lincoln; Last Sermon in Plymouth Church; Beecherisms, Eulogies, etc., etc.

The Life of Our Blessed Lord and Saviour Jesus Christ,

By Rev. John Fleetwood, D.D., with notes by Rev. T. Newton Brown, D.D. Illustrated with 14 full-page steel engravings. 8vo, cloth.......................... $2 00

Poems of Passion,

By Ella Wheeler, author of "Maurine" and other poems. (32d edition.) The most salable Book of Poems published this century. Small 12mo, red cloth.. $1 00

Maurine, and Other Poems,

By Ella Wheeler, Author of "Poems of **Passion.**" Small 12mo, red cloth, with Portrait................**$1 00**

Studies in Social Life,

A review of the Principles, Practices and Problems of Society. By George C. Lorimer, LL.D. 12mo, cloth $1 00

"No one can read this book without obtaining a better insight into problems underlying the social fabric."—*Chicago Herald.*

"The lectures are marked by a breadth of thought, and a minuteness of observation that show the author to be a man thoroughly abreast of the times."—*Chicago News.*

"The author's fairness of discussion and clearness of treatment commend the work to a careful reading."—*Binghamton Republican.*

Elmo's Model Speaker,

For Platform, School and Home, arranged on an entirely new plan, providing programmes for Twelve Evening Entertainments; Selections suitable for Juvenile Gatherings; Brief Responses to Encores; Addresses for Weddings, Presentations, Farewells and Welcomes. Compiled by Thomas W. Handford. (16th edition). 12mo, cloth, gold and black........ $1 25

Two Thousand and Ten Choice Quotations,

In Poetry and Prose, from the Master Minds of all ages. Arranged for daily use by Thos. W. Handford. (10th edition.) 12mo, cloth, gold and black. $1 25

Mes Amours, Poems Passionate and Playful,

By Selina Dolaro. 1 Vol. small quarto, illustrated.... $1 25

"This is one of those books that it is impossible adequately to describe. It is extremely lively and entertaining. The book is certainly bound to become popular, if only for its entire uniqueness."—*Baltimore American.*

"Selina Doloro, a charming actress, receives a number of poems, some passionate, some playful, and having enjoyed many a good laugh over them, gives some of them to the public with interpolated comments."—*The Argus.*

"These verses are full of spirit and life, and the merry mood plays and sings between the lines like the contented streamlet between wind-swept hillsides."—*Albany Journal.*

Ashes of The Future: The Suicide of Sylvester Gray,

By Edward Heron-Allen. 1 Vol. 12mo, paper covers. 50

"Is the work of a very vigorous and cultivated pen as well as of a deep thinking and fervid brain."—*Brooklyn Eagle.*

Anti-Poverty and Progress,

By Sister Frances M. Clare, the Nun of Kenmare. 1 Vol. 12mo, paper covers....................... . 50

"The good sister alternately deals effective blows against Mr. George's impracticabilities and urges upon the rich, alike ecclesiastical as lay, the inauguration of true anti-poverty from the top of society. . . . The author evidently thinks religion more of a remedy for poverty than science."—*Brooklyn Eagle.*

Forty Years on the Rail,

By Charles B. George. Reminiscences of a Veteran Conductor. Illustrated, 12mo, cloth............... $1 00
Paper cover.. 50

The Politics of Labor,

By Phillips Thompson. 1 Vol. 12mo, cloth.......... $1 25

"This book will mark an epoch in American thought. It is fully up with the times. . . . It is the prophet of the New Era."—*The People, R. I.*

"One of the most valuable works drawn out by current discussions on social and economical questions, and one that is sure to take a high place in the permanent and standard literature of the times."—*Opinion, Rockland.*

"This book is enlightening and inspiring; every thoughtful man and woman should read it."—*Tribune, Junction City.*

"Mr. Thompson presents the whole question of land and labor reform as clearly as could be desired."—*Mail, Chicago.*

Prince Coastwind's Victory, or the Fairy Bride of Croton Lake,

By Mrs. Niles H. MacNamara. 1 Vol. illustrated. Cloth... $1 00

"This is a genuine American fairy tale, and, so far as we can remember, the first and only one that can lay claim to the title."—*Daily Times, Troy, N. Y.*

"It is fanciful and fresh, and written out delightfully."—*Philadelphia Press.*

"The story is well told and cleverly illustrated in strong and delicate pen and ink drawings."—*Brooklyn Eagle.*

"A dainty little volume, describing the fate and fortunes of a Fairy Bride."—*Times-Democrat, New Orleans.*

The Truth about Tristrem Varick,

By Edgar Saltus, author of "Mr. Incouls Misadventure," "The Philosophy of Disenchantment," "Balzac," etc. 1 Vol. 12mo, cloth..................... $1 00
Paper covers.. 50

In this novel Mr. Saltus has treated a subject hitherto unexplored in fiction. The scene is Fifth avenue, the plot a surprise. "There is," some one has said, "as much mud in the upper classes as in the lower — only in the former it is gilded." This aphorism might serve as an epigraph to *Tristrem Varick.*

It is the Law,

A story of marriage and divorce in New York. By Thomas Edgar Willson. 12mo, cloth........... ... $1 00
Paper covers.................................. 50

"It is the Law" is a unique novel. That it contains a libel in every chapter is probably an exaggeration, but it certainly conveys that impression to the average reader. If the law on divorce and marriage of New York state is in the complex muddle that Mr. Willson depicts it, then there are extenuating circumstances for Mr. Willson placing in our hands a novel which shows that a man may have, and does have, as many legal wives as his sense of propriety or pleasure desires. The same state of things also applies to women. It is indeed strong meat, dished up in a fearless too plain manner —*A Critic.*

Man and Labor,

A Series of short and simple studies, by Cyrus Elder. 12mo, cloth.. $1 00
Paper covers.. 50

"So excellent a manual of sound, economic philosophy ought to be widely circulated. . . . It is not a book written by a capitalist nor by a workingman. But it gives good advice to all classes, and gives it in a most attractive manner."—*Philadelphia Evening Bulletin.*

"Mr. Elder's book is a compound of sound argument, apt illustration, noble sentiment and vigorous language."—*Inter Ocean, Chicago.*

A Boston Girl. At Boston, Bar Harbor and Paris,

By Rev. Arthur Swaze. 1 Vol. 12mo, cloth.......... $1 00

"Those who read 'A Boston Girl' will like it and those who do not read it will, if they only knew it, miss spending an agreeable hour or two."—*San Francisco Call.*

"Those who are pining for an original American Novel will be gratified upon reading this volume."—*Kansas City Times.*

The Confessions of a Society Man,

A novel of absorbing interest. 1 Vol. 12mo, cloth.... $1 25
Paper covers.. 25

"This is the novel of the year. The love-making in it is charming and it is interesting up to the very end. It gives ad picture of lives of the men of the present day in our large cities, particularly in New York and Philadelphia. Like Thackeray's *Barry Lyndon*, it is an elaborate study of selfishness."—*The World, New York.*

Princess Sophia-Adelaide.

The deserted daughter of Queen Victoria and Prince Albert. 1 Vol. 12mo, paper covers, illustrated..... 50

"The authoress asserts in the most emphatic way, that she is Sophia-Adelaide, Princess Royal of England and Duchess of Saxony, and that she was born in Windsor Castle, on November 21, 1840, that her father was Prince Albert Edward of Germany, and that her mother is Queen Victoria. The portrait of the author printed in the volume bears an unmistakable resemblance to Queen Victoria."—*Minneapolis Tribune.*

Divorced,

A Novel. By Madeline Vinton Dahlgren, author of "Lights and Shadows of Life," "South Sea Sketches," "A Washington Winter," "Memoirs of Admiral Dahlgren," etc. 1 Vol. 12mo, cloth.......................... $1 00

"This is a masterly discussion of one of the burning questions of the age, dealt with according to the logic of facts. The plot is most ingenious. The characters are sketched with a powerful hand."—*Tribune.*

Two Women in Black,

By James Mooney. Mooney & Boland Detective Series. Profusely illustrated by True Williams. 12mo, cloth, gold and black.......................... $1 00
Paper covers.. 50

Shadowed to Europe,

By James Mooney. A Chicago Detective on two continents. By James Mooney. Mooney & Boland Detective Series. Illustrated by True Williams. 12mo, cloth.................................$1 00
Paper covers.................................50

The Vanderbilts,

By W. A. Crofutt. Illustrated with portraits of the Vanderbilt family and their various residences. The work reads almost like a fairy tale, giving as it does an accurate history drawn from authoritative sources of the methods by which the great Vanderbilt fortune was built up. 12mo, cloth, black and gold.....$1 50

Her Desperate Victory,

By Mrs. M. L. Rayne, author of "Against Fate," "What a Woman Can Do," etc. Illustrated by True W. Williams. In this work Mrs. Rayne deals in her own effective and trenchant manner with the power of a gentle life to overcome the greatest difficulties. Every mother and daughter in America should read this book. 12mo, cloth, black and gold............$1 00

Love's Ladder,

A Novel. By W. DeWitt Wallace. 1 Vol. 12mo, cloth, gold and black..............................$1 00

"This story is a powerful one and rivets the attention from beginning to end. The movement is rapid and reminds one throughout of the onward march of a drama."—*Chronicle, Washington, D. C.*

"It is vigorous and original."—*Herald, Indianapolis.*

The Veteran and His Pipe,

Being the famous articles from the Chicago *Inter Ocean*. 12mo, cloth..............................$1 00
Paper covers.................................50

"Of even more importance than many of the more pretentious volumes which aim to set aright the story of a campaign."—*Chicago Times.*

Legends and Superstitions of The Sea,

By Lieut. Bassett of the U. S. Navy, with numerous fine illustrations. 12mo, cloth, gold and black.....$1 50

"A valuable work of reference."—*United Service Magazine, New York.*

"It is a collection of Folk-lore of the Sea so comprehensive, and so systematically arranged, as to be of encyclopedic usefulness."—*Literary World, Boston.*

"Entertaining to read and valuable as a book of reference." —*The Critic, New York.*

Ingersollia,

Gems of Thoughts from the Lectures, Speeches and Conversations of Col. Robert G. Ingersoll, with portrait. 12mo, cloth..........................$1 00
Paper covers.................................50

The Kentucky Housewife,

A collection of Recipes for Cooking. By Mrs. Peter A. White. 1 Vol. 12mo, cloth........................ $1 00

The Every-Day Cook Book,

By Miss M. E. Neill. Economical, Reliable, Excellent. 1 Vol. 12mo, oilcloth covers (Kitchen Style)........ $1 00

Ten Minute Sketches—Essays Humorous, Satirical, Sentimental and Burlesque,

By Chas. H. Ham. 1 Vol. 12mo, cloth.............. $1 00

A Man of Destiny. Letters to Grover Cleveland, President Elect,

By Siva. 12mo, cloth.................................. $1 00
Paper covers.. 50

Why We are Democrats; Or, the Principles and Policies of the American Democracy,

By S. S. Bloom. Containing a concise statement of the leading principles of the Democratic party of the United States, as taught by the Fathers of the Republic, enunciated in the National Platforms, and proclaimed by representative Democrats from the foundation of the Government to the present day.
12mo, cloth.. $1 00
Paper covers.. 50

Seneca's Morals: "A Happy Life," "Benefits," "Anger," and "Clemency,"

Translated by Sir Roger L'Estrange. I Vol., 12mo, cloth.. $1 00

A History of the United States,

In Chronological Order from A. D. 432 to the present time (1886). Fully illustrated. 12mo, cloth $1 25

The Truth about Alcohol,

By Robert Alexander Gunn, M.D., Square 32mo, cloth.. 40

"There is much common sense in 'The Truth About Alcohol.' The author is a well-known New York physician who has made a specialty of the subject of stimulants. He demonstrates by conclusive evidence that spirits are of great value in many cases and that the temperance advocates wilfully pervert the truth. Increasing age brings with it less capacity for enduring mental strain and worry, and spirits act as a recuperative influence. The same is true in regard to taking of wine or liquors by brain-workers with their meals. Digestion is aided and the lassitude so frequently experienced is removed. The little book demands a wide circulation, as it contains information vouched for by the best medical authorities, both here and abroad, which is of great practical value."—*San Francisco Chronicle.*

Needles and Brushes, and How to Use Them,

Directions for Embroidery and Fancy Work, with 150 illustrations. 12mo, cloth, black and gold 75

Tennyson's Birthday Book,

Edited by Emily Shakespeare. 32mo, cloth, full gilt edges, gilt side and back........................ $1 00

The Tariff.

12mo, paper covers.. 25

The surplus, and the reduction of the tariff, are the political issues of to-day, and will remain the absorbing ones for many years. Very few persons know what the tariff rates are on the thousands of articles imported. This volume gives all the information wanted. Being reprinted from Governmental Authorized Reports, it is reliable. The index is the beauty of this little work; any person can, by turning to it, find in an instant of time the duty on every article. Those who take an interest in the present tariff fight will find this volume invaluable.

Bancroft's History of the Colonization of the United States,

By George Bancroft. Two vols. in one, 12mo, illustrated, cloth.. $1 50

"Since Ranke's death George Bancroft is the greatest living historian. The American citizen who has not read his history of the United States is a poor patriot, or an unfortunately ignorant person. We fear there are too many of them as there are of those who have never even read the constitution of their country. It is not too late for these delinquents to buy a copy of this great book and learn something that will be of interest and profit the remainder of their lives."—*The Churchman.*

Fifty Years a Queen; or, Great Britain under Queen Victoria,

By Mrs. Katherine Hodge. 12mo, cloth.............. $1 00

Justin McCarthy's "History of Our Own Times" is deservedly the most popular history of our times. It has passed the Rubicon and is now an interesting classic. "Greater Britain under Queen Victoria," which should be the title of "Fifty Years a Queen," is less pretentious to the above masterpiece, but it is a succinct, concise and accurate account of the history of the past fifty years. Those who do not care to give the time to the larger history will find this book a valuable substitute."—*London Academy.*

Eating and Living,

Diet in relation to Age and Activity. By Sir Henry Thompson, Small 16mo, cloth... 40

"If those ailing would buy a copy of the world-renowned physician, Dr. Thompson's work on the preservation of health, fewer drugs need be bought and more cheerful men and women would walk the earth. It is concise, simple and effective."—*The Lancet.*

Treasures New and Old; or, Many Thoughts For Many Hours,

Selections in Prose and Poetry. By Alice L. Williams. Illustrated with 54 full-page illustrations, by Irene Jerome. Quarto. Richly bound, title and gold ornamentation. Cloth........................ $4 00
Full morocco.. 8 00

Laurel Leaves,

Poems, Stories and Essays. By Henry W. Longfellow and others. With 75 illustrations by Eytinge Jr., Birket Foster and others. One handsome volume, 4to, cloth extra, full gilt, gilt edges. Cloth........ $4 00
Full morocco.. 8 00

Lotus Leaves,

Original Stories, Essays, and Poems. By some of the most popular American and English authors. Edited by W. F. Gill. New and improved edition. Beautifully illustrated with engravings from designs by Fredericks, Lumley, Lyell and others. One handsome volume, 4to, full gilt, gilt edges. Cloth... ..$ 4 00
Full morocco.. 8 00

Papyrus Leaves,

A companion to "Laurel Leaves" and "Lotus Leaves," comprising Poems, Stories, and Essays by Longfellow, O. W. Holmes, Whittier, Bryant, Lowell, Wilkie Collins, Edward Eggleston, James T. Fields and other eminent authors. Fully illustrated with fine engravings by eminent artists. One handsome volume, 4to, cloth extra, full gilt, gilt edges. Cloth $4 00
Full morocco.. 8 00

New Stories from an Old Book,

(Biblical Characters with Modern Titles.) By Rev. H. L. Hammond ("Laurens"), with an introduction by Rev. John H. Vincent, D.D., Chancellor of Chautauqua University, with 25 original full-page illustrations by True W. Williams.
Small 4to, full gilt edges.............................. $2 50
12mo edition.. 1 50

Painters of the Italian Renaissance,

By Edith Healy. Illustrated by 25 original copper-plate engravings or choice masterpieces of the leading Italian painters, executed in the highest style of art by the famous French engraver, M. De Mare. Small 4to. Richly bound, extra cloth, gold title and ornamentation.............................. $5 00
Full morocco.. 4 00
Cloth, school edition.............................. 1 25

The Story of Manon Lescaut,

From the French of L'Abbe Prèvost. A new translation, by Arthur W. Gundry, from the French edition of 1753, with over 200 full-page and other illustrations, by the great French artist, Maurice Leloir and others. Reproduced by photogravure, wood engraving and photo-engraving processes from the superb edition de luxe, published in Paris in 1885. 4to, cloth, extra, gold and red, in a neat box.... ... $3 00

[N. B.—The price of the French edition, with same engravings, is $20.]

THE MOST POPULAR LINE OF HUMOROUS BOOKS PUBLISHED.

Bill Nye's Chestnuts, Old and New,

The Latest Gathering. A Fountain of Perpetual Merriment. Richly Illustrated, by Williams, Opper and Hopkins. 12mo, cloth........................ $1 00
Paper covers.................................. 50

Bill Nye and Boomerang,

By Bill Nye. Illustrated. 12mo, cloth............. $1 00
Paper Covers.................................. 25

Baled Hay,

By Bill Nye. Illustrated. 12mo, cloth............. $1 00
Paper covers.................................. 25

Forty Liars and Other Lies,

By Bill Nye. Illustrated. 12mo, cloth............. $1 00
Paper covers.................................. 25

A Book by "Peck's Bad Boy,"

Peck's Irish Friend, Phelan Geoheagan. By Geo. W. Peck, Jr., the original of Peck's Bad Boy. Richly illustrated by True Williams. (30th thousand.) 12mo, Cloth, gold and black........................ $1 00
Paper covers.................................. 25

GEO. W. PECK'S POPULAR BOOKS.

How Private Geo. W. Peck put down the Rebellion;

Or, The Funny Experiences of a Raw Recruit (40th thousand), with 16 full page illustrations. 12mo, Cloth, black and gold........................ $1 00
Paper covers.................................. 50

OUR FAMOUS

CAXTON LIST

—OF—

POPULAR BOOKS.

200 VOLUMES.

PRINTED ON GOOD PAPER FROM CLEAR TYPE, AND TASTEFULLY BOUND IN CLOTH, WITH INK AND GOLD DESIGN.

PRICE 75 CENTS PER VOLUME.

WORKS OF ADVENTURE.

Adventures Among The Indians. By W. H. Kingston.
Beauchampe. By W. Gilmore Simms.
Border Beagles. By W. Gilmore Simms.
Cast Up By The Sea. By Sir Samuel Baker.
Charlemont. By W. Gilmore Simms.
Confession. By W. Gilmore Simms.
Deep Down. By R. M. Ballantyne.
Deerslayer (The) By Fenimore Cooper.
Don Quixote. By Miguel Cervantes.
Erling, The Bold. By R. M. Ballantyne.
Eutaw. By W. Gilmore Simms.
Fire Brigade, The. By R. M. Ballantyne.
Forayers (The). By W. Gilmore Simms.
Giant Raft (The). By Jules Verne.
Guy Rivers. By W. Gilmore Simms.
Hunting In The Great West. By G. O. Shields.
Katharine Walton. By W. Gilmore Simms.
Last of The Mohicans (The). By Fenimore Cooper.
Mellichampe. By W. Gilmore Simms.
Mysterious Island, (The.) By Jules Verne.
Partisan (The). By W. Gilmore Simms.
Pathfinder (The.) By Fenimore Cooper.
Perilous Adventures, By Land and Sea. By John Frost, LL.D
Rifle and Hound In Ceylon. By Sir Samuel Baker.
Richard Hurdis. By W. Gilmore Simms.
Robinson Crusoe. By Daniel Defoe.
Scout (The). By W. Gilmore Simms.
Secret Dispatch (The). By James Grant.
Southward Ho! By W. Gilmore Simms.
Spy (The). By Fenimore Cooper.
Swiss Family Robinson. By Wyss & Montolieu.
Thrilling Scenes Among The Indians. By T. M. Newson.
Tour of The World In Eighty Days. By Jules Verne.
Twenty Thousand Leagues Under The Sea. By Jules Verne.
Vasconselos. By W. Gilmore Simms.
Woodcraft. By W. Gilmore Simms.
Wigwam and Cabin (The). By W. Gilmore Simms.
Young Foresters (The). By W. H. Kingston.
Yemassee. By W. Gilmore Simms.

DETECTIVE STORIES.

File 113. By Emile Gaboriau.
Gilded Clique (The). By Emile Gaboriau.
In Peril Of His Life. By Emile Gaboriau.
Lerouge Case (The). By Emile Gaboriau.
Monsier Lecoq. By Emile Gaboriau.
Mystery of Orcival. By Emile Gaboriau.
Other People's Money. By Emile Gaboriau.

ESSAYS AND BELLES LETTRES.

Alhambra. By Washington Irving.
Astoria. By Washington Irving.
Crown of Wild Olive and Queen of The Air. By John Ruskin.
Ethics of The Dust and A Joy Forever. By John Ruskin.
Heroes and Hero Worship. By Thomas Carlyle.
Sartor Resartus. By Thomas Carlyle.
Sesame and Lilies and Unto This Last. By John Ruskin.
Sketch Book. By Washington Irving.

ETIQUETTE, ETC.

Complete Letter Writer. By Thomas W. Handford.
Ladies' Etiquette.
Ladies' Family Physician. By Pye Henry Chavasse.
Needles and Brushes, Embroidery and Fancy Work.
Stoddard's Readings and Recitations. By R. H. and Elizabeth Stoddard.

FABLES AND FAIRY TALES.

Æsop's Fables, 100 Illustrations.
Andersen's Fairy Tales. By Hans Christian Andersen.
Arabian Nights (The)
Grimm's Popular Tales. By The Brothers Grimm.
Gulliver's Travels and Baron Munchausen. By Dean Swift and R. E. Raspe.

FICTION.

Adam Bede. By Geo. Eliot.
Admiral's Ward. By Mrs. Alexander.
Airy Fairy Lilian. By "The Duchess."
All In A Garden Fair. By Besant & Rice.
Arundel Motto (The). By Mary Cecil Hay.
Beauty's Daughters. By "The Duchess."
Belinda. By Rhoda Broughton.
Beyond Pardon. By Bertha M. Clay.
Broken Wedding Ring (A). By Bertha M. Clay.
Called Back and Dark Days. By Hugh Conway.
Cardinal Sin (A). By Hugh Conway.
Children of The Abbey. By Maria Roche.
Daughter of Heth (A). By Wm. Black.
Doris. By "The Duchess."
Dora Thorne. By Bertha M. Clay.
Dick's Sweetheart. By "The Duchess."
Dunallan. By Grace Kennedy.
Earl's Atonement (The). By Bertha M. Clay.

East Lynne. By Mrs. Henry Wood.
Eugene Aram. By Bulwer Lytton.
Endymion. By Benjamin Disraeli.
Faith and Unfaith. By "The Duchess."
Felix Holt. By Geo. Eliot.
For Lilias. By Rosa N. Carey.
Green Pastures and Picadilly. By Wm. Black.
Great Expectations. By Chas. Dickens.
Heart and Science. By Wilkie Collins.
Henry Esmond. By Wm. M. Thackeray.
Her Desperate Victory. By Mrs. M. L. Rayne.
Her Mother's Sin. By Bertha M. Clay.
Ione Stewart. By Miss E. Linn Linton.
Ishmaelite (An). By Miss M. E. Braddon.
Jane Eyre. By Charlotte Bronte.
John Halifax, Gentleman. By Miss Mulock.
Kenelm Chillingly. By Bulwer Lytton.
King Arthur. By Miss Mulock.
King Solomon's Mines. By H. Rider Haggard.
Ladies Lindores. By Mrs. Oliphant.
Lady Audley's Secret. By Miss M. E. Braddon.
Lady Branksmere. By "The Duchess."
Love Works Wonders. By Bertha M. Clay.
Macleod of Dare. By Wm. Black.
Madcap Violet. By Wm. Black.
Maid of Athens. By Justin McCarthy.
Margaret and Her Bridesmaids. By Julia Stretton.
Mental Struggle, (A). By "The Duchess."
Mill On The Floss. By Geo. Eliot.
Molly Bawn. By "The Duchess."
Mrs. Geoffrey. By "The Duchess."
New Magdalen (The). By Wilkie Collins.
Old Myddelton's Money. By Mary Cecil Hay.
Oliver Twist. By Charles Dickens.
Our Mutual Friend. By Charles Dickens.
Parisians (The). By Bulwer Lytton.
Paul and Virginia, Rasselas and Vicar of Wakefield. By St Pierre, Johnson & Goldsmith.
Phantom Fortune. By Miss M. E. Braddon.
Phyllis. By "The Duchess."
Portia; or, By Passions Rocked. By "The Duchess."
Princess of Thule (A). By Wm. Black.
Repented at Leisure. By Bertha M. Clay.
Romola. By Geo. Eliot.
Rossmoyne. By "The Duchess."
Shandon Bells. By Wm. Black.
She. By H. Rider Haggard.
Strange Story (A). By Bulwer Lytton.
Strange Adventures of a Phaeton. By Wm. Black.
Sunrise. By Wm. Black.
Sunshine and Roses. By Bertha M. Clay.
Tale of Two Cities (A). By Charles Dickens.
That Beautiful Wretch. By Wm. Black.
Three Feathers. By Wm. Black.
To The Bitter End. By Miss M. E. Braddon.
Tom Brown's School Days. By Thomas Hughes.
Tom Brown At Oxford. By Thomas Hughes.

Two On A Tower. By Thos. Hardy.
Under Two Flags. By Ouida.
Vanity Fair. By Wm. Thackeray.
Wanda. By Ouida.
Wilfred Cumbermede. By Geo. Macdonald.
Woman's Temptation (A). By Bertha M. Clay
Wooing O't. By Mrs. Alexander.
Yolande. By Wm. Black.
Zanoni. By Bulwer Lytton.

HISTORICAL ROMANCES.

Bride of Lammermoor. By Sir Walter Scott.
Guy Mannering. By Sir Walter Scott.
Heart of Midlothian. By Sir Walter Scott.
Ivanhoe. By Sir Walter Scott.
Kenilworth. By Sir Walter Scott.
Last Days of Pompeii. By Bulwer Lytton.
Redgauntlet. By Sir Walter Scott.
Rienzi. By Bulwer Lytton.
Rob Roy. By Sir Walter Scott.
Scottish Chiefs. By Jane Porter.
Thaddeus of Warsaw. By Jane Porter.
Waverley. By Sir Walter Scott.
Willy Reilly. By Wm. Carleton.

HISTORY AND BIOGRAPHY.

Dickens' Child's History of England.
Washington and Marion (Life of).
Webster (Life of). By Samuel Smucker, LL.D.

HUMOROUS FICTION.

Charles O'Malley. By Charles Lever.
Handy Andy. By Samuel Lover.
Harry Lorrequer. By Charles Lever.
Rory O'More. Samuel Lover.

RELIGIOUS AND DEVOTIONAL.

From Year to Year. By Alice Carey.
Imitation of Christ. By Thos. á Kempis.
Is Life Worth Living. By W. H. Mallock.
Pilgrim's Progress (The). By John Bunyan.

SEA TALES.

Cruise of The Black Prince (The). By Commander Cameron.
Five Years Before The Mast. By W. B. Hazen.
Jack In The Forecastle. By Hawser Martingale.
Mark Seaworth. By W. H. Kingston.
Midshipman (The). By W. H. Kingston.
Peter The Whaler. By Sir Samuel Baker.
Pilot (The). By Fenimore Cooper.
Pirate (The). By Sir Walter Scott.
Red Eric (The). By R. M. Ballantyne.
Round The World. By W. H. Kingston.
Salt Water. By Sir Samuel Baker.

Sea Queen (A). By W. Clark Russell.
Tom Cringle's Log. By Michael Scott.
Two Years Before The Mast. By R. H. Dana, Jr.

SHORT STORIES.

Dickens' Christmas Stories.
Dickens' Shorter Stories.
Dickens' Story Teller.
Ethan Brand. By Nathaniel Hawthorne and others.
Fern Leaves. By Fanny Fern.
Half Hours With Great Authors.
Half Hours With Great Humorists.
Half Hours With Great Novelists.
Half Hours With Great Story Tellers.
Poe's Tales. By Edgar Allan Poe.
Shadows and Sunbeams. By Fanny Fern.
True Stories From History. By Hugh DeNormand.

TRAVEL.

Eight Years' Wanderings In Ceylon. By Sir Samuel Baker.
Hyperion. By H. W. Longfellow.
Outre Mer. By H. W. Longfellow.

Some New and Popular Books.

A Dream and a Forgetting.
By Julian Hawthorne. 12mo, cloth.............................. $1 00
Paper covers.............................. 50

Rents in Our Robes.
By Mrs. Frank Leslie, a brilliant review of modern society and manners by one of their most noted exponents. 12mo, cloth 1 00
Paper covers.............................. 50

A Slave of Circumstances.
By E. DeLancy Pierson. 12mo, cloth.............................. 1 00
Paper covers.............................. 50

The Romance of a Quiet Watering Place.
An extraordinary study of human nature, by Nora Wardell. 12mo, cloth.............................. 1 00
Paper covers.............................. 50

His Way and Her Will.
A pen-and-ink miniature of Eastern society, by A.X. 12mo, cloth 1 00
Paper covers.............................. 50

The Land of the Nihilist: Russia.
By W. E. Curtis. Illustrated with over 100 drawings. 12mo, cloth 1 00

The Lone Grave of the Shenandoah.
By Donn Piatt. 12mo, cloth.............................. 1 00
Paper covers.............................. 50

The Political Oratory of Emery A. Storrs.
From Lincoln to Garfield.
By Isaac E. Adams. 12mo, cloth.............................. 1 00
Paper covers.............................. 50

The Protective Tariff.
What it Does for Us! By Gen'l Hermann Lieb. 12mo, cloth.... 1 00

www.ingramcontent.com/pod-product-compliance
Lightning Source LLC
Chambersburg PA
CBHW030348270326
41926CB00009B/1013

* 9 7 8 3 3 3 7 0 2 7 0 0 1 *